Best Canadian
ESSAYS
1989

· · · · · · · · · ·

DOUGLAS FETHERLING, EDITOR

FIFTH HOUSE PUBLISHERS
SASKATOON

Canadian Cataloguing in Publication Data

Best Canadian Essays 1989
ISBN 0-920079-43-1
1. Canadian essays (English) - 20th century*
I. Fetherling, Douglas, 1949-

PS8373.B48 1989   C814'.54   C89-098041-1
PR9197.7.B48 1989

"The Creative Approach" © *The Royal Bank Letter* 1988
Reprinted with the permission of The Royal Bank of Canada

"The Moral Status of Pity" © The *Canadian Journal of Philosophy*, University
of Alberta, Edmonton

This book was published with the assistance of The Saskatchewan Arts
Board and The Canada Council.

Design: Robert MacDonald, MediaClones Inc.,
Saskatoon Saskatchewan and Toronto Ontario.
Cover Photograph: Copyright © Piotrek B. Gorski

FIFTH HOUSE PUBLISHERS
20 – 36th Street East
Saskatoon Saskatchewan
S7K 5S8 Canada

Printed in Canada

Contents

· · · · · · · · · ·

Foreword

• • • • • • • • •

People insist that the essay as a literary form is dying. People have been saying so for decades, centuries almost. The essay's disappearance is thus one of the longest most drawn-out death-scenes in the history of melodrama. In actuality, the essay is in a state of relatively robust health, no less so in Canada than in Britain or the United States, though somewhat differently. The existence of *Best Canadian Essays 1989*, the first in a series of what will be annual volumes of this type, should illustrate the point. This is a browser's book, intended as a diverse choice of the most intriguing, most thoughtful or best-crafted essays published by Canadians in the 12-month period just ended. Perhaps simply by existing at all, it points up the source of the doom-saying.

Even in a selection as brief as this, there is all manner of prose, from traditional to experimental, from the light and graceful to the long and complex. Yet none of it resembles what might have been found in such a sampling even one generation ago. When people contend that the essay is on the way out they are only showing unintentionally that it continues to change and mutate, as it always has done in the past. If this ongoing process is what gives the essay its resilience, it's also what makes this type of writing so slippery. It's not difficult for speakers to announce that the essay as they remember it is obsolete or obsolescent. It takes more effort to pinpoint what stage the essay is at in its perpetual evolution. That is the crux of the matter surely.

Not that anyone desires to make a state-of-the-essay address, full of quotations from the past and balanced caution. It will suffice to emphasize that the essay has always been first and most importantly a type of periodical writing. The study of English literature has often blinded us to one of its more brutal realities: the fact that Addison and Steele, Dr. Johnson, Hazlitt, Lamb, De Quincey—all of those figures were busily attempting to fill up the pages of magazines. In American literature the situation was the same. Emerson's famous essays are no less topical for the fact that he wrote many of them to give as lectures, for he needed fresh material to take on the road each performing season.

What of the Canadian tradition? It's certainly similar without being tautologous. Hugh MacLennan was once known and loved no more for his fiction than for his "familiar essays" (an old-fashioned term, but they were old-fashioned essays even then). If today only a very few Canadian writers, such as B.W. Powe, have made their reputations as essayists, this is only because writers are not often called by that name any longer. They are thought of instead as some manner of journalist. Historically this is as it should be, though it carries its own kind of vagueness and confusion.

As Val Clery, a Toronto editor, noted some years ago in his introduction to a collection of magazine pieces, Canada's general-interest magazines "have provided—for writers with an itch to write with style and with a need to think twice about what they write—a temporary limbo of opportunity between the well-paid tyranny of daily journalism and the ill-paid longeurs of literature." It's a nicely turned phrase, "limbo of opportunity." It speaks to the fact that the way to success in periodical publishing is thought to lie in sophisticated visual presentations of unsophisticated editorial content—poor writing with pretty pictures. To survive, the contributors with the itch Clery describes have had to become clever and infinitely facile stylists and even, on occasion, innovative thinkers. Out of their necessity has come the contemporary essay in all its variety.

What's the difference between an "article" and an "essay"?

Some pieces of writing declare themselves essays by the way they hark back to older definitions of the word. Those which are formalistic—that is, ones important for their style and mood, not their factual content—are easiest to identify. They often affect a rustic flavor, in deference to the old-fashioned occasional essays ("On the Occasion of the Visit by HRH the Prince of Wales"—by any of half a hundred forgotten writers) or familiar essays ("On Friendship"—ditto). It was by means of such pieces that American literature clung to its British roots for so long. The New England tradition, it's sometimes called, with no play on words intended. Its Canadian adherents have tended to be city folks masquerading as country folks. They range from the late Gregory Clark, whose false effusions about huntin' and fishin' were part of growing up for two or three generations of *Star Weekly* and *Weekend* readers, to Robertson Davies, who in his Samuel Marchbanks columns, still read today with pleasure, exploited the old-timer's pose better than anyone else. Such essays, especially ones about country ways, still have a following, to judge from writers as different as Noel Perrin in the US or Bruce Hutchison in Canada. In their proper setting, such as *Harrowsmith*, they are still a source of enjoyment. But they're also an anomaly, perhaps an aberration.

The essay is the instrument of independent journalism, not of corporatism, and mostly what distinguishes it from the article is the skill of the writer has used in sneaking something of higher than average quality into the publication for which he or she is working: something whose diction isn't totally corrupted by journalese, whose level isn't so limited by the need to inform as actually to preclude the possibility of thought. Writing or rather publishing an essay in the world of commercial journalism is thus a subversive act. By finding the means to make quality acceptable to the editors and the readers, the writer scores a victory over mediocrity. The Canada Council refers to this and related activity as "creative non-fiction" but I am attracted by another term. It comes from a secondhand bookshop that I used to frequent in Toronto. The proprietor tended to create his own categories for arranging the inventory; one of the labels on his shelves read INSPIRED JOURNALISM. I knew just what he meant.

The criteria for *Best Canadian Essays 1989* have been simple ones. To be considered, material must have been published by a Canadian in any domestic or foreign periodical during calendar year 1988. I attempted to monitor an almost absurdly wide range of such publications myself. As much as I'm pleased to note that there are contributions from unknown writers as well as from famous ones, I'm even happier to see that the span of publications runs from the *Canadian Journal of Philosophy* to *The Edmonton Journal* (with which it is so seldom confused). I fancy that few if any subscribers to *This Magazine,* the leftwing magazine, are also supporters of *Canadian Defence Quarterly,* for example, and so I hope that by keeping an eye on both periodicals, along with scores of other diverse journals and newspapers, I have given readers some sense that they are getting a digest of sorts. Certainly they're receiving a broad range of opinion, as well as a subliminal rundown on many of the year's concerns and issues.

Even so, this series, beginning with the next book, *Best Canadian Essays 1990,* can move forward only if readers alert me to material that I am likely to have missed and if publishers, editors and the essayists themselves make submissions directly. Remember, the potential contributions must be Canadian and must be appearing in a periodical or newspaper between 1 January and 31 December, 1989. The address is: Douglas Fetherling, Best Canadian Essays, Box 367, Station F, Toronto Ontario M4Y 2L8. Material cannot be acknowledged or returned, but the writers whose work is chosen will be contacted by the publisher well in advance.

Thank you.

Ed.

The Soul of an Old Machine
ROBERT FULFORD

. . . .

They're like a Chinese army pouring over the hill in waves, the word-processor people. They come rushing at you, full of smugness and jargon, eager to tell you how word processors changed their lives. They love to describe the mistakes they've made ("so then I pushed the wrong button and lost three chapters") and they're so intoxicated by the delirious masochism of their experience that they fail to see how it terrifies people like me. Every horror story I hear puts my own purchase of a word processor back another five years: now I'm not scheduled to buy one until at least 2038.

It's no use trying to drive away the processor people with insults; there'll always be more of them coming over the hill. And like all cultists, they yearn to make converts. In my case they suggest that, since I do a fair amount of writing, a word processor will save me time. "It makes your life so much easier," they always say. (Funny: they never *look* like people whose lives have been made easier.) They especially love to point out that with a word processor you can take a paragraph from here and move it to there, "simply." When I reply that as it happens I am already quite capable of taking a paragraph from here and moving it to there (you just cut the paper with the edge of a ruler and stick it together again with Scotch tape), they look at me with pity in their eyes.

What they don't understand is that my 40-year-old relationship with the typewriter has emotional overtones I can't easily ignore. For one thing, mine is a manual—I've never got used to working regularly with an electric. I like the clatter (it reminds me of the newsrooms of my youth) and I like the idea of my machine operating entirely on the power of my hands. It seems intimate and natural; it provides me with a pleasant sense of living in the

Robert Fulford (born 1932) was the editor of Saturday Night *for 19 years, as described in the autobiography he published during 1988,* Best Seat in the House: Memoirs of a Lucky Man. *The essay reprinted here first appeared in* The Financial Times of Canada, *5 Dec., 1988.*

mechanical age, when many people actually understood the machines that surrounded them. And there is a certain pleasure in being independent of everything outside your office, including the power grid. A few years ago an electricity failure hit the company where I worked and my typewriter was the only one still operating. Two people in the office, desperate to get letters out by the end of the day, came in to borrow my machine. (They had to *beg* me.)

But these considerations are secondary. The more important truth is that my affection for my typewriter is based on an emotion that's embarrassing to acknowledge—gratitude. Those who have sometimes endured unrequited passion will recall the grateful warmth they later felt when finally someone accepted their love and returned it. In my case, I'm grateful to my typewriter because it's the only machine that never resisted my advances. When I was 15 years old I already knew that I couldn't repair a bicycle, build a model airplane, or figure out what went on under the hood of a car. But a typewriter turned out to be a different matter.

In Grade 10 my typing teacher liked to say, "Respect your typewriter and it will respect you." He thought that anyone who ripped a sheet of paper out of the typewriter without loosening the carriage was, well, a vicious person, possibly headed for the penitentiary. Those were more serious times. It was 1948, at Malvern Collegiate Institute in the East End of Toronto. Above the teacher's head hung a photograph of King George VI, typing on his own portable, an inspiration to us all.

We learned on typewriters with blank keys, so that we wouldn't be tempted to peek. We were continuing (though we didn't know it) a grand tradition founded, more or less spontaneously, by a Salt Lake City court reporter named Frank McGurrin. In the late 1870s, working with one of the first Remingtons, McGurrin somehow got the inspired idea of memorizing the keyboard and began giving public demonstrations of his ability to type, literally, blindfolded. All by himself, he invented touch typing, something the inventors of the machine had never imagined. Along the way, against the conventional wisdom of his time, he proved that it was better to use 10 fingers than four.

Like McGurrin, we students learned the Qwerty keyboard, named for the first six letters on the second row. Unlike McGurrin, we knew Qwerty was a truly wretched system—as our teacher said, almost any other arrangement (including most of those that would result from throwing the letters across the room at random) would produce more efficiency and less fatigue. Qwerty was devised by an American mathematics teacher of limited imagination who, through a mishap of history, was the brother-in-law of one of the inventors of the Remington. The math teacher responded to the inventor's request that he devise a keyboard that would prevent jamming, and did so; alas, his system also called for the maximum output of human energy. Hundreds of attempts to revise it have failed, mainly because no one can think of a way to persuade all the typists in the world to submit to retraining. Qwerty persists even on word processors, one of the great human mistakes that humanity just doesn't feel like correcting, a permanent source of encouragement to anyone—like me—who thinks efficiency an overrated virtue.

My first few days in typing class were difficult—my fingers seldom respond readily to instructions, and I lack patience. But something about those blank grey keys attracted me, and I began caressing them. Soon I found that running through the first finger exercise the teacher gave us—;lkj— was a pleasure. In a couple of months I was as fast as anyone in the class. Ever since, I've been the fastest typist (though not necessarily the most accurate) wherever I've worked. I realize that among typists I'd be considered a clod. Once Kildare Dobbs said he'd like to match me, *mano a mano*, with Northrop Frye, but I'd never get caught in a trap like that. Frye is a real typist—his first trip to Toronto was to take part in a national typing championship—whereas I'm good only when set down among journalists and other non-pros.

I now understand why my typewriter and I bonded so quickly: like many lovers, I used it in the early stages as a projection of my fantasies. At age 15 I had ideas about being a war correspondent, so in our free-practice periods in typing class I'd compose despatches from abroad. "Cairo, Oct. 18— (AP)—Widespread fighting broke out here today between groups of dissident ..." The boy at the next desk liked to look over and read what I was writing. He kidded me about it—"Where's the war today?"—but he envied me too. He was a natural athlete, from whose fingers a football would fly accurately for 40 or 50 yards, but he negotiated the keyboard only with the greatest difficulty. All he lacked, I see now, was love.

The typewriter I use today, my main squeeze, is an Underwood Rhythm Shift Model, a descendant of the inventions of Franz Xavier Wagner (1837-1907), a German-American genius who designed the earliest Underwoods. I acquired it in the mid-1950s, which means I've known it longer than my wife, my children, and most of my friends. It's scarred and worn, like a piece of old farm machinery you'd find in a barn, but it works like a charm. As back-up I have a relatively modern Adler Universal 300, the gift of a friend when he moved to word processing; for travel I have a cute little Smith-Corona Viceroy De-Luxe, which I picked up a decade ago for $60.

Wilfred A. Beeching, director of the British Typing Museum at Bournemouth, says in his standard text, *Century of the Typewriter*, "It is a complicated piece of machinery but it has not captured the imagination or affections of men." He clearly doesn't know about my Underwood and me and all that we've shared. But how could he? How could he understand what we've had together—the tears, the triumphs, the hours of lonely frustration, the miraculous (so they seemed at the time) moments of breakthrough when at last the murky idea became clear or the incomprehensible anecdote straightened itself out on paper.

It's harder to work with an Underwood manual than with a word processor, my processing friends insist. They're right, probably. But a certain difficulty in writing, a relationship with the physical facts of paper and ink, may not be a bad thing. One reason my Underwood and I have grown closer together in recent years is that I've observed what word processing has done to other writers. In my view it hasn't improved any of them, and it has harmed some. At least in their first few years with a w-p, they've become prolix—the kind of writer who used to send me a two-page letter began writing three- or four-page letters after acquiring a word processor. It's easy, apparently, and it's fun, and they just like to go on and on. Moreover, they don't know how many mistakes they make. On the video display screen their words appear perfect to them, and once they have a printout they send it off without re-reading. I receive letters and manuscripts containing far more typos than in the pre-processing days.

Perhaps this is all sour grapes on my part, though. Certainly there was something of that in my reaction to a newspaper column written recently by my old friend Harry Bruce. It began: "One sultry summer Sunday, lightning zapped my beloved Chedabucto Bay, shot into my office, sabotaged my computer, barred me from my own files, stole two pieces of half-written work, and left me with a heartburn of panic." The rest of the story described how Harry had to load his lightning-crippled computer into his car and drive a long way to get it fixed, at considerable cost. It was a melancholy story. Why, then, did I laugh so much when reading it?

The word-processing propaganda never stops, of course—it flows into my office in magazines, sales brochures, in the letters of friends. Sometimes I sense that it makes my Underwood insecure. After all, even the oldest and best-established relationships can come unstuck. But not this one. Don't listen to them, my sweet. We'll never be parted.

Return of the Battle of the Monster Trucks
TOM HAWTHORN

• • • • • • • • • •

Up there atop Bigfoot sits Ken Koelling, strapped into seven tons of mean machine, his Missouri butt just inches from a 429-cubic-inch boss Ford hemi V-6 power plant. The Crunch Bunch in the stands are on their feet in delirium over The Clash of Titans, which begins as soon as this Monster Truck does some righteous damage to those eight dead sedans parked door-to-door on the floor of the hockey arena. Rest assured, Ken knows his bruising beast sometimes flips and sometimes careens crazily into the seats, but all he can think about as he looks out on those cars is, "I sure wish that were a mud pit."

A mud pit is a challenge to a man of Koelling's skills. They make this giant bog of mud and muck for the Monster Truck drivers to plow through. Only slick handling saves a driver and his rig from sinking into the goo, but this here dinky rink at Copps Coliseum in Hamilton is simply too small for a quagmire. All Ken has to do tonight is stomp on dead cars in Bigfoot, a task he finds about as sporting as squirrel hunting with a cannon. "From what I understand," he had said in his slow Midwest drawl, "we're going to go out there and crush cars just to crush 'em."

A Mercury Monarch is the first to go. Koelling slips Bigfoot into gear, rocketing his mutant truck towards the cars. Four huge tires start their climb onto the Monarch's roof with a jolt. A roar louder than Bigfoot's engine goes up from the stands, and cameras flash. The Monarch caves in easily, followed in quick succession by a Cordoba, a Galaxy, a Capri, an Aspen, some big boat of a Chrysler and pair of LTDs, each crunch raising another cheer from the Crunch Bunch. Bigfoot turns around and drives over them again to complete the freestyle portion of the program. That done, Koelling backs his

---

Tom Hawthorn was born in Winnipeg in 1960 and worked on the Vancouver Sun. *He is now a freelance writer in Toronto and appears frequently in* The Globe and Mail, *though this piece was first published in* This Magazine, *May 1988.*

truck against the end boards, pops the clutch, puts the pedal to the metal, and as his tires hit the first car he soars into the air, landing in a cloud of paint chips on the roof of an LTD 28 feet from where he became airborne.

• • • • • • • • • •

It is ten o'clock Friday evening in Steeltown, the first of two nights of The Return of the Battle of the Monster Trucks. Top ticket costs $18.50 and it's a poor night for Hamilton's babysitters. Eight thousand fans, maybe half of them kids, are revved up for some gear-grinding, axle-busting, flame-throwing fun. The kids are here for the Monster Trucks, lured by their fascination for things that are big, loud and powerful. The adults, who better appreciate the rear-wheel dragsters and modified four-wheel-drive Hot Rods that haul 50,000-pound sleds to open the show, are here for the same reason. "The power of the machines ... I think that gets everybody," says a carpenter, his Ford cap pushed back on his head. "I have a four-wheel-drive of my own ... and I'd just love to get behind the wheel of one of *those*, to feel that power under me."

You can see it now, the man's sensible Ford Ranger chassis plopped precariously atop a giant rubbery block of Super Terra-Grips as tall as a man. The hulking mass of metal would be the greatest status item in the neighborhood, besting even the humongous satellite dish in the front yard down the street. The other guys with trucks would park near by to gawk. "Hell, I wouldn't mind driving that thing in a traffic jam," one'd say. But you'd need more than just big tires. Big engine (preferably on the outside where the flywheel and the header could shine in the sun), nice hand-rubbed lacquer paint job, a pair of thin racing stripes painted along the panels and maybe even a sword-wielding babe with billowing science-fiction breasts—but no, the wife wouldn't go for that. And after you'd finished hopping up the truck, a slow cruise would be in order, elbow out the window, the steering wheel controlled by the open palm of your right hand. And in that rumbling truck, with a two-four of Molson on the floor and burger in hand, a little bit of hot-rod heaven will have been discovered.

The temptation would be to unleash the 400 horsepower straining under the hood, but it's embarrassing to lay smoke when you're 38, an age better given to burning leaves than burning rubber. So the carpenter just uses his truck to haul the occasional load of wood, and tonight it's brought him and his 11-year-old son to the arena where he can dream of being in Ken Koelling's place, with all that liberating internal-combustion power underneath.

It is garish spectacle, and the snooty can seek all form of explanation for its meaning. Some would see this as clear evidence of Western bourgeois decadence, the purposefully wasteful destruction of goods with wanton disregard for all those who lack cars. Others would see it as a product of worker alienation, all the riveters from the Ford assembly line in nearby Oakville here to wreak vengeance on the oppressive monster that forced them to create the cars now getting crunched. Still others would see the horror of gladiator culture, a celebration of Road Warrior Rambos tooling about in two-ton phalli.

It is, however, none of these. Where road racing is still a serious sport— with its specter of imminent spectacular death—Monster Trucks are the punchline of car culture. They are the Liberace, the Elvis, the Shrine of Ste. Anne de Beaupre of four-wheel drive.

Bigfoot is the Hulk Hogan of Monster Truckdom, but new heroes are making the scene. The Virginia Beach Beast and Bear Foot Trax are two trucks with tank treads instead of tires. Where Bigfoot stomps cars dead, these monsters shred them open like tin cans. When tank trucks jump, they land with a spray of sparks. Everyone says the tank trucks are the next big thing in the world's fastest growing motorsport.

Monster Trucks have all the making of becoming one of the great good ol' boy sports, like Indy racing or stock cars. Racing the Indianapolis 500, a 500-mile road race run round and round an oval track, is a matter of sticking the biggest engine imaginable on the sleekest body engineers can design, strapping some nut to the works and telling him to keep turning left. Monster Trucks work on a similar principle, except speed is replaced by brute force. But it's all too lowbrow for the sports pages, because the big tire and car companies haven't yet thrown their full financial weight behind Monster Trucks, and until they do the sport is not going to have the status that would permit the sports pages to ignore its humble beginnings. The sons of Alabama were racing their monster stock cars across dirt tracks all over the South for years before Goodyear and Quaker State and Valvoline and STP twigged on that millions of car-driving Southerners identified with the Junior Johnsons and Lee Pettys risking their necks at 160 mph. The cars nowadays are mobile billboards, and TV provides up to eight different angles—camera in the pits, camera on the blimp, camera behind the driver, even a Bumpercam—for the big crashes. Monster Trucks are far from the big time, although The Sports Network airs regular weekend truck- and tractor-pull shows for Canadian audiences.

"The kids can watch more of it on TV than they've ever been able to," says Jim Harris, a promoter. "And they have access to fan clubs of the trucks. Boys and trucks. Boys and trucks, that's what it is."

Harris, 31, books the trucks, puts in the dirt track and inspects the vehicles to make sure no one is accidentally barbecued. For four years, he has been running SRO Pace Promotions, which created the U.S. Hot Rod Association, out of Hot Springs, Ark. He designs formats for the shows and brooks no talk of his competitions being choreographed like wrestling.

"We could put a bit more character into this sport if we wanted to stage it all, know who was going to do what, know who was going to win the event before it even started. That way you could always put on a better show. With this, I don't even know who's going to do what when they get out there."

Like the time in Maryland when the Monster Truck crushed a bunch of cars, and everyone was hooting and hollering even as the damn thing headed into the seats. "It was someone who just couldn't stop," Harris shrugs. His job during showtime is to make sure no such mishaps occur, so as the trucks and the tanks turn the beater cars into so much scrap metal, he scurries along awful close to the jumping machines. "If a throttle sticks on one of those trucks, he's gonna go up into the stands. He'll climb to the middle level. So they have kill switches on them that are accessible to the driver inside the truck and to someone outside the truck. Like myself. That's why I stand close to the trucks when they're going over the cars. There's a kill switch on the back bumper with a two-inch diameter ring on it that I can pull to stop the truck. I'm there to protect the people in the seats to make sure somethin' doesn't happen. A driver can get knocked out even with a helmet on."

· · · · · · · · · · ·

Thrills, chills, spills, and the whole freaking concept was an accident. Fellow out of St. Louis by the name Bob Chandler ... ah, announcer Brent Kepner knows the story. "Ladies and gentlemen," he says, standing on the floor of the arena with a microphone on a long cord, "back in 1973, he decided to create a four-wheel-drive pickup truck that would draw attention to his off-road shop. Not even Bob Chandler had any idea of what he was creating. What he created was an entire sport. Were it not for that man, and the trucks he has produced since then, we would not be here tonight watching these machines. Those trucks have gone on to appear in virtually every country in front of the Iron Curtain." Where, undoubtedly, slave-labor Monster Trucks are inferior to free-enterprise Monster Trucks. No matter. Bob Chandler is the Abner Doubleday of Monster Trucks, the visionary whose gimmick has become a favored pastime for millions, who has added another chapter to the history of car culture. Bob Chandler now has six Bigfoots, so on any given night six American cities are being converted to his cause. Ken Koelling, the man who misses his mud pit, usually drives the original Bigfoot, but tonight he's handling Bigfoot III. Each machine costs $125,000 (U.S.), but what with poster and T-shirt sales, and sponsors in Ford and McDonald's restaurants, and the $50,000 he'll earn when Bigfoot III finishes its current 12-city tour, not to mention how all the attention hasn't hurt business at Chandler Auto Sales back home, Bob Chandler is not wanting for money.

It only take the Monster Trucks about 20 minutes to finish squishing, so The Return of the Battle of the Monster Trucks is padded by more than two hours of sled pulls. The program is the same as the tour travels its circuit from Anaheim, Calif., to Alexandria, Va. The announcer is perhaps the most important participant, as his steady patter keeps things moving. Brent Kepner has been doing this for ten years. He's both barker and pitchman, though sometimes his rhetoric hits the wrong note.

"I ask you to stand," he says, "as we salute the greatest country on the face of the earth—our national anthem." The anthem is "The Star-Spangled Banner." In the garage beneath the stands, mechanics and drivers doff their caps to place them over their hearts.

"How many Chevrolet fans do we have here? How many Ford fans? Come on, Fords, I wanna hear you yell." The world thus divided, the competition begins. A black truck called the Tasmanian Devil bucks across the dirt. It is the first of a dozen modified 4WDs that will be attached to a sled with an adjustable weight. They start at 50,000 pounds and will end at 80,000. The sled is called the Humiliator. The object is to drag it all the way across the floor—Full Pull!—without causing the engine to seize. Where farmers once competed by hauling heavy logs with a team of horses, their modern counterpart does the same with horsepower.

The cognoscenti wear industrial earmuffs from home. Others stuff their ears with yellow plugs. Those without protection soon suffer from a skull-splitting ache, as this motorized extravaganza takes its toll. Kids cry. And on the floor of the arena, the Tasmanian Devil is kicking up a bejeezus spray of sand as the Humiliator lives up to its name. Tires spinning and steam spraying, the truck is stranded 15 meters from its goal. "One thing's for sure," shouts Kepner, "the Devil's driver wasn't afraid to keep his right foot planted!" The parade continues. There's Charlie's L'il Angel out of Michigan lugging 604 cubic inches; Positively Wicked from Rhode Island with a 454 stock block inside the body of a '49 Chevy pickup; and Wild Child from Connecticut, a '53 Chevy found rusting in a field, which body-shop-owner Rob Peradi has home-built with steely-grey dual fuel injectors jabbing out from under its crimson hood. "It probably broke his heart to cut open that hood," Kepner sympathizes, the crowd roaring as twin blue flames burst from the injectors. One driver comes within a hair of an engine meltdown in a futile effort to snag a share of the purse. "It doesn't take a nuclear physicist to figure out why that pull didn't work. The young man was *brutalizing* his equipment!" A '68 military jeep with camouflage coloring called Gone A.W.O.L. finally pulls the 80,000-pound sled more than 155 feet to win the pull-off.

In between sales pitches for the hot rod association's "official wall-quality calendar" and its most recent video (*Blood, Sweat and Gears*), a trio of funny cars struts its stuff. One has four rear wheels and two front ones. It rears on its back tries as it tries to pull the sled. "What a beautiful and outrageous wheelie by War Lord!" Kepner says. Another has a hydraulic flip-top mechanism that raises the entire chassis of the truck to expose its engine parts in all their shiny splendor.

The funny cars are a throwback to the glory days of hot rodding and customizing. Detroit was cookie-cutting millions of lookalike cars after the war. They had engines big enough to power a tank—no problem there—but the '55 Mercury you bought was exactly the same as the one your old man brought home. The young went for baroque, adding dynamic curvilinear ornamentation to their Motown wheels. Jack the back, Mac. Chrome! Decorate the Mae Wests up front with a line of hand-painted flame in yellow and red, and maybe a manic cartoon character. But that's all show, no go. So boost the HP to blow your old man's doors in. Then that awful day came when factory options killed the hot rod. Detroit would do all the custom work and all the engine revamping for a few C-notes, and suddenly any squirrel boy with a see-through mustache was tearing down the highway. Hell, they *bought* their decals. Even the local Canadian Tire was selling those angry Woody Woodpeckers chomping on a cigar.

But in small towns like Latrobe, Pa., and Rockville, R.I., and Amelia, Ohio, and Hope, B.C., and Cayuga, Ont., the car and truck lovers can be found covered in the black grease of their hobby. They work on their wheels and dream of tearing down the never-ending blacktop that rushes past their garage. Once they make it on the truck show circuit, travelling the black ribbon becomes as much as part of their day as another's bus ride.

"It's a busy life," says Ken Koelling. "You drive all night, come here and you put it together and you wait. After the show, you tear down and head back home."

After Bigfoot wins the Battle of the Monster Trucks, mechanics and drivers gather in the concrete garage to swig brew and suck back methanol exhaust. It's well below freezing, but this is one of the rare nights when the roustabouts don't have to take the trucks apart for the long haul to the next stop. There is a lot of chatting and story-telling going on.

"I remember when Freddie rolled Bear Foot," Bigfoot's mechanic is telling a driver from Rhode Island. "Oh, hell, he turned that sumbitch over. I ran over and pulled him out. He was upside down when he landed, so it took a little while to get him out 'cause the shoulder harness had him. He was shakin' so hard you coulda used him for a vibrator."

Rhode Island doesn't cotton to talk about getting hurt: "Don't say that in no concrete building when there ain't no pieces of wood to knock on." He doesn't laugh.

Gene Fanning stands off to one side, his pockets filled with beer cans. He wears a full-length camouflage suit to match that of his truck, Gone A.W.O.L. It took almost three years to build the truck, a project he started after getting laid off from a steel factory in Derby, Pa. "I haven't been looking for another jobs with any heart," Fanning admits. "I'm just trying to make a go of this pulling. I'm tryin' real hard for sponsors, but it's tough. I've made a pretty good enough name for myself, but I just cain't get no money out of anybody." His latest brainstorm is to contact the brewers of Rolling Rock beer in nearby Latrobe, which was bought recently by a Canadian brewer. "I'm a local boy," he says. "I can do a lot of good for them."

Fanning, 26, has been working trucks since he graduated from high school. Gone A.W.O.L. cost him $30,000 to build, which some spend on an engine alone. He's tempted to invest in another pulling truck, or perhaps a funny car. "You got exhibition, you got guaranteed income. Funny cars, you know that money's coming in."

It's a precarious and not very lucrative life, but it suits Fanning fine. He likes trucks, and he likes it when others like his trucks. "I have another truck that I run on the streets of Derby. It's camouflage, a beater truck, just a snow-plowing, four-wheel-drive, hunting truck. It turns heads, and I figured if that ugly thing could turn heads, then I just had to get a nice one."

Roar from the Sea
HARRY BRUCE

· · · · · · · · · ·

When I moved from Ontario to Nova Scotia in 1971, the relentlessness with which the Maritime press carped about the shafting the region got from greedy "Upper Canada" made me think I'd parachuted into the 1890s. Were these people *still* whining about the deal struck in 1867? Where were the gas lanterns, horse-drawn streetcars, hoop skirts, and brigantines? In July 1977, the Halifax *Chronicle-Herald* marked the 110th birthday of Canada with a six-part series entitled "The True Story of Confederation." For any "Come From Away," as some Maritimers call outsiders who've settled among them, the series offered a wonderfully educational analysis of one of the sturdiest grudges in Canadian history. The writer was Alexander P. Paterson of Saint John, N.B., and to document Canada's betrayal of the Maritimes *The Chronicle-Herald* gave him space for no fewer than 9,000 words.

The gist of Paterson's argument was this: before Confederation, the Maritimes were prosperous, self-sufficient colonies, while Canada "writhed in the travail of many troubles of dire combination." Equal representation by Ontario and Quebec had deadlocked their government, and cancellation of reciprocity with the United States threatened their economy. War with the Americans loomed, and Canadian trade through U.S. ports was in danger. In England, and even Canada, many favored giving the whole nuisance to the Americans. Canada had no winter ports, and without safe rail connections to Atlantic seaports it "could hope for no real future as a British community." Thus, it was *Canada* that wanted Confederation. Indeed, Confederation was "imperative to her very existence." The Maritimes didn't need it or want it. "The suppliant was in travail, while the supplicated basked in the sunshine of substantial prosperity."

Harry Bruce (born 1934) has turned his hand to a remarkable variety of writing tasks, always with a felicitous style that sets him apart. He has been an editor or staff writer at Maclean's, Saturday Night, The Star Weekly *and* Atlantic Insight, *and has published 10 books, including two collections of essays,* The Short Happy Walks of Max MacPherson *(1968) and* Movin' East *(1985). His most recent book is* Down Home: Notes of a Maritime Son *(1988). He lives in Port Shoreham, Guysborough County, Nova Scotia. This essay appeared in the July 1988 issue of* Saturday Night.

Canada wanted Confederation so badly, "she literally forced it upon the Maritimes, having actually enlisted the assistance of the Imperial Government to that end." Maritimers were citizens of the Dominion of Canada not out of choice but because Upper Canadians seduced some of their leaders, and Britain shoe-horned the region into Confederation. (On this point, even so eminent a lover of all things bright and British as Nova Scotia politician Joseph Howe complained, "Even French girls who would have no objections to being married don't like to be ravished.") But, Paterson continued, "misleading propaganda" soon led Central Canadians to believe a monstrous lie: "that, in 1867, Canada *permitted* Nova Scotia and New Brunswick to join her, and that, ever since, she has found these provinces a very heavy burden. In the hazy distance, beyond the blue hills of Quebec, such people see in the Maritimes a strange folk who, when not fishing or lumbering, are insistently clamouring for financial aid from the Federal Government."

Central Canada soon confirmed the worst fears of the wise herring chokers and bluenoses who'd fought Confederation. The British North America Act was supposed to have been an agreement, but Canada "speedily lost sight of her sacred obligations to the Maritimes," and "shattered sacred pledges." The most important pledge was to build the Intercolonial Railway and to run it not as a commercial line but as "a National Work" to enable Maritime goods to flow profitably into Upper Canadian markets, and to bring the foreign trade of the new nation through Maritime ports. Sir John A. Macdonald himself had promised that Ontario and Quebec would "cheerfully contribute to the utmost extent in order to make that important link without which no political connection can be complete ... Build the road and Halifax will soon become one of the great emporiums of the world. All the great resources of the West will soon come over the immense railways of Canada to the bosom of your harbour."

Later generations of Upper Canadians, however, betrayed Macdonald's dream by insisting that "the Maritimes should be compelled to pay freight rates that would render the Intercolonial a commercial success ... During the [First World War], and under the plea of patriotism and the need of money, these Confederation rights were wholly cancelled. Freight rates that discriminated against the Maritimes were established; and finally, the old ICR ceased to exist as such." There were other injustices, and one of them was the lie that the Maritimes were indebted to the rest of Canada.

Paterson insisted the exact opposite was the truth, that the Maritimes had contributed millions more to "the Confederation Scheme" than they'd ever received from it; that the feds had pumped tens of millions of Maritimers' dollars into projects from Quebec to British Columbia, while allowing Down Home industries to die; and that Maritimers had been forced to help finance transportation improvements, such as the St. Lawrence Seaway, that spelled their own economic ruin. "The obvious unfairness of this is pathetic," Paterson wrote, and he rolled on from there to a resounding summary of grievances:

"The people of the Maritimes have been compelled to the conclusion that, for many years, there has been continued, consistent action to sacrifice their industrial and commercial future for the benefit of the middle provinces which, by reason of their financial and political dominance, have most certainly achieved that end.

"As a result, Maritime industries have languished and died, so that most of the present Maritime consumption of industrial products emanates from the tariff-protected factories of Central Canada. The shattering of Confederation pledges, upon the inviolate fulfilment of which the Maritimes innocently confided, is accomplishing their economic strangulation. The whole tragic circumstance is the direct outcome of a self-centered disregard for the sacred interests of three Provinces by the political dominance of Central Canadian financial and commercial interest."

Ploughing through "The True Story of Confederation," I gathered Paterson had not written it to any deadline *The Chronicle-Herald* had imposed. The newspaper acknowledged the series was written by the *late* Alexander P. Paterson, but neglected to say when. Clues lie in the text. It appears that, when *The Chronicle-Herald* published his exposé in 1977, roughly half a century had passed since he had written it. I found this weird. The job of a newspaper, I thought, was to tell what happened yesterday or this morning, not to trot out long-winded opinions that a dead man had written back when older Maritimers could still remember flags at half-mast on the first Dominion Day. But the longer I would live in the Maritimes the better I would understand that, when it comes to the treacherous nature of Upper Canadian power, the news is never old.

Many Maritimers still blame the betrayals that followed the Confederation deal for the flight of their people and capital, the collapse of their industries, the feebleness of their economy, and the fact that their social services are poorer and their pay cheques smaller than those other Canadians get. They know they live in a dependent colony of the Canadian empire, and that their plight is a direct result of a gigantic double-cross.

It is as though X had sold a house to Y, granting Y a long-term mortgage. Y moved into the house, then quit making mortgage payments. X was too weak to force payment, or to dislodge Y, and was therefore reduced to endless begging at what had once been his own door. After a century of this, big Y sees little X as a whiner who can be safely ignored. The Atlantic provinces, Premier Frank Moores of Newfoundland said in 1978, remain "the only region in Canada that hasn't the affluence to do much else but be indignant." And to remind Ottawa, decade after decade after decade, of old and broken promises.

For the first 70-odd years of Confederation, the forgotten promises were not part of a master plan to torpedo the Maritimes. The federal government prompted immigration to settle the West, but it did not deliberately arrange Canada's population growth so that it would sap the Maritimes' influence in Parliament. Central Canadian greed and competitiveness undermined the Down Home economy, but no one specifically orchestrated them for the destruction of East Coast industry. With the arrival of the Second World War, however, came a federal-government policy not just to let the Maritimes slide backwards but to shove them backwards. The villain in this scheme, from a Maritimes view, was the American-born minister of Munitions and Supply, C.D. Howe.

He is often celebrated as the strong man who put Canadian industry on a war footing, and reconstructed the country's postwar economy. But he was so determined to fatten Central Canadian industry with government money, while starving Maritime industry, that he did so even at the cost of bungling the war effort. One historian, Ernest R. Forbes, writing in the journal *Acadiensis*, has described part of the dismal story.

The Dominion Steel and Coal Corporation was the largest industrial employer in the Maritimes, and one of Canada's "big three" steel producers. The other two were the Steel Company of Canada and Algoma Steel. While granting these two Ontario firms huge subsidies to modernize and build new mills, the feds were so tightfisted with DOSCO that its president, Arthur Cross, complained to Howe in 1941 that it was "the only primary steel producer in this country which is receiving no government assistance." Cross suspected Howe's team had "deliberately formulated a policy which is bound to discriminate against the postwar future of this corporation and in favour of its Central Canadian competitors."

As Howe's gang concentrated steel making, shipbuilding, and even the repair of fighting vessels in Central Canada, skilled workers flowed inland from the Maritimes. Having caused a labor shortage in the Maritimes, the feds now used it as an excuse not to bolster Maritime war industries. Another excuse was "distance." But it wasn't the Maritimes that were distant from the battle of the North Atlantic, it was Central Canada. Howe's anti-Maritime bias, along with the political clout of Montreal, forced warships to go for repairs not to convoy headquarters in Halifax but all the way up the St. Lawrence. "The navy," Forbes wrote, "was reduced to the desperate expedients of leaving some vessels frozen in St. Lawrence ports for the winter, routing others to British Columbia, and sending still others on the dubious gamble of breaking into refit schedules at American ports."

Some argue that Canada's failure to set up an efficient, strategically located repair center turned the Canadian navy into a bystander, while British escorts beat the Nazis on the North Atlantic. As early as 1940, British naval authorities objected to Canada's policy of building vessels at inland yards. Ice barred the new ships from the ocean for almost half the year, and winter damaged them even before they could be launched. Moreover, the British specifically asked Ottawa to build a decent repair center at Halifax, with graving docks for their biggest vessels. "The Americans, too, were surprised by Canadian nonchalance at the state of their repair facilities," Forbes wrote. U.S. investigators surveyed the port of Halifax, and told their government to "send tugboats to Halifax to rescue 'vessels of all nationalities ... detained for an unreasonable length of time in Canadian waters awaiting repairs.'" The U.S. survey irritated Howe, but it did not get Halifax the repair center the Allies needed.

If Maritime industry did not draw its share of government investment during arrangements for war, neither did it draw it during arrangements for peace. In 1944, Howe took charge of the new Department of Reconstruction, which made sure government assistance went only to profitable companies that showed promise of a successful transition to peacetime production. By 1 July 1945, 5% of the funds had gone to the six maritime and prairie provinces; Ontario had received 48%, Quebec 32, and British Columbia 15. It wasn't the Maritimes who'd hogged the blessings of the plump federal teat, it was Central Canada.

Maritime industries, such as DOSCO, survived the war but, thanks to the government-fueled expansion and modernization of Ontario competitors, found themselves badly weakened in the market place. Over the next quarter-century, DOSCO would be taken over by British interests, milked of its capital, and dismantled. Forbes concluded that, in the long run, the impact of the government's wartime policies on the Maritimes was negative.

Howe was so antagonistic to DOSCO that in 1944 he told his steel controllers to use it "to the minimum extent possible, even if we have to buy the steel from the United States." He had close ties with Sir James Dunn, the head of Algoma Steel, and Dunn's empire collected more than 80% of the government's direct wartime grants to the steel industry. Dunn buttressed the powerful lobby on behalf of Great Lakes ports with his own anti-DOSCO lobby, and touted the concentration of Canadian manufacturing on the shores of the Great Lakes. Howe was the M.P. for Port Arthur, and had earned much of his substantial private fortune by building grain elevators on the lakes. He shared the vision of "a centralized manufacturing complex closely integrated with the United States"; but the vision, Forbes continued, "apparently did not include the Maritimes in any significant role."

Some Maritime grievances never die. During debate over a jump in railway freight rates in 1975, the former premier of Nova Scotia, G.I. Smith, sounded exactly like Alexander P. Paterson half a century earlier: "Our railways are not simply commercial enterprises. They were a basic instrument of national policy in creating this country." Both the violation of that national policy and the preservation of another national policy, guaranteeing tariff protection of Central Canada, had enriched the center and impoverished the east: "Between 1956 and 1965 ... Nova Scotians paid more than $18 million to support the protection policy, on cars alone. There are similar examples in scores of fields, such as electrical appliances, industrial machinery, chemicals."

While richer provinces feel that the money flowing from them, through the federal government, to the Maritimes proves their generosity, Maritimers have never regarded federal aid as charity. They see federal grants as neither hand-outs, nor some sort of dole, but as rights, and as inadequate payment on the tremendous debt Canada owed them for having sacrificed Down Home interests to Toronto and Montreal. "I find something quite unreal about the Bay Street friends of mine who say the Atlantic provinces are a bottomless pit of federal funding," Donald Jamieson said in 1986. "There is no necessity for any underdeveloped or disadvantaged part of this country to feel like some kind of mendicant when it starts looking for benefits from the government in Ottawa." An eloquent Newfoundland politician who had served as Canada's minister for external affairs, Jamieson spoke for four provinces when he added, "The next time, I say, don't bail out the banks, bail out Atlantic Canada." Nothing annoys Maritimers more than the hoary notion that they are the alms-seekers of Canada. "Too often ... we are stereotyped as recipients, as needers rather than givers," Premier John Buchanan of Nova Scotia told the Canadian Club in Toronto in 1979, "as part of the baggage of Confederation." The idea is particularly repulsive in light of the billions the feds have poured into Central Canadian benefits such as the St. Lawrence Seaway, the Mirabel Airport boondoggle, fast trains on the Windsor-Montreal corridor, and assorted subsidies and tax breaks for auto plants, aircraft factories, paper mills, and other industries sprinkled about southern Ontario and Quebec.

For the image of the Maritimes as the leeches of Confederation, their people have blamed Upper Canadian propagandists. "Unfortunately," Paterson wrote, "Central Canadian publications have teemed with just such singularly unfair mis-statements." Thus, Upper Canada was guilty not only of betraying the Maritimes but of slandering them as well. Like other evil forces in the world, Upper Canada distorted history to promote its own imperialism.

If all Maritimers feel in their bones that Central Canadians have a distorted view of them, experts in Maritime history have begun to document the distortions. They've taken to exposing the way Canada's best-known historians twist the Maritimes story while jamming it into the national story. J.M. Bumsted, for instance, analyzed the picture of Prince Edward Island at Confederation, as it appeared in works by W.L. Morton, D.G. Creighton, and P.B. Waite. Lumping together descriptions by these national historians, one learns that Islanders were complacent, yet somehow bitter, feuding, and violent. They were isolated, parochial, narrow-minded, self-obsessed, smugly self-sufficient, and so immersed in a weird kind of local patriotism that they were incapable of larger loyalties. In the grand national perspective, Islanders were simply too stupid to recognize their glorious chance to join Confederation.

But Island ships were sailing round the world, Island farm products had good markets in the United States, and Island manufacturing was mushrooming. As Bumsted wrote, "The self-sufficient attitude of the Island's politicians in the Confederation debates, therefore, had a sound basis in reality." Moreover, feelings of local patriotism "were not, as the national historians would suggest, curious, but legitimate responses to circumstances." Big-shot historians trained west of the Maritimes couldn't see this. They didn't know enough.

Maritime scholars repeatedly complain that general histories and textbooks about Canada betray disgraceful ignorance about the region. Before writing about the Maritimes, Central Canadian historians often neglect to read even the easily available research by East Coast scholars. The historian John G. Reid assessed nine recent books about Canadian history. He found most gave short shrift to the Maritimes, and some made stupendous mistakes about the most elementary facts in the region's history. Discussing *The Structure of Canadian History* by J.L. Finlay and D.N. Sprague (1984), Reid wrote, "The figure of 1,000 for the Acadian population at the time of the conquest ... is a serious underestimate. Was the population in the Maritime colonies in the 1830s really 'extremely homogeneous by class and ethnicity'? Many regional scholars would disagree with such a sweeping assertion." They would also disagree with almost every sentence of the summary of Acadian history that Desmond Morton offered in *A Short History of Canada* (1983):

"Most Acadians were heirs of the few French who had remained in the area when Champlain had chosen to move up the St. Lawrence. Tossed, for a few turbulent years, between French adventurers and New England pirates, the Acadians were then left to themselves for a century. They learned to dyke the rich bottom land of the Minas Basin against the Fundy tides. In 1713, when the Treaty of Utrecht transferred Acadia to the British, perhaps sixteen hundred Acadians were included. It seemed to make no difference to them."

Reid, however, argued that the Acadians were *not* heirs of Champlain's clonists but descendants of French families who arrived years after Champlain had gone; that the Acadians were *not* left to themselves for a century but dealt regularly with both French assertions of power, and military and economic interference from New England; and that they did *not* learn their dyking skills on Minas Basin, but, decades before any settlement there, had learned them in the Annapolis Valley. Moreover, he continued, "To say that the conquest made no difference to the Acadian population ignores important and long-published evidence of postconquest migrations, demographic trends, and cultural changes ..."

But none of this was so annoying to Reid as *Twentieth Century Canada.* It was the work of five of the biggest guns among Canadian historians: J.L. Granatstein, Irving M. Abella, David J. Bercuson, R. Craig Brown, and H. Blair Neatby. Yet it offered the amazing news that, *before Confederation*, Nova Scotians were struggling "to break free of the superior power and economic strength of the Canadas." This was codswallop, and Reid skewered it: "To be sure, 'Empire Canada' was in full operation by the turn of the twentieth century, but to date its emergence before 1867 seems fanciful at best."

From *Twentieth Century Canada*, Reid reported, "We learn that 'in the Maritime Provinces the Depression made less of an impact ... only because these provinces had experienced an almost continuous depression since Confederation.' After that revelation, the region mercifully disappears from the text for a hundred or so pages." From start to finish, Reid stated, *Twentieth Century Canada* portrayed the Maritimes as a laggard and poor cousin. "To see this tired and misleading nonsense trotted out again in 1986—and by five historians of national reputation at that—is not so much infuriating as saddening."

· · · · · · · · · ·

Like the attitude of a child towards a capricious parent, the attitude of the Maritimes towards the federal government swarms with contradictions. No matter how hostile the Maritimes' opposition to granting Quebec special status within Confederation, they saw only good in the idea that they themselves should enjoy such special privileges as free trade with New England, and exclusive rights to funds from the Department of Regional Economic Expansion. No matter what wrongs Confederation imposed on them, Maritimers regard their own separatists as kooks and cranks. No matter how callously Ottawa treats the Maritimes, and no matter how vigorous the lip service their politicians and newspapers pay to the virtues of provincial autonomy and self-reliance, the region remains Canada's staunchest supporter of strong central government.

The federal government may never have shared the wealth fairly, but at least it knows that sharing the wealth is part of its duty. One recent survey indicated that 80 to 90% of Maritimers and Newfoundlanders felt Confederation had been good for Atlantic Canada. "Only Ottawa Can Turn the Tide," declared an editorial in the Moncton *Times* in 1970. "Despite all their well-worn grievances," Maritimer Carman Miller wrote in 1982, "the Atlantic provinces editorial writers remain firmly wedded to the Canadian option, if only because existing economic exigencies seem to make it the best bargain available."

That's why the Halifax *Chronicle-Herald* was suspicious of the Meech Lake accord: "For Nova Scotia, the most serious aspect is its general concession to the rising power of the provinces ... Nova Scotia and its sister Atlantic provinces, so dependent on transfer payments from Ottawa, must be concerned about the erosion of federal power. As frustrated as we sometimes are by the federal government's insensitivity to the region, most Atlantic Canadians would rather appeal to Ottawa in times of need than to provincial premiers in Victoria or Toronto."

No one understood this unpalatable line of reasoning better than Alex Campbell when he was premier of Prince Edward Island. If Quebec pulled out of Canada, Campbell told me in 1978, "We'd be alone on the Atlantic coast, and we're *not* self-sufficient. Ever since Confederation, there's been a decline in our self-sufficiency. We've allowed the region to become a market of Central Canada. You know, forty per cent of all the personal income in Prince Edward Island comes directly from the federal government. We'd be without that. The population of the Atlantic provinces would drop by at least half, and you know who'd leave first. The workforce, and the entrepreneurs. We'd be left with the very young and the very old. We'd face half a century of doubt and uncertainty. Even united as an Atlantic nation, it would take us fifty years to turn things around and get back just to where we are right now."

· · · · · · · · · ·

Resentment against Central Canada and its selfish manipulation of the federal government is as natural to Maritimers as muddy roads near Montague, P.E.I., or a storm-stayed basketball team at Campbellton, N.B. Indeed, it's part of the regional identity, just as bitching about the CBC is part of the national identity. It expresses itself not only when a federal shipbuilding job goes to Sorel, Que., rather than Saint John, not only when a federal contract for the maintenance of fighter planes goes to Montreal rather than Halifax, not only when tens of millions of federal dollars go into jazzing up the Toronto waterfront while wharves rot throughout the Maritimes, but also in every field from transportation to culture to sports:

When a blizzard imprisons ferry boats at Cape Tormentine, N.B., any Prince Edward Islander with an ounce of constitutional knowledge can tell you that, for at least the 3,000th time, Canada has reneged on her ancient pledge to the Garden of the Gulf. The Island sourly joined Confederation in 1873 and, to sweeten the deal, hadn't Canada promised "efficient steam service" to the "mainland of the Dominion, winter and summer, thus placing the Island in continuous communication with ... the railway systems of the Dominion"?

When the Canada Council refuses grants to a Maritime dance company, the troupe complains that this is not because its performances are less than excellent but because a narrow-minded clique in Upper Canada controls the council's funding, and funnels the money to friends up there.

When the Canadian Intercollegiate Athletic Union chooses a fullback from Ontario as the most valuable college player in Canada, rather than a star tailback at Acadia University, a Halifax sportswriter says the CIAU has "once again snubbed its nose" at Maritime football. Moreover, "this latest snub by the CIAU" may not be as old as Confederation, but it is certainly "nothing new." The superior player from Acadia is too classy to complain, "But deep down, it has to hurt. Just as the latest slap in the face must hurt all the players, coaches and fans in the Atlantic Provinces."

Such items are not exceptional. They're typical of a strain of anger and resignation about the Maritimes' status in Canada that's as routine in the regional press as weather reports and the funnies. But even worse than snubs and injustices is the feeling that Canada has forgotten the Maritimes, and acts as though they've disappeared under the ocean. When Albertans flaunted bumper stickers saying, "Let the eastern bastards freeze in the dark," it didn't comfort Maritimers that the target was Ontario, because that meant western- ers didn't even know where the *real* east was. The real east was Down Home, and its people would rather be bastards than nobodies. Nothing arouses apoplectic editorials in Maritime newspapers more surely than a description of a "coast-to-coast" trip that starts in Montreal and ends in Victoria, or fed- eral-government travel bumph that gives short, inaccurate shrift to the East Coast.

The Maritimes have long felt that Ottawa's attitude towards them has been "out of sight, out of mind," and they dislike the old feeling. They also dislike the Upper Canadian notion that because they're far from Toronto they are, by definition, isolated. Halifax was an international port when Toronto was a Mississauga encampment. The Maritimes built much of their early economy on world trade, and each summer their offspring still flood back Down Home from distant cities. You won't find many spots in the Maritimes more out of the way than Port Shoreham, where I write in the par- lor at The Place, and if you were to zip through it on your way to Cape Breton, you might naturally assume it was as insular as a community could be. You'd be wrong, and in *Saturday Night* 30 years ago my father explained why. Describing a midsummer gathering in another parlor, at the second farmhouse up the road, he wrote:

"For here were men and women from Alberta, from Saskatchewan, from Ontario, from California and Massachusetts, and what they had to talk about was people. The expatriates, home for a week or a summer or a day, must bring themselves abreast of Time as measured by deaths and marriages, births and departures. The stay-at-homes must hear about others who had gone away ... The thought that occurred to me was that things hadn't changed. When I was small, the talk in our parlour on a Sunday would often as not be about events in Somerville or Lynn or Glou'ster. Mother and father had lived in the States before I was born ... Their circle of acquaintance took in not only a local radius of a dozen miles, but swept outward to include brothers and sisters, sons and cousins, who had gone away. In as sense the neighbourhood we lived in was a neighbourhood that reached the southern borders of New England, and far to the west and east and south and north."

• • • • • • • • • •

Many Maritimers believe it's not they who are parochial but Torontonians. Born in Cape Breton, raised in Halifax, and celebrated everywhere as a pioneer of Canlit, Hugh MacLennan once told me he endorsed his fellow novelist Robertson Davies' opinion of Toronto: "Rob says 'a Toronto audience won't laugh at a joke unless they've got a written guarantee that it's already been laughed at in New York.' They're a terribly narrow, provincial people. Nova Scotians aren't like that." MacLennan, it's true, had never forgiven Toronto critics for crucifying his novel *Return of the Sphinx*, but even so, those who describe the city as provincial have a point. Toronto wraps her own in a careering ball of energy, ambition, desire, and images of their own excellence. A cloud of self-interest insulates the ball and prevents Torontonians from grasping that, all across Canada, there are other spheres in which millions of Canadians are very much in touch with everything that's important to them. "Oh, yeah, I forgot," a Toronto newspaper editor told me by phone. "You're so out of touch down there, aren't you?" While watching the seagulls glide over Chedabucto Bay, I had confessed to him that I knew nothing about an impending strike at his paper. His response griped me a bit. What did he know about the oil rigs abandoning offshore exploration, or pollution in Halifax harbor, or the renovation of the Saint John waterfront? What did anyone in that self-satisfied, self-absorbed, self-mesmerized city know about the latest blow to the steel plant in Sydney? Who, really, was out of touch? And with what? Who in the hell was Toronto to define for Port Shoreham the things with which it was important to be in touch? One night I poured another rum for a fierce and native son of the Nova Scotian soil, and I told him about all this, and he said, "My God, Harry, you're becoming a Maritimer."

About Home
CAROLYN SMART

. . . .

A number of years ago I attended a poetry reading at Harbourfront, in Toronto. The place was packed: the headliner for the evening was Czeslaw Milosz who had just been announced as the winner of the Nobel Prize for Literature. And as usual, the headliner was slotted for the end of the evening. Before he began there were two previous readers, and the first was a man named Adrian Henri, described in the press as a Liverpool poet. Adrian is probably best known for his contributions to a Penguin paperback called *The Mersey Sound* which sold millions of copies in the 1960s. The timing was right for three Liverpool poets. Incidentally they *were* friends of the Beatles. However, this is the 1980s and Adrian wasn't just reading about how he wanted to be Paul McCartney anymore, he was reading about growing up. It was so familiar to me. It seemed as if he was writing about my family too. He read a poem that night, "Autobiography Part I 1932-51," and in the break before Milosz began, I found Adrian outside in the hall, buying a drink at the bar. I asked him if that poem had been about Wallasey, where some of my first memories are from, of my grandfather with a club foot, of my granny sitting in the parlor, of the loo at the end of the garden, the smell of damp grass and the tree of Paradise, my Auntie Clarice widowed in the First War and never the same. Adrian never expected to come to Toronto, to read on the same night as the winner of the Nobel Prize, to suddenly be met by someone who also knew Wallasey, knew those long streets that angled down towards the harbor, those streets that at night looked like the docks from the air and therefore the Nazis bombed as much as they could of them night after night. To hear Adrian read that poem that night was like coming home for me, to a home I can never return to with my North American education, to a home that is probably not home at all anymore.

And that's what I want to write about here, about home, about a sense of exile from one's home, about loss and memory and life.

Carolyn Smart (born 1952) is a poet who lives outside Sydenham, Ontario, near Kingston. Her third collection of verse, Stoning the Moon, *was published in 1986. *About Home *is taken from the March 1988 issue of* Quarry, *a literary quarterly.*

My mother's name was Jane Van Tress. She was born in Paris to American parents who traveled so extensively that she attended 14 different public schools before Grade Nine. During the Second World War she began to work as a textiles expert for the British Embassy in Washington, met my father, married him in Washington and moved to England. She had two children there, moved to Canada, lived in Mexico for a while, eventually died in Canada at the age of 57.

My father was born in Wallasey, moved to the States when he was 22 because he had won a Commonwealth scholarship to study at Harvard, moved to Canada a few years later to teach at the University of Saskatchewan in Saskatoon, moved to Washington, D.C., to work for the British Embassy during the war, met my mother, moved back to southern England, and from there to Ottawa as a diplomat, bringing his family with him. His daughters at 10 and six did not really understand what he meant the day he told us in the car that we were going to move to Canada, if we wanted to. Of course we agreed. A couple of years before I had thought Switzerland was a chocolate bar. What did I know at six about exile? What did any of us know? So we went, and from there, like good little diplomat's children, we went back to boarding school in England and finally settled down to high school in Toronto after my father resigned from the diplomatic service and became a merchant banker on Bay Street.

My mother had what they call a transatlantic accent, meaning wherever she was her accent conformed to the norm. My father always sounded more British, although early on in life he had made sure his northern Wallasey accent was lost. He even changed his name from a good northern Ted Smart to a more affluent-sounding Angus Smart. It was only towards the end of his life that he began to admit, at first reluctantly, but eventually with fondness, that he was a northern lad. He'd even use a lot of the slang he'd grown up with, not quite Liverpool scouse, as Wallasey had always been proudly across the water from Liverpool, across the Mersey River, a little removed but close enough. I remember riding the ferry 'cross the Mersey with my granny. They don't operate anymore. Now you go by tunnel under the water, either by car or train.

Immigration: what a concept. It was all a barrel of laughs for my sister and me: first, the boat train from London to Southampton, then boarding the *Queen Elizabeth* at the docks—at that time there was nothing like the name *QE1* or even *QE2*. There *was* no *QE2* then. But then there was the *Queen Mary* and there was the *Queen Elizabeth* and they were glorious boats. We sailed into New York harbor past the Statue of Liberty, with the tug boats all around the hull shooting jets of water into the air as a greeting. To me this was not just some huge foreign city but it was also my mother's hometown, where her remaining family lived, where some of her fondest memories grew from.

And she seemed to know it so well. We had such fun there. After a few days we got on a train which took us up to Montreal, and then someone picked us up there and drove us to Ottawa. We hadn't a house to live in for a while, so we stayed at an apartment hotel. It was about 20 below in my first December in Canada. We got lost one day going for a walk outside. None of us was speaking, I remember feeling very afraid, rootless. I think we all did. I lived in Ottawa for five years, moving in the diplomatic corps circles. It was a group of exiles all together, a pack of like-minded souls who every three years got what was known as "home leave," meaning you could go back to the place you started from and stay for a couple of months, paid for by the government. We'd go back to England, live in a furnished apartment. My parents would travel on the continent. My sister and I would stay with Granny and Grandpa, ride the double deckers, eat icelollies on the ferry.

By the time I was sent to boarding school on the coast of Sussex, I had learned to write in a North American script, I was quite fluent in French, I was enamored of the Kennedys. In England I was taught to write a different way, I forgot my French so as not to appear different, I achieved an English accent again within two months. When Kennedy was assassinated I was the expert in the school. By the end of the year I felt totally British. Then I was called back to Canada and had to start all over again. In high school I was teased for my accent, my handwriting was judged unacceptable, I was way behind scholastically. I discovered the Beatles and held on to them for dear life all through high school. At the same time my North American education was truly sinking in: I discovered hockey—Frank Mahovolich, Dave Keon, Mike Walton—my other idols. I watched *Ed Sullivan* and *Bonanza, 77 Sunset Strip* and *Hawaiian Eye.* At night I'd lie in bed with my transistor radio and listen to the Motown stations from Detroit. As my friends in England were encouraged to leave school and attend cooking classes and secretarial courses, we were encouraged to attend university and make a career for ourselves. The people I was still in touch with from boarding school married quite early and moved all over the world. I stayed put in Toronto, went through university, started work in publishing, started to write and eventually to publish.

But I went back to England after high school by myself for the summer, feeling somehow that I had to see it again and make some kind of choice. I remember the sight of the ground just before landing at Heathrow. As the clouds parted and I could see the hedgerows and those giant trees, tears came to my eyes. I knew it was home. I went to visit the Beatles' houses, I spent lots of time in the village of my childhood, I went up north to Wallasey to stay with my aunt and uncle, and acted like the absurd teenager I must have been at 17, eating nothing but grilled cheese on crackers and always nipping out for a smoke. But they put up with me and have since forgiven me, although they still tell my husband and my new friends how obnoxious I really was, just to get a laugh.

But by the end of the summer I was so enchanted with a life that I found suited my temperament, a life in a small village within easy reach of London, that I asked permission of my parents to stay for a year. Permission was denied, and unwillingly I returned to Canada to begin my studies at university. But every summer thereafter I returned to England to work in London at various jobs and to travel on the continent with money that I'd save. Still, it was different once I began university. There was a gap suddenly between my life as a student and the lives of my female friends living on their own in flats in London and working as secretaries. I read a great deal; they went out to the clubs.

I found social life very different in England suddenly, and realized it was not going to be so easy to live there after all. I had a real perception of "the upper class twits of the year" and didn't want to hang around them. No one seemed to have any political interests or an awareness of regional differences, of class barriers and divisions, of racial tension. No one had grown up with the same television news showing kids our age going off to fight in Vietnam or getting beaten up on the streets of Chicago at the Democratic convention. These were things that I'd watched sitting next to my mother who never gave up her American citizenship, who expected her daughters to become educated and traveled and sophisticated in many different ways. In England I'd watch my friends' mothers judging which boy would be a more suitable marriage partner for their little darlings.

Going into Foyle's bookshop in London, expecting the store that had a reputation for carrying more books than anywhere else in London or New York to carry just about anyone I cared to find, I noticed that they didn't carry any northern writers—no Adrian Henri in other words, although they did carry Ted Hughes. I guess they overlooked the fact that he is a Yorkshireman (after all, he's now the poet laureate). There was no Brian Patten, there was no Roger McGough, no Adrian Mitchell, no Carol Ann Duffy. Quite the opposite situation presented itself when Adrian Henri took me 'round the bookshops in Liverpool five years ago. There were no southerners on the shelves, not unless you consider T.S. Eliot an Englishman, as I guess some people do.

So—where does all this leave me? Feeling half way between two worlds, in a sense, being drawn by my emotions to England and being attracted in my intellect to North America, feeling at home in neither place. For many years I felt cheated by the fact that my father and mother chose to remove my sister and me from our home and leave us rootless. I used to feel jealous when I'd have conversations with friends in Canada who could pinpoint places where they'd spent time with their grandparents and could trace their history in that same spot continuously to the present day: a sense of personal history with traceable roots in the same land. I can't ever hope to have that experience nor can I offer that to my children. But I hope my children can offer it to their children, if that is what they wish for themselves. I've grown in the last few years to a new kind of understanding about home, and I think as my confidence has grown in my work, in my poetry, I feel I have placed my sense of home in that, in poems. In a way I guess I could say home is my head, my imagination. My poetry offers me a chronology and a journal of my creative life and intellectual growth in a way nothing else can approach. I can trace the threads of my upbringing and the various places I've lived with their accompanying influences: whether it be a description of the rain in Liverpool, the vision of an Aztec dancer in a cathedral in Mexico City, or the strange sight of antique crop dusting airplanes flying over our house near Sydenham, Ont.

My particular style of writing is influenced by both North American and British work, although on the whole I'd say my rhythm, my line lengths and my rather open-ended current style tends more towards North American poetry than British, which I find unnecessarily formal at times.

A contemporary British poet, Carol Ann Duffy, once told me that Canadians were always writing about their grandparents. She wondered if on the whole they didn't really know who they were. Carol Ann has never been interested in writing her own family history in the same way as I might be, perhaps, because she has remained in the country of her ancestors. She doesn't need to "pay back that sacred debt," as Katharine Mansfield would put it. But home is not only in my writing, it is also in my children, my husband. Home is the family and without the support of my family I would lack the courage to continue with much of the work that I do. Without love it would be much more terrifying to write of anger; without children I would find it more difficult to face the future.

In the Introduction to *Juno and the Paycock*, Sean O'Casey stated, "In order to write, you must be free. In order to be free you must smash three things, faith, family and fatherland, not necessarily in that order." Although in many ways I'm glad I don't have the same perception, I perceive some truth in this statement. Many other writers feel that same way.

Katharine Mansfield was born in Wellington, N.Z., in 1888. At the age of 14 she began school in England and was reluctant to return to New Zealand. When she did return, she was confirmed in her feeling that her own country could not offer the kind of life she wished to lead. Two years later she talked her parents into allowing her to live in London and pursue her ambition to be a writer. In a journal entry of 22 January 1916, shortly after the death of her brother Leslie in the First World War, she wrote:

Now, really, what is it that I do want to write? Now—now I want to write about my own country. Yes, I want to write about my own country till I simply exhaust my store. Not only because it is 'a sacred debt' that I pay to my country because my brother and I were born there, but also because in my thoughts I range with him over all the remembered places. I am never far away from them. I long to renew them in writing.

Ah the people—the people we loved there—of them, too, I want to write. Another 'debt of love': Oh, I want for one moment to make our undiscovered country leap into the eyes of the Old World. It must be mysterious, as though floating, it must take the breath.

Sylvia Plath originally went to Cambridge on a Fulbright scholarship, returned to the United States and then back to England with her husband Ted Hughes for the birth of their first child. Even after the break-up of her marriage, she chose to stay in England, and in a letter to her mother dated 4 February 1963, she stated:

I have absolutely no desire ever to return to America. Not now, anyway. I have my beautiful country house, the car, and London is the one city in the world I'd like to live in with its fine doctors, nice neighbours, parks, theatres, and the *BBC*. There is nothing like the BBC in America—over there they do not publish my stuff as they do here, poems and novels.

Seven days later she committed suicide, working on what she felt were her finest poems, as well as a novel that Ted Hughes later destroyed.

One of the major differences between what happened to Mansfield, and Plath, and what happened to me is that *they* chose to leave the countries of their births as adults and move to places that they considered more conducive to their chosen work. For me as a child there was no choice involved. As an adult rethinking my future there didn't seem to be any choice either—I was too North American to be comfortable living in English society, yet there is too much of England in me to feel as if Canada is my homeland.

Over the years I've lived in this country I've moved 15 times. Originally I settled in Ottawa, then Toronto (following boarding school in England), then Winnipeg, back to Ottawa, back to Toronto, to Elginburg and finally to Sydenham where I now live, about 30 kilometers from Kingston. In an attempt to make a home for myself I have become very attached to particular places and spaces where I've lived. One of my strongest connections (and perhaps my closest physical connection with this country) is with the Gatineau Hills outside of Ottawa/Hull where my parents rented a cottage for two years when I was nine and 10. The smell of the pines, the mixture of deciduous trees and evergreens, the rocky landscape surrounding the clear lakes is the Canada I carry in my memory, the part that I miss when I am abroad or in unfamiliar surroundings. And for these reasons I am always stunned to find these landmarks changed, the houses torn down, the vista altered, as if it is a personal attack on my history, a robbery from my experience. The house we rented when I was a child, where the novelist Elizabeth Smart grew up (unrelated to me, unfortunately), has been torn down now, and to visit the spot you would never know there had ever been a house or a vibrant series of lives lived there.

My attraction for the Shield country, that mixture of rock and water and pine, has led me indirectly to Portland Township where I live now—poor farming land but visually stunning. If I close my eyes I can smell the same warm smell of pine, feel the same kinds of breezes off the water, have a sense of connection with this land, this country.

The poet and novelist Lawrence Durrell offers a complex and fascinating personal history of exile. An Irishman born in India, Durrell was the third generation of his family to be born there. When he was sent to school in England at the age of 12, neither his mother nor his father had ever seen England. Yet Durrell stayed on in England until his schooling was complete and went on to spend the next 20 years in various Mediterranean countries (Greece, Egypt, and Yugoslavia) before finally settling in France. In an interview with Marc Alyn that took place in 1970, Durrell had this to say about his childhood in India:

I am, and I remain, an expatriate. That vague sense of exile has never quite left me. But at the same time it has meant that I can feel at ease anywhere, given a minimum of sunshine. The expatriate carries his country within him, inside him: everywhere belongs to him, because he belongs nowhere.

I have felt increasingly as I grew into adulthood that in many ways my parents had given me a gift of adaptability by the life they offered us, the sense of rootlessness my sister and I share.

Hamilton As It Should Be
ELLIOTT HALPERN

. . . .

I.

In which Y. bares his soul of steel in a foreign city, & no one gets to eat dinner.

Things got crazy in a sedate West Hollywood restaurant the other day. The three diners were just recovering from the waiter's recitation of the specials, coming out of their defensive postures, stretching neck muscles and dabbing their foreheads with spritzer.

The L.A. entertainment lawyer asked Y., the newly arrived visitor, where he came from in Canada.

"Hamilton."

Y.'s Australian-born hostess tried to interject, but Y. cut her off, again addressing himself to the lawyer.

"I'm from Hamilton."

The lawyer nodded. "Yes, a suburb of Toronto."

"No, it's not."

The lawyer had grown up in Rochester and had often driven to Toronto. Surely Hamilton was the smelly suburb on the western flank of the tidy metropolis.

Y. hung on. "It's not a suburb, it's a city. Hamilton's a city!"

And then he began to rave.

"Why is Toronto so rich? Toronto doesn't make anything, at least nothing

Elliott Halpern was born in the city he writes about (in 1956) and grew up in its West End. He studied law at the University of Ottawa and was called to the bar but is now a screenwriter and film producer in Toronto and an editor-at-large of The Idler, *where this piece first appeared (September-October 1988).*

you can see. Where does all the cash come from?"

Heads turned in the quiet restaurant. The hostess's cheeks were burning as her eyes met the lawyer's. His sheepish grin said, It's not your fault, who could have known?

The torrent continued. "But Hamilton. Hamilton makes something. When times are good, you can *see* the reason, you can hold it in your hands. Steel. The product of the honest labor of working men. Something useful. Something the world needs. Something to be proud of."

The waiter approached, but passed on. The lawyer gestured wildly. The hostess knew it was pointless; clearly, Y.'s behavior had been observed. An Angeleno knows a madman when he sees him. The waiter would never come now.

"A suburb of Toronto! Thank God no! Toronto's soft and flabby and smug. Hamilton's tough. It's got serious Mob. *Gangsters.* None of this new-generation Harvard B. School we're-investment-bankers-now, riding around town in dude jeeps. But then Toronto doesn't have the North End. In the North End, the bosses have the guts to wear Brylcreem. They're the real thing, Blue Stratos men in shiny blue serge suits and handmade winkle-pickers. They always 'pack.' They don't have PR guys to deal with the press, you know, guys who are always saying: 'Mr. G********s resents the recent suggestions in the press—.' Hamilton bosses deal with reporters personally: 'Hey Face! You! Get out a here with that camera before I make you eat it.' And they're modest. They always tell you they earn their living buying the produce for the family grocery store. They know fruit. The Buffalo people started to get a little embarrassed, tried to bring in some new blood, but the old ways are best.

"It's a football town. Even the buses are yellow and black, the team colors. The team's made up of real heroes, the best. They play for the City, not money. Hamilton's the cheapest team in the league and proud of it. The players are loyal. They're not just overpaid bums like the Argonauts who retreat south to their homes at the end of the season and disappear for good after two. Torontonians have their favorite NFL team. Hamiltonians don't give a shit about the NFL. How can you adopt another city? Tiger-Cats move their families to the City, start steak houses, sell insurance, wrestle, anything to stay in Hamilton. They whip those Toronto bums every Labor Day. What do Torontonians know about *Labor Day*? That game is more important to Hamilton than the Grey Cup. It's an annual reminder of what every Hamiltonian knows: Money never motivated anyone, love of your city does."

"Just let it run its course," whispered the hostess to the lawyer.

Y. didn't notice.

"Civic Stadium, where they play the game, is in the East End. So are the steel mills. The East End is the soul of Hamilton. Every game day, East Enders open their driveways and lawns to the rest of the City, they make parking for everyone. East Enders really follow city politics. They've got the goods on all the politicians. But they really loved John Munro. They used to call him Johnny Mun-ro, like he was an honorary Italian or something. They love talking about old scandals. City Hall was so corrupt, its marble facing began falling off; the first white slab took out a visiting reeve. East Enders have a strong sense of public duty; the election of school board trustees is serious business. In Toronto, only real estate developers give a damn about city politics; there's no civic-mindedness, just the yip-yap of selfish tenants.

"Do you remember the Mackenzie Brothers, the Great White North? Remember the slang? 'Hey, hoser'? That's pure Hamilton. *Hosebag, hoser, hosero*. Both those guys used to live in Steeltown. But they only touched the surface. They never talked about 'shooting the boots' in a fight: 'He was really pissed off, shot both boots.'

"You called Hamilton 'smelly.' Well what do you know, watching the City pass from the Skyway as you drive by? 'Verdant mountain and sparkling bay,' to quote a local poet. The best natural harbor in the Province, the Hong Kong of Lake Ontario. Hamiltonians aren't scared of a little pollution. They have a 'fuck-off' attitude about it. If you're stupid enough to go swimming in the bay, you get what you deserve. And the stuff in the air makes for the most beautiful sunsets. Once, on Christmas Day, I remember looking out my bedroom window: the City was covered in a soft blanket of fine red dust.

"Prudhomme's was just outside town. It had live theater, restaurants, and caged monkeys. It was always burning down and being rebuilt. Fisher's Hotel on York Street was dark and mysterious; the creme de menthe glowed, lighting up your family's faces from below. The live peacocks on the grounds of Dundurn Castle looked like they needed a good hairdresser; Dundurn Castle itself looked fake. The Ontario Hospital, the 'OH,' on the Mountain brow, looked like a real medieval castle, and the insane were locked up there under real medieval conditions. On a quiet summer night, you could hear their screams waft over the City. I never heard them myself; maybe the soundproofing got better in the early '50s."

Briefly, Y. paused, as if listening for something, and the others looked hopeful. Then suddenly he sprang to his feet and began to sing in a sweet tenor:

White hot are the fires in our furnaces,
Forging a city strong,
A link uniting the nation,
Hamilton, Hamilto-on.

The Moun-tain is our refuge,
The Bay our soo-thing balm
Between them lies the City,
Hamilton, Hamilto-on.

He trailed off, leaving out the remaining 11 verses, to slump down in his chair. No one had joined in. He hadn't sung the Marseillaise, and this wasn't Rick's Cafe. It wasn't even Hanrahan's. The hostess signaled the all-clear to the waiter. It was unnecessary; the waiter was heading towards the table. Clearing her throat, the hostess said, "I think we're ready to order now."

"I'm sorry, the kitchen is closed."

The waiter withdrew a few feet to watch.

Y. looked across at his hostess. She hissed at him: "*You* never lived in the East End, you ungrateful little shit. You grew up in Westdale, a *suburb* of Hamilton. Didn't you? Didn't you?"

Y. put up little resistance. In a barely audible voice, he replied, "The West End, not Westdale."

"Same diff, wanker," she spat. "Westdale, West End. Same soft middle-class neighborhoods, tough guy. And you stopped following the Ti-Cats when Faloney retired and Zuger replaced him as quarterback in '64."

It wasn't just me, Y. wanted to say, no one could relate to Zuger.

The hostess was unrelenting: "And you left when you were 14. What do you know about Hamilton? You've been living in Toronto most of your life."

Y. rubbed his eyes. Zuger, Faloney? Had she really said all that? She's Australian, how could she know? He blinked and looked at her again. Her face was all care and concern. So was the waiter's. Y. concluded that he had been hallucinating. Anyhow, she was right.

The lawyer loudly cleared his throat, what in Hamilton would be called horking. Here, it was a demand for an apology.

"Sorry," said Y., "must be jet lag."

A week later, on the plane back, Y. closed his eyes and began to think.

II.

In which Y. crosses a continent, trying to recall where things were & how they got there.

What did he really know about Hamilton? It is at the western end of Lake Ontario. Toronto is 40 miles to the east. The United States is south, on the other side of the lake. The Mountain is in the opposite direction from the water, north. Simple enough.

The City has a West End, East End, North End, and—no, there is no South

End. There is the Mountain. People live there too now, but no one knows anything about them. Then there is Westdale, which isn't really part of Hamilton.

Y. grew up in the West End, not Westdale. He always made this distinction. At least the West End was Hamilton proper, not a '30s subdivision with irrationally curving streets and an ersatz village center.

Y.'s throat tightened. There was something askew in what he had just said about the Mountain. Now it is well known that the City is disorienting to strangers. If they venture off the Skyway at all, attracted by the comforting sound of York Street, they get lost in the planned maze of one-way streets. Had Y. become one of them?

He ascended to first principles.

The concern with orientation arises in earliest childhood. The sense of direction, like the other senses, is innate. Some are said to have a good sense of direction, others a poor one. Orientation is knowledge of one's place in the world: the solid basis for well-being. In the past, people were ashamed of a weak sense of direction. It was accepted that the disoriented man had a disoriented soul. The confusion of desires in such a soul was often compared to a mass of iron filings that had never been subjected to the discipline of a magnet. Now people boast of this deficiency; it is admired as a sign of creativity.

A child orients himself within his small world. As he gets older and his world grows, the challenges of orientation increase. Once he is of school age, he turns his mind to such practical problems as how to traverse the distance from school to home by a route that passes a candy store.

Soon the child confronts the difficult matter of north and south, the standard for terrestrial orientation. He learns to associate north with up and south with down. He tries to murder his sister on a hot summer-car ride Up North. His parents abandon him to a desiccated maiden aunt while they go Down South in the winter. When he examines a globe for the first time, he is not surprised to find that North is Up and South is Down.

He takes special interest in the location of his own country on the globe. It is north, above the United States. If he lives near the Great Lakes, he will observe that generally he and his fellow countrymen of that region live along the northern shores, looking down across the waters at the Americans.

The United States is a Going Down, like the Going Down of the Children of Israel into Egypt. The child develops the basis for the adult's smug feeling of moral superiority to his neighbors to the south.

If the child lives in Toronto, experience will bear out what he has learned, ensuring correct orientation and a high level of smugness. In that city, the land slopes gently south to the lakeshore. One literally goes Up North and Down South. Across the lake, south where it should be, lies the United States.

The Torontonian reacts with palpable anger to the observation that Toronto is further south than, and therefore "below" a good chunk of the United States. "No, you must be thinking of Windsor. Anyhow, head north from Toronto, you won't find the United States."

In Hamilton, too, the land slopes down to the water from the foot of the Mountain. A child of the City assumes that Up the Mountain is north and Down to the Lake is south. On the other side of the lake is the United States. One goes east to Toronto.

Then the child notices things that disturb him. One travels to the Buffalo Zoo, and rest of the States, from the East End of the City, and to Toronto from the West End. His bedroom window faces the Mountain, which must be the North; so the sun rises over the OH, to the left of his house, in the West, and sets to the right, in the East. The North End is down at the Harbor, where the missing South End should be. And the Royal Botanical Gardens have the habit of popping up everywhere, in three different cities, Hamilton, Dundas, even Burlington.

His disorientation is so complete, so deep, that he cannot articulate it. He ignores it.

The City is in a zone of transition between two different regions of forest. Tree species from the boreal and Great Lakes-St. Lawrence reach their southern limits near the City. Similarly, a number of species from the deciduous forest to the south range no further north. Even the flora grow up confused.

The confusion of Nature gave way to the confusion of man. The land at the head of Lake Ontario was once inhabited by a large Indian nation, known to the French as *Les Neutres*, and to their Huron neighbors as the Attiwandaronks, or "they are those whose language is awry."

The north shore is a steep bluff. Access to the waterfront was impossible from there, and shale slopes made development unpractical. Topography dictated that the town be on the south shore.

For almost 200 years, the center of the town remained unchanged. The original survey was finished in 1788. The lines defined Lot 14 in Concessions II and III of Township no. 8 at the head of Lake Ontario. In about 1820, Lot 14 appeared on a map as the City's townsite.

Its boundaries were the "Present Road from Queenston to Burlington" (King Street), or the "Road to Hughson Landing" (James Street), and King and Hunter Streets. The Third Concession Road is Main Street. The "Road up the Mountain to Ancaster" would become John Street. The old site near the shoreline, a low-lying plain then fretted with marshy creeks, still constitutes the center of the City.

But this means isolation. The town was not on the East-West axis of the province, Simcoe's road from York through Dundas to London (now

Dundas Street in Toronto). It was shut off from the lake by a sand barrier at the mouth of the bar (Burlington Bar or Beach Strip). The southern lakeshore was for the most part swampy, and expansion to the south, inland, was hindered by the Mountain. Expansion westwards was limited by a swampy creek. The City was on the wrong side of the lake.

Despite the apparently impossible location, the town was chosen in 1816 as the center of the newly created District of Gore, over Dundas, Crook's Hollow (above Dundas), Ancaster, and Burlington.

Dundas did not give up its dream of dominating the region. It formed the ambitious scheme of building a canal through the marsh of Coote's Paradise and a channel through the Burlington Bar, hoping to be the port at the head of the lake. In this Dundas failed; the bar was cut before the canal was completed, and Hamilton got most of the benefit. To this day, beneath the placid surface of Coote's Paradise, lies the submerged canal, a way to nowhere.

Hamilton left Dundas far behind. From 1834 to 1841, its population increased two and a half times. In 1851, there were 10,000 people; six years later 25,000. A map of 1866 entitled "Hamilton As It Should Be" has railway lines and sea routes spewing out in all directions: to Saginaw, Chicago, Sarnia, Toledo, Cleveland, Erie, Dunkirk, Buffalo, Rochester, Kingston, Toronto, and Europe.

The City's businessmen were adept at promotion, and attracted great American businesses. Heavy industries, like steel, settled in Hamilton, partly because of its access to raw materials through the Great Lakes, still more because of its extraordinary hydroelectric enterprise. The operation of the Welland Canal produced a flow of surplus water from Lake Erie through a channel to the top of the escarpment. The daring Hamiltonians bought the surplus, dropped it down the escarpment, and used the power generated to electrify the City 30 miles away.

At the beginning of the 19th century, Hamilton had four taverns. By mid-century, there were three breweries, 11 beer shops, and 65 taverns. Towards the end of the century, the OH was established as an asylum for "inebriates." They were kept away from the town, on the brow of the Mountain.

The plane descended towards Toronto. Y. resolved to go to Hamilton at once.

III.

In which Y. has an involuntary panorama.

Y. ran to the first telephone booth in the airport, and called information for the number of an old friend who still lived in the City. They hadn't spoken in almost 20 years. B. Answered the phone. Y. identified himself. Before B. could express his surprise, Y. launched into a long discourse on disorientation, ending, "I have to know: Is it just me? Do you feel the same way?"

There was a pause, followed by a nervous laugh and denial.

"Look," said Y., "can I drop by?"

"Sure. Sure."

"How do I get to your place?"

B. started to give directions, then broke down in confusion, admitting that, yes, he had always had a problem with directions, though he had never dared to think about it before. Y. decided to take the bus. As it labored towards Hamilton, Y. thought of a time his mother had made this journey down the Queen Elizabeth Way. The driver had got lost, and ended up on the service road.

The bus terminal looked the same. Y. walked to the old center of town. The turn-of-the-century buildings on King Street still surrounded the Gore, a wedge-shaped bit of park in the heart of the City. But its merchants' shops were deserted. The magnificent statue of Victoria, "Queen and Empress, Model Wife and Mother," at the James Street tip of the Gore, was covered in nylon. The glorious Palace Theater was no more. Now there was a "Palace Theater—Two Cinesex Cinemas and Peepshow." Y. fell in with the thousands of glazed-looking pedestrians going by the abandoned shops and the convoys of idling buses.

He saw the Stelco Tower in the distance. When the Steel Company of Canada built the tower, it was bright orange. At the time, the company prophesied that soon it would turn a pleasing shade of brown. For years, the City watched, anxiously searching for signs of change. The company moved its corporate offices to Toronto. Now, the prophecy had been fulfilled; the tower was a pleasing shade of brown. Perhaps the company would come back.

The crowd was still pushing Y. forward. A large suburban mall had been dropped on the corner of King and James. The Lloyd D. Jackson Square (named after a former mayor) was sucking in pedestrians by the hundreds as they passed. Y. found himself at the entrance of the mall (pronounced "maw"), then within a dark maze of discount jeans emporia and record stores, with floors a pleasing shade of brown. He came up for air on a rooftop "people place," a large empty concrete piazza.

From this vantage point, Y. saw a vast array of buildings: a theater, an art gallery with bad art, a library, a farmer's market, a convention center, an insurance tower, a bank tower, a hotel, and the Copps Coliseum (named after a former mayor). The entire city had been moved indoors and the buildings joined by a series of public squares, a level above ground, a place

to shop and attend more and more cultural events. A now hoary wunder-
kind, still claiming he had heard a cello playing while he was in his mother's
womb, conducted the "philharmonic" orchestra in the Great Hall.

The old patterns of movement had been changed out of recognition to
serve this complex. Traffic planners had developed terminal obsessions
about bi-directional flow, critical intersections, turning frictions. They had
broadened the narrow, turning York Street into a giant funnel; they had
straightened the crooked, subjugated the Mountain with slashes of road,
enlightened with the sign of the One Way. The City's grid had been
transformed from a grating over meandering streams into a great river of
cars.

In the distance, Civic Stadium (renamed Ivor Wynn, after a former
mayor) stood empty. The football team was now made up of the same
professional transients as other teams, and the owner was a Torontonian.

The number of men working in the steel mills had been drastically
reduced. Stelco had built its new works in Nanticoke, on the shore of Lake
Erie. McMaster University, once resented for being standoffish, was now the
third largest employer; it was said to have created 15,000 jobs and injected
$84 million into the economy. Ivy had detached itself from the walls.

The City had embarked on a plan to recover the waterfront, and clean up
the bay, formerly home only to the odd rubber tire.

Recently, *The Globe and Mail* had reported that the City paid James F.
Hickling Management Consultants Ltd. of Toronto to tell it that Hamilton
had "a poor self-image," that "while downtown renewal, improved cultural
facilities and events and a more diversified local economy had made the city
'more dynamic,' citizens suffer from an inferiority complex and do not
accept criticism well." In the same article, an alderman was quoted as
chirping, "We have come a long way. And we have a long way to go before
things work the way they should. The point is we have an idea of ourselves
now." For all the City's straining, self-definition had been nothing more than
self-deception. The City's new idea of itself was the idea of another city.

Life in the impossible city continues. No one will give directions anywhere. No one knows or wants to know anything about Westdale or the
Mountain, where once the OH stood. There is a general denial that there is
such a thing as the South End. People take no notice of the sun through the
heavens; all are glad of the smog that obscures it. No one really wants access
to the Bay; as long as access is difficult, they can go on believing that it is not
really down there beyond the North End. It's better to retreat into the bowels
of the Square that is no square. Other cities have "busstops," points marked
on streets, meaning Here the bus will stop. Hamilton has "bus areas": it might
stop Here, but then again it might stop over There.

IV.

In which Y. returns to Toronto, is no longer the swaggering Hamiltonian in the decadent Cosmopolis, just doesn't have it in him any more, & lives in fear someone will call him on his West End origins again.

B. phoned a few months later to report a chain reaction. All over town, the disoriented were coming out of the closet, gathering at the bus areas.

Y. thought of it as a reconciliation with Nature. Had She not long ago chosen the place for the City? The swagger in his walk began to come back.

Trotsky in Amherst
SILVER DONALD CAMERON

· · · · · · · · ·

British officers and armed bluejackets boarded the Kristianiafjord and in the name of the officer commanding the port called upon me, my wife, my two boys and five other passengers to leave the steamer. The reasons, they told me, would be given to me at Halifax. We answered that the demand was illegal and that we would refuse to comply. Thereupon the armed sailors, amid shouts of "shame" from a considerable number of passengers, bodily carried us aboard a naval cutter, which took us to Halifax under escort of a cruiser. A dozen of the sailors were busy with my struggling person when my elder boy ran to my assistance and planted his tiny fist in the officer's face, crying, "Shall I hit him again, Father?"

He was eleven years old: it was his first contact with British democracy.

The ironic voice belongs to Leon Trotsky: height 5'8½"; weight 170 lbs.; eyes and hair black; moustache and beard black; complexion dark; age 37; captured at Halifax, 3 April 1917; citizenship Russian; profession, journalist.

The details were recorded by Col. Arthur Henry Morris, officer commanding Internment Camp Amherst in Nova Scotia. Trotsky, whose adult life had been divided between prisons and exile, had reached Nova Scotia from New York, where he had been living since mid-January, writing for the Russian-language newspaper *Novyi Mir* (New World), giving speeches to exile groups, and preparing for the revolution he felt sure was imminent.

He was right. On 15 March 1917, Czar Nicholas II abdicated and a provisional government under Prince Georgy Lvov took office. Trotsky hurried to the Russian Embassy and obtained visas. On 27 March, with his petite wife, Natalya, his sons, Sergei, 9, and Lyova, 11, and five other revolutionaries, Trotsky sailed aboard the Norwegian-American liner *SS Kristianiafjord* bound for Russia. Three days later, the ship arrived in Halifax.

Silver Donald Cameron (born 1937) was a university professor before turning to full-time writing in 1971. His books range from literary interviews and criticism to essays and fiction, including a young adult novel, The Baitchopper. *He lives in Nova Scotia.* Canadian Geographic *published this article in its April-May 1988 number.*

As Hugh MacLennan notes, Halifax thrives in wartime. It is the Canadian navy's chief Atlantic base, and the closest to Europe of all mainland North American ports. In both world wars, it was the major point of departure for troops and war materiel; enemy submarines harried the harbor approaches because Halifax was the assembly point for transatlantic convoys. It was thus a geographical as well as an historical accident that brought Trotsky's ship to Nova Scotia, where it was to unload cargo and await its convoy.

But a British secret agent had notified London of Trotsky's plans. Russia was allied to Britain, but British authorities were concerned about the unstable situation in Russia and its impact on the Russian war effort. The day after the *Kristianiafjord* arrived in Halifax, a message flashed from the British Admiralty to the Naval Control Officer in Halifax, Capt. O.M. Makins of the Royal Navy, bidding him remove the little band of Russians and hold them "pending instructions." These, said the cable,

> are Russian Socialists leaving [the United States] for the purpose of starting revolution against present Russian government for which Trotsky is reported to have 10,000 dollars subscribed by socialists and Germans.

Makins' men boarded the ship and questioned the Russians vigorously. In his report, Makins confirmed that "they are all avowed Socialists, and though professing a desire to help the new Russian Govt. might well be in league with German Socialists in America, and quite likely a hindrance to the government in Russia just at present. It is therefore proposed to remove them ... on Tuesday morning ..."

Trotsky, of course, remembered the interrogation more vividly: the Russian travelers were not given "the treatment accorded other passengers not so unfortunate as to belong to a nation allied to England." Instead, they were

> submitted to a thorough cross-examination as to their political convictions and affiliations. I declined to enter into a political debate of this sort, and declared that while I was ready to answer any questions or submit any evidence as to my identity, I would do no more: Russia's internal politics were not yet under the control of the British naval police.[1]

---

1. Trostky may have occasionally confused British and Canadian military officials in these accounts of his internment, as both countries worked in close co-operation. Although Canada had its own navy as of 1910, officers of the British Royal Navy were seconded to Canada during the First World War.

Though the other Russians wrote a protest, Trotsky did not deign to sign. "I saw little use," he noted acidly, "in complaining to Beelzebub about Satan."

Trotsky's wife and sons were held in Halifax, first at the Market Street home of the port's official Russian translator, Dave Horowetz, and later in a nearby hotel. Trotsky and his comrades were shunted off to Amherst by train, where that evening they were duly inducted into the camp by Colonel Morris.

A reviewer of Robert Fothergill's recent play about this episode, *Detaining Mr. Trotsky*, describes Trotsky as "a devotional figure of the left wing because he was an idealist, and because he died before he could betray his idealism." Not exactly. Trotsky was exiled by Stalin in 1929 and he was 60 when the KGB assassinated him in Mexico. But he retains a special magnetism. He was a remarkable human being: energetic, eloquent, devoted, impassioned, a citizen of the world graced with a delightful sense of humor.

By 1917, Trotsky was a seasoned revolutionary, a veteran not only of prison and exile, but also the former leader of the Petrograd Soviet during the brief revolution of 1905. When that rebellion was quelled, soldiers surrounded the building in which the Soviet executive committee was meeting, and a police officer barged in to read the warrant.

"Please do not interfere with the speaker," said Trotsky, the chairman. "If you wish to take the floor, you must give your name, and I shall ask the meeting whether it wishes to hear you."

Thunderstruck, the officer waited. Trotsky then invited him to read the warrant "for the sake of information," after which he suggested that the meeting acknowledge the statement and pass to the next item on the agenda.

The policeman protested.

"Please do not interfere," Trotsky scolded him. "You have had the floor, you have made your statement, we have acknowledged it. Does the meeting wish to have any further dealings with the policeman?"

"No!" cried the other committee members.

"Then, please, leave the hall," said Trotsky—and the policeman left.

He soon returned, however, and Trotsky was imprisoned in the Peter and Paul Fortress. He was not unduly perturbed.

"I feel splendid," he told another prisoner. "I sit and work and feel perfectly sure that I can't be arrested. You will agree that under the conditions in Czarist Russia, this is rather an unusual sensation."

Trotsky took the same approach in Amherst—even in prison, he had work to do—but he considered that Colonel Morris gave him worse treatment than the minions of the czar.

We were put through an examination the like of which I had never before experienced, even in the Peter-Paul Fortress. For in the Czar's fortress the police stripped me and searched me in privacy, whereas here our democratic allies subjected us to this shameful humiliation before a dozen men.

Nor did the camp itself impress him: "The Amherst concentration camp," he notes in his autobiography,

was located in an old and very dilapidated iron foundry that had been confiscated from its German owner. The sleeping bunks were arranged in three tiers, two deep, on each side of the hall. About 800 of us lived in these conditions. The air in this improvised dormitory at night can be imagined. Men hopelessly clogged the passages, elbowed their way through, lay down or got up, played cards or chess. Many of them practised crafts, some with extraordinary skill. I still have, stored in Moscow, some things made by Amherst prisoners. And yet, in spite of the heroic efforts of the prisoners to keep themselves physically and morally fit, five of them had gone insane. We had to eat and sleep in the same room with these madmen.

At the time of Trotsky's arrival, the former buildings of the Canadian Car and Foundry Company contained 851 German prisoners of war. Of these, said Trotsky, about 500 were captured sailors and another 200 were "workers caught by the war in Canada," while 100 or so were German officers and "civilian prisoners of the bourgeois class."

The officers and the bourgeois in the camp considered the Russian revolutionaries to be enemies—but not the sailors and workers. At the time, Germany had the largest Communist party in the world, and Trotsky was a genuine internationalist who believed that the Russian example would spark a worldwide revolution, ushering in a new era of liberation for people everywhere. A brilliant linguist and a happy traveler, he made himself at home wherever he found himself—even in a prison camp.

"The whole month I was there was like one continuous mass meeting," Trotsky later recalled. "I told the prisoners about the Russian Revolution, about Leibknecht, about Lenin, and about the causes of the collapse of the old International, and the intervention of the United States in the war." In addition to the public speeches, there were "constant discussions in smaller groups." In effect, Trotsky seems to have turned the camp into an improvised college of socialist studies.

The prisoners had been isolated from the war and from other news for several years, and Trotsky was happy to bring them up to date in his own style. The revolutionary proletariat, Trotsky told the prisoners, would not only end czarism but would also put an end to the war. The Russian revolutionaries would seek a quick peace, and German socialists were organizing the workers to overthrow Kaiser Wilhelm and end the war. The only newspaper the prisoners were permitted was the Halifax *Chronicle*, laying it out before him on a table, Trotsky would read it aloud, translating it on the fly into German and Russian.

He was a great speaker and organizer—Lenin later marveled at his ability to conjure whole armies out of thin air—and he was eloquent on behalf of the prisoners, and vigorous in his complaints about the defects of the camp administration. This led Colonel Morris, who had served in the British colonial service and was a veteran of the Boer War, to mutter, "If only I had him on the South African coast!" This, Trotsky recalled, "was his pet expression."

Within days, Trotsky had become a hero to the prisoners—to the extent that he had some difficulty persuading them that he should take his own turn in the food lineups and do his share of such chores as sweeping floors, washing dishes, peeling potatoes and cleaning the lavatories. Trotsky was not permitted to communicate with his wife unless he agreed not to attempt to send messages through her to the Russian consulate. He angrily refused. In Halifax, Natalya Sedova was also angry. She spoke French, German and Russian, but her English consisted of just one sentence: "Speak you French?" A devoted revolutionary herself, she had been cheerful throughout the years of exile, not even complaining when in Vienna her household belongings had to be pawned to finance the publication of a revolutionary newspaper. In Halifax, she lost no opportunity to discuss socialist themes with anyone with whom she shared a language; her acquaintances were impressed by her knowledge of the French socialist movement and the Industrial Workers of the World in the United States.

Natalya agreed that she and her husband were (in Trotsky's words) "irreproachable Russian revolutionaries returning to our country, liberated by the revolution." They had committed no crime, and as allied citizens traveling on legitimate passports, they believed they were being victimized by agents of the czar. One day Natalya went shopping with Fanny Horowetz, the translator's daughter, looking for a notepad. At Connolly's Book and Stationery Store on Barrington Street, she was offered a pad whose cover was decorated with the flags of the Allies.

"I want none of them," cried Natalya in Russian. "I have no use for any flags but the flag of real freedom!"

"If I ever get back to my own country," she said on another occasion, "I will talk, I will write, I will let my country's people know that Canada is not free, that the United States is not free ..."

Throughout April, messages flew back and forth across the Atlantic and across Europe. Many British and some Canadian officials wanted a pretext to continue the internment, recognizing the danger that a new Russian government influenced by Trotsky might well sue for peace, leaving Germany free to concentrate her armies against the Allied Forces on the Western Front. The longer Trotsky could be kept in Amherst, the better.

Trotsky himself had been prevented in his attempts to cable British Prime Minister Lloyd George in London and the provisional government in Petrograd. "The Czar's gendarmes never acted so arbitrarily," he grumbled. The British Foreign Office had notified the Russian government of the arrest, and must have been disappointed when on 8 April the foreign minister, Paul Miliukov, requested that the party be released. But Miliukov was no friend to Trotsky—he had coined the term "Trotskyism" as early as 1905—and two days later he asked the British ambassador to Russia, Sir George Buchanan, to cancel the request pending "further information." Buchanan thus blamed the Russian government "for their further detention until April 21."

In Amherst, meanwhile, Trotsky's mini-revolution was coming along very nicely. "He was a man who when he looked at you seemed to hypnotize you," remembered Capt. F.C. Whitmore, an officer at the camp. "He gave us a lot of trouble at the camp, and if he had stayed there any longer ... would have made Communists of all the German prisoners."

Alarmed by Trotsky's success, the German officers protested to Colonel Morris. "The British colonel instantly sided with the Hohenzollern patriots," Trotsky scornfully commented, "and forbade me to make any more public speeches. But this did not happen until the last few days of our stay at the camp." Morris eventually put Trotsky in solitary confinement, and the prisoners responded with a petition bearing 530 signatures—a sign of success that Trotsky considered "more than ample compensation for all the hardships of the Amherst imprisonment." On the telegraph cables, the diplomatic flurry continued. As early as 6 April, the Russian consul-general in Montreal had protested to the British military authorities in Canada. Canadian concern increased when the story was published in *Novyi Mir* on 10 April. The editors attempted to cable Trotsky; receiving no response, they cabled Alexander Kerensky, then minister of justice in the provisional government. Protests took place in New York, Pittsburgh and Petrograd.

Canadian officials, such as Deputy Postmaster General R.M. Coulter, had been discreetly voicing their objections to the arbitrary actions of the British military authorities, and they were perceptibly relieved when, on 20 April, the Admiralty cabled that the "Russian Socialists should be allowed to proceed." A British Foreign Office file notes regretfully that "we must permit, but need not expedite, their journey."

We were ordered to pack our things and proceed ... When we demanded the why and wherefore, they refused to say anything. The prisoners became excited because they thought we were being taken to a fortress. We asked for the nearest Russian Consul; they refused us again. We had reason enough for not trusting these highwaymen of the sea, and so we insisted that we would not go voluntarily until they told us where we were going. The commander ordered forcible measures ... It was only when the convoy was faced with the task of carrying us out bodily, just as we had been taken off the steamer a month earlier ... that the commander relented and told us, in his characteristic Anglo-Colonial way, that we were to sail on a Danish boat for Russia. The colonel's purple face twitched convulsively. If only it had been on the African coast!

And so Trotsky left Amherst—his route lined with hundreds of cheering German sailors, while an improvised band played the "Internationale." With his family and his comrades, he sailed for Russia on 3 May 1917.

A few months later, Trotsky was Russia's foreign minister, negotiating peace with Germany. A German diplomat noted Trotsky's "burning hatred of the English" stemming from his imprisonment in Canada. By 1918, Trotsky was leading the Red Army in the infant Soviet Union's successful defense against both internal insurgency and invading armies from the United States, Japan, Czechoslovakia—and Britain (with the participation of Canadian soldiers).

He had vowed vengeance on the English-speaking nations. Did he feel a certain grim glee as he defeated their armies on Russian soil? He had certainly evened the score for Amherst.

Suppressing Rebellion In Lower Canada: British Military Policy And Practice, 1837-38

ELINOR KYTE SENIOR

· · · · · · · · · ·

In the event of insurrection—whether in Ireland, in Jamaica or in Canada—the usual British military practice in the early 1800s was to seize the papers of rebel chiefs, burn their homes and imprison leaders when caught. Rank and file insurgents were less likely to have their homes burnt unless those buildings had been used by insurgents to fire upon Crown forces. "Free quartering" of troops was often imposed on a disaffected populace as part of the punitive measures, but exile or hanging of rebel leaders were measures of last resort. Imposition of martial law meant the suspension of civil government, a step contemplated with as much anxiety by loyal citizens as by disaffected elements. Government and military authorities clearly believed that rebels had to be punished, and that such punishment should be evident, not only to the loyal part of the population but to the neutral and wavering elements as well.

Most British officers and soldiers of this period who served abroad were familiar with coping with disturbed areas. It was then usual military practice to send regiments to Ireland prior to a posting overseas, as the Irish station was considered an excellent training ground both for use of troops in aid of

Elinor Kyte Senior, a military historian, was an associate professor at McGill when this essay was published in the Spring 1988 number of Canadian Defence Quarterly, *a year after it was first delivered as a paper at a symposium in Scotland, at the University of Edinburgh Centre of Canadian Studies. She is now visiting professor of military and strategic studies at Acadia University. Her hobby is fencing.*

civil power and for training in ceremonial procedures. Colonel George Cathcart of the 1st King's Dragoon Guards, for instance, had served in Ireland and then in Jamaica during the slave revolt there in the 1830s. When faced with insurrection in Lower Canada, he made use of his experience, particularly with regard to combined police-military operations. His expertise in these matters enabled him to exercise great influence in the reorganization of the Montreal police both during and after the rebellions.[1] Similarly, Colonel Charles Grey of the 71st Highland Light Infantry urged civil authorities to make use of the Irish Insurrection Act of 1798 to compel each Montreal householder to post on the front door a list of all residents and order them to be within the house by a certain hour each night.[2]

Even before the first actual battle of the 1837 rebellion occurred in Lower Canada, the British military command had formulated a policy of home burning as a punitive measure. This policy was instituted as a reaction to the rescue of arrested *Patriote* chiefs by a body of armed *Patriotes* under Bonaventure Viger. These insurgent leaders had been arrested in Saint Jean on 16 November 1837 by Montreal bailiffs, who were escorted by troopers of the Royal Mounted Cavalry under the command of Lieutenant Charles Oakes Ermatinger, an Ojibway chief. Lieutenant Ermatinger was hit by the first shot of the first rebellion, a shot fired by the insurgent son of a half-pay Scottish officer, Patrick Murray.[3] In the ensuing melée, the men of the Royal Montreal Cavalry were scattered, their prisoners freed, and authorities faced the first open defiance of government and military forces. The commander of the British forces in Canada, Sir John Colborne, immediately sent a strong contingent of regulars back to the spot where the cavalry had been attacked, with orders to arrest the men who had fired on the troopers. "Should they resist the civil power or fire on the troops, you will fire on the rebels, also destroy any house from which they may fire."[4] On returning to Saint Jean, however, the troops found the houses deserted, the women and children hiding in the woods. The men had gone to Boucherville to reinforce insurgents ranks there under Bonaventure Viger. Some prisoners were taken, but no homes put to the torch.

This rescue of the Saint Jean *Patriote* chiefs was, however, the incident that triggered Sir John Colborne to move against the radical centers of Saint Denis and Saint Charles, on the Richelieu River, with some 800 troops, ostensibly as "an aid to civil power." The troops were to accompany magistrates with warrants to arrest the *Patriote* leaders Louis-Joseph Papineau, Dr. Wolfred Nelson, Thomas Storrow Brown and others, who were then forming armed camps on the Richelieu.

Colborne's military policy was to move swiftly against the armed camps. In a two-pronged pincer movement, one brigade was to move south from Sorel toward Saint Denis, and a second would march from Chambly against the armed camp at Saint Charles. It was expected that the brigade headed to Saint Denis would pass through that small village with little opposition. When put into practice, however, this plan proved only partly successful. Bad weather and bad tactics on the part of Colonel Gore allowed rebel reinforcements to get to Saint Denis during the battle. The regular troops were exhausted after an all-night march in the frightful November weather, and victory ultimately went to the insurgents, who fought vigorously from a strong defensive position.

By contrast, two days later, good weather and effective military leadership enabled the Chambly brigade to move decisively against Saint Charles in a triumphant two-hour battle. Following this battle the first of the punitive military measures began—the burning of houses and barns from which rebels had fired on Crown forces. The armed camp at Saint Charles was destroyed, except for the manor house of Pierre-Dominique Debartzch, which the insurgents had used as their main headquarters.[5] Some 20 buildings were put to the torch immediately. Prisoners were rounded up and lodged in the parish church until sent to jail in Montreal, where they joined those *Patriote* chiefs from Montreal who had already been arrested since 16 November.

With the suppression of the rebel camp at Saint Charles, a brigade of some 500 regulars, with field artillery and a cornet's detachment of the Royal Montreal Cavalry, returned to Saint Denis on 1 December. They entered the village unopposed, and there was no sign of Dr. Wolfred Nelson, Papineau or other rebel leaders. The officer commanding the regulars, Colonel Gore, lost no time in putting the torch to the fortified stone building which a week earlier the rebel forces had defended so effectively that regular soldiers had been unable to storm it.

In his first report to Colborne on 1 December 1837, Gore stated, "The fortified house has been burned and several others from which we were fired on." He added, "Wolfred Nelson's property will be destroyed tomorrow."[6] The destruction of Nelson's property and of other buildings was thus carried out as a punitive and as a repressive measure—to punish rebels and to prevent future uprisings. The British succeeded in the first, but failed in the second.

During and immediately after the first military engagements in Lower Canada, some 184 homes were burned. About 30 of these were disciplined military acts. The rest represented plunder and vengeance. After the battle of Saint Eustache, for instance, troops were ordered to "free quarters." This was a euphemism for plunder, as officers and soldiers fully understood. One regular officer described the pillaging at Saint Eustache as "equalling or surpassing that which followed the sack of Badajoz in Spain."[7] Only two homes were ordered burned in Saint Eustache—those of the local *Patriote* leaders, the merchant William Henry Scott and Dr. Jean Chénier.[8]

When "unofficial" fires broke out after the battle, troops were ordered out to protect property, but without much effect, and some 60 houses were gutted.[9] There was probably a certain element of calculation on the part of the military authorities with regard to these unofficial burnings. Colborne had warned the men of nearby Saint Benoit that their village would be put to fire and the sword if a single shot was fired as the Crown forces approached the village. Not a shot was fired, but the village was gutted nonetheless. Colborne had ordered three homes burnt in Saint Benoit, those of the three principal *Patriote* leaders—Notary Jean-Joseph Girouard, Dr. Luc Masson and J.B. Dumouchel. The rest were put to the torch by local volunteers and residents. The church at Saint Benoit was set on fire three times; twice troops put out the flames, but the third time the church burned to the ground. Regular troops then marched through the disaffected area of the Lake of Two Mountains for three days. On orders, they burned two homes, took up surrendered arms and received the oath of allegiance from rural inhabitants. Their final duty was to escort to Montreal some of the 361 political prisoners that crowded the jails over that winter.[10]

Arrested rebels were expected to give depositions before magistrates about their part in the uprisings. Floggings and half-hangings, so much a part of the Irish rebellion scene in 1798, did not, however, form part of the repressive measures in Lower Canada in 1837. Rather, an atmosphere of terror was temporarily created by widespread police interrogation carried out under Pierre-Edouard Leclère, head of the newly raised police. No one could know to what extent a neighbor's testimony might implicate one in treason, and there was thus a continual flight over the American border of rebels and their sympathizers. They were undoubtedly frightened, but they were not so terrorized that they refrained from engaging in border raids from their safe haven in the United States.

The military reaction to these first border raids was to order the Glengarry Highlanders to move from Upper Canada in the spring of 1838 to police areas south of the Saint Lawrence, and regular officers were brought over from England on "particular duty," that is, to act as intelligence officers. They were scattered in a number of small towns south of the Saint Lawrence, with the task of reporting to Colborne any suspicious behavior of the *habitants* and those suspected of disaffection. It was no wonder that *Patriote* chiefs over the border spoke uneasily of "spies being sent throughout the agricultural districts." [11]

By May 1838 additional troops from Great Britain were pouring into Lower Canada. The Grenadier Guards and the Coldstream Guards, along with two cavalry regiments, arrived under the command of Sir James

Macdonell. In addition, three other regiments were brought in from the Maritime colonies. This brought Colborne's regular force up to a strength of 5,000 and, with his local volunteer troops numbering about 4,000, this combined military force exceeded the peacetime strength of the army of the United States.

In spite of the increasing size of the regular garrison, the *Patriotes* over the American line began preparations for a second uprising, this time through the agency of a secret society, *Les Frères Chasseurs.* Border raids were called off temporarily. With this lessening of border tension, Colborne released 200 of the lesser rebels from jail, a move that provoked considerable resentment on the part of the well affected populace. Colborne went even farther. He agreed to a policy of general amnesty, expecting that such leniency would remove from the border the more turbulent spirits thought to be plotting another insurrection. Thus, six months after the first rebellion, all political prisoners had been released except for eight leaders who were sent into exile in Bermuda. Disaffected elements had accurately predicted this release of prisoners, and openly boasted that government dared not bring any of them to trial. Exile there was, then, for eight *Patriote* chiefs, but no executions. In fact, the only execution during the first rebellion in Lower Canada was that of a loyalist French-Canadian volunteer, executed by rebel forces who accused him of being a government spy.[12] This was in sharp contrast to what had happened in the upper province, where civil authorities promptly hanged two captured rebel leaders.

When the second insurrection broke out in Lower Canada in November 1838, it faced a well prepared government which suppressed it within a week. The rebellion, and its suppression, had something of a Scottish tone about it. The leader of the *Chasseur* conspiracy in Montreal was John de Bélestre Macdonell, son of a half-pay Scottish officer who had settled in Glengarry County and married into the prominent de Bélestre family. It was out of Macdonell's law office in Montreal that the head lodge of the Chasseurs operated and funneled money to Dr. Robert Nelson, leader of the insurgent forces south of the American line.

On the other side of the coin, the officer in charge of the harsh repressive measures after the second insurrection was Major-General Sir James Macdonell, brother of the late Highland Chieftain from Glengarry. It was thus not surprising that Colborne had no hesitation in ordering Glengarry Regiments from Upper Canada to cross the provincial line and surround insurgent forces in the Beauharnois area. Numerous Macdonells and other volunteers from Glengarry were delighted to join forces with their kinsman as he moved west from Quebec City with a brigade of Guards, doubly indignant that a man by the name of Macdonell was numbered among the rebel leaders.

The insurgents' fear of the Scots was clearly stated by one of them, himself half-Scot. Pierre Reid claimed that the reason the insurgents tried to disarm the Caughnawaga Indians just prior to the second uprising was because they feared "the Indians were coming with the Scotch to massacre us." [13] Reid's fear contained some element of reality: Captain Edmund Thomas Campbell of the 7th Hussars was in charge of suppressing the insurgents at Chateauguay; Colonel George Cathcart of the 1st King's Dragoon Guards scoured the area around La Prairie; and still another Campbell, Major John Campbell, commanded the Huntingdon Volunteers as they moved down the Chateauguay River against a rebel encampment at Baker's Farm. It is no wonder then that the pipers of the Stormont Highlanders gaily played "The Campbells are Coming" as they marched into the Huntingdon camp, accompanied by 60 warriors from the Indian village of Saint Regis, just opposite Cornwall. The combination of the Scottish bagpipes and the Indian warcries proved to be too much for the insurgents a short distance away: they silently slipped away overnight.

On their march from Beauharnois towards the major rebel encampment at Napierville, the Glengarries boasted that they left a trail six miles wide as they came along "burning and pillaging."[14] The Scottish wife of Edward Ellice, *seigneur* of Beauharnois, described them as a "wild set of men—very like what one imagines the old Highlanders in Scotland and equally difficult to manage." She concluded that the rural *habitants* were less afraid of the Indians than of the Glengarries, and with reason. The Highlander who rowed her and her husband to safety at Lachine after they were rescued from the insurgents laconically told them "the houses they had spared in coming down the country, they would surely burn going back."[15]

A border raid on the windmill at Prescott sent the Highlanders scurrying back to defend their own province. Having come as infantry, most of them returned as cavalrymen, mounting, as they claimed, "stray French ponies they found on the wayside."[16] The horses were on the loose because the *habitants* had freed their animals, fearing that their properties would be burned as part of the repressive military measures. The use of the Glengarries and the Indians was part of a military policy of instilling terror among the rebel forces, a policy that succeeded, for fighting took place only briefly at Lacolle and Odelltown, on the frontier, and at Baker's Farm and Beauharnois. In none of the areas that rose during the previous autumn was a shot fired, evidence of the efficacy of the repressive measures by the military in those areas.

This second revolt, coming so swiftly on the heels of the first, faced a harsher military policy. Colonel Charles Grey, son of a former British prime minister, expressed the common military attitude. "You certainly cannot allow people to give you all this trouble and to act as they have towards the loyal part of the population, and then go to their homes without any punishment."[17] Once the second insurrection was suppressed, a policy of "dragooning" was adopted, designed to check any possible attempt at a third uprising. The spectre of a third rebellion was indeed raised by Curé François-Xavier Bellamin Ricard of Ile Perrot. Identified as one "well acquainted with all the secret plans and designs of the late revolt," Curé Ricard visited Beauharnois in the wake of the troops on Sunday, 11 November 1838. He was horrified by what he saw, just as Jane Ellice was as she "stood watching the village in flames—an awful sight."[18]

As soon as Curé Ricard returned to his own parish from Beauharnois, he predicted that "they would revolt again next year and would be unsuccessful, but that in the year 1840, they would rise again in rebellion and be revenged for their injuries." Strangely, Ricard said this before a housefull of people, among them two loyalist volunteer officers who immediately informed military headquarters of the priest's speech. "The prediction is the ground-work of a future insurrection."[19]

Military authorities did not need evidence of continuing disaffection in order to initiate a harsher policy. Having, as they believed, treated disaffection with great leniency the previous year—no executions, and all but eight of the prisoners freed—they concluded that their former policy had been interpreted as weakness. Many of the loyalists repeatedly insisted that a lenient policy would lead to fresh outbreaks of rebellion. Henceforth, troops were quartered south of the Saint Lawrence, some 3,000 regulars and 1,000 volunteers. Homes were searched for rebels and arms, arrests made and oaths of allegiance exacted. Houses of suspected insurgent leaders and of those thought to be still consorting with sympathizers across the American border were burnt.

At Napierville, a village of about 80 houses, military authorities at first intended to burn all rebel homes. Non-commissioned officers from regular regiments were selected for the task, and had actually begun when the order was countermanded by Sir John Colborne. Colonel Charles Grey claimed that the countermand order arrived too late "to prevent several homes being burnt, among them Dr. Côte's which we saw in full blaze after we left the place."[20] Grey was heading towards Saint Edouard, accompanied by Captain Sydney Bellingham of the Royal Montreal Cavalry; their objective was to "burn the houses of the leaders of the insurgents." Bellingham described how the policy of burning had been adopted. It was largely the work of Attorney-General Charles Richard Ogden. "He [Ogden] discovered the authors of the outrages to which the loyal inhabitants had been exposed, and as the principal actors took refuge beyond the frontier, and secretly returned to excite the population, Mr. Ogden came to the conclusion that the best method of punishing them was to burn their homesteads. The officers in command of troops merely obeyed orders."[21] A Montreal newspaper dolefully reported that not a single rebel home was left standing south of the Saint Lawrence. This was far from the case. At least 1,500 men took up arms in the second insurrection and there were as many as 7,500 among the disaffected, yet the number of homes burnt in the second uprising, even counting those burned at Beauharnois and Chateauguay immediately after military engagements, was probably under 100.[22]

Not all burnings were, however, authorized by the military. At Beauharnois, for example, a village of about 45 homes, some 23 houses were burned by loyalists, who reasoned that it was the only punishment the rebels would receive.[23] The Lachine Volunteers were responsible for at least 10 homes out of the 20 that were burned at Chateauguay. These were unauthorized burnings, and the Lachine Volunteers involved were put under military arrest.

By early 1839 the military burnings had ceased. But by then disaffected elements over the border had renewed raids and had started to burn properties themselves. In most cases, the border burnings were confined to barns, but in two cases homes of loyalist volunteers were set on fire. With regard to "free quarters," or pillaging, regulars and volunteers engaged in both with equal gusto, sometimes legitimately, as in the case of the church funds of Napierville, where insurgents had confiscated them from the local priest. In their haste to clear out of Napierville as regular troops neared, the rebels left the cart containing the funds behind. They took time out only to set fire to the house they used as their arms depot. Soldiers of the 71st Highland Light Infantry pulled the cart out of the way and, as they did so, it upset. The chest containing the "sacred silver" broke open, whereupon the delighted soldiers helped themselves. Colonel Grey regarded this as legitimate plunder, but he had harsh words for other incidents of pillage. "The sort of plunderers that the Guards, the Artillery and the 7th Hussars are, I think I never saw. There was this excuse for killing animals to eat, that no rations were issued to the men ... but the slaughter of poultry of all sorts by the Guards and the Hussars in particular I never saw equalled."[24] His own regiment was not totally innocent, and pillaging ceased only after five men had been sentenced to 12 months imprisonment for plundering.

The effect of this persecution, together with the courtmartial of some 111 prisoners and the hanging of 12 insurgents in Montreal, drove at least 3,775 Patriote sympathizers over the border by 1838. [25] Some of these political refugees continued to think in terms of limited border raids, hoping to provoke war between Great Britain and the United States. But this new round of border outrages caused such negative reactions in the United States that *Chasseur* leaders as far away as Baltimore wrote to insurgent leaders on the border deploring the raids. "Tell our friends to cease these martial excursions," one wrote. "They do only harm to our cause."[26] Moreover, the firm stand by the American Generals John Wool and Winfield Scott convinced military leaders in Montreal that the American government was anxious to avoid war.

By 1840 only a few desultory border raids were made. But the refugee communities were quick to denounce them as "individual private acts, not being pushed by the chiefs."[27] Many over the border were longing for home. Others had found work and established their families over the line, and were now anxious to raise the image of French Canadians in the eyes of their fellow American citizens.

By creating an atmosphere of terror, dragooning had done its job. Those disaffected elements who had sought safety across the American border soon learned that there was no chance of American military aid. And without such aid, they recognized the folly of continued resistance, for all hopes of a successful insurrection were predicated on an uprising *en masse* of the *habitants*, coupled with American aid. Thus, directly or indirectly, military policy and practice stamped out insurrection in Lower Canada.

Notes

1. Elinor Kyte Senior, *British Regulars in Montreal: An Imperial Garrison 1832-1854* (Montreal, 1981), pp.28-30.
2. Lt. Col. Charles Grey to his father, 5 November 1838, in William Ormsby, *Crisis in the Canadas 1838-39* (Toronto, 1964), p.155.
3. Elinor Kyte Senior, *Redcoats & Patriotes: The Rebellions in Lower Canada 1837-38* (Stittsville, 1985), pp.54-55.
4. Deputy Quarter Master General Sir Charles Gore to Lt.-Col. George Wetherall, 17 November 1837, PAC: MG11/Q239/2/p.10.
5. Wetherall to Gore, 28 November 1837, PAC: RG4/S390/A1/II/147; Pierre Meunier, *L'Insurrection à Saint-Charles et le Seigneur Debartzch* (Quebec, 1986), p.216.
6. Gore to Major Goldie, 2 December 1837, PAC: Colborne Papers, MF24/A40/8043.
7. Statement of Captain Joseph Swinburne in PAC: Wily Memoirs, PAC: MG29/E1/94.
8. *Gazette*, Montreal, 16 December 1837.
9. Lord Charles Beauclerk, *Lithographic Views of the Military Operations in Canada*, (London, 1840), p.12.
10. *Transcript*, Montreal, 18 December 1837; Maitland to Gore, 16 December 1837, PAC: Q239/346-7; Colborne to Somerset, 22 December 1837, PAC: RG8/C1272/57.
11. E.B. O'Callaghan to Thomas Falconer, 24 June 1838, PAC: Chapman

Papers, MG24/B31/i/37-44.

12. For details see Senior, *Redcoats & Patriotes*, p.101.

13. Pierre Reid's testimony, in *Report of the State Trials* (Montreal, 1839), i, pp.42-44.

14. Grey to his father, 13 November 1838, in PAC: Grey Papers, MG24/A10/ii/127.

15. Ellice Diary, PAC: MG24/A2/50, see entry 14 November 1838.

16. John Fraser, *Canadian Pen and Ink Sketches* (Montreal, 1890), p. 105.

17. Grey to father, 11 November 1838, PAC: Grey Papers, MG24/A10/ii/124.

18. Major J.A. Mathison's deposition, 12 November 1838, in Archives nationales de Québec: Documents relatifs aux événements de 1837-38, #2953; Ellice diary, PAC: MG24/A2/50, entry dated 10 November 1838.

19. Captain Edward Jones' deposition, 23 November 1838, ANQ: Documents relatifs aux événements de 1837-38, #2951.

20. Ormsby, *Crisis in the Canadas*, p.147.

21. Bellingham Memoirs, PAC: MG24/B25/ii/126.

22. This figure is estimated from *First Report of Commissioners to enquire into losses occasioned by the troubles during the years 1837-38, Appendix to the Journal*, 1846, no. 2, app. x, see claims for over £100; see also, Robert Sellar, *History of Huntingdon* (Huntingdon, 1888), p.604; Fraser, *Pen & Ink Sketches*, p.91; F.S. Prieur, *Notes of a Convict*, 1838 (Australia, 1949), pp.49-55.

23. Ormsby, *Crisis in the Canadas*, p.150.

24. Grey to father, 11 November 1838, PAC: Grey Papers, MG24/A10/ii/124.

25. For figures see Elinor Kyte Senior, "The Presence of French Canadians in American Towns Bordering Lower Canada 1837-1840: Disaffection, Terror or Economic Pulls", in *Journal of the Northern New York American-Canadian Genealogical Society* (Plattsburgh, N.Y.), iv, no.2, fall, 1987, pp.17-30.

26. Dr. Henri Gauvin to Louis Perrault, 5 April 1839, PAC: Duvernay Papers, MG24/C3/iii/1351.

27. Assemblie de comité de l'association des Refugiés Canadiens d'état de Vermont, 29 août, 1840, PAC: Duvernay Papers, MG24/C3/iii/1860.

On Being Motionless/On Refusing the Story
RUDY WIEBE

· · · · · · · · · ·

The Inuit understanding of all visible phenomena is expressed by their language as two dimensional: the very grammar of Inuktitut identifies all phenomena as either equal in size—things (an igloo, a ball, a human being) are about as broad as they are long, that is, they are *areal*, or as unequal—they (a harpoon, a rope, a river) are longer than they are broad, that is, linear. This understanding explains why it is really impossible for a living being to be ultimately lost on the vast expanses of the Arctic landscape, either tundra or ice.

Two corollaries expand this linguistic understanding and further explain it: (1) any areal thing (a ball, a human being) changes dimension and becomes linear when it moves, and (2) any area without easily observable limits (a field of ice, the sea, an expanse of tundra) is automatically classified as long and narrow—that is, as linear also. Now in order to live a human being must move; to live in the Arctic a human being must, generally speaking, move quite a bit to acquire food; that is, in order to live he/she will become a linear dimension in a linear space. That means another moving person (also linear) will certainly find them because even in the largest space their moving lines must at some point intersect. The very rarity of those lines in the "empty" Arctic makes them all the more conspicuous.

All this changes radically of course when the human being's dimension changes back to areal, that is, the person becomes motionless. A body may take years to find; Sir John Franklin's, some of his sailors', took 12 or 13 years; Andree, the Swedish lighter-than-air balloonist and his two assistants

---

This essay by Rudy Wiebe (born 1934), from the Spring 1988 issue of Brick, *a Toronto literary journal, bears an obvious relationship to* The Mad Trapper *(1980), one of his many works of fiction, the best known of which is the 1973 novel* The Temptations of Big Bear. *Wiebe teaches English and creative writing at the University of Alberta and has won the Governor General's Award and numerous other prizes.*

who began their airy drift for the North Pole on 11 July 1897, were not found until 9 July 1930, and only by accident. A body in the Arctic may be lost forever. But on the so-called empty barrens it is actually impossible for a living person to stay lost. By the same token, it is impossible to hide.

Aklavik (a word which means the place of the brown bear) is a cluster of 750 people almost invisible in the enormous Mackenzie Delta. The Anglican Church Cemetery there contains the grave of a man who tried to hide in the Arctic. Albert Johnson, as he is called, should have known better. He never saw Aklavik alive; he was brought there only to be buried on 9 March 1932, and since he had killed one policeman and almost killed two others, he was interred as far away from the tiny log church as possible, on the very edge of church property. However, since 1932 the town has grown; the old brown church has become a museum and a new prefab structure stands there bluer than the sky; the town is now so large that the main street with its two stores, hamlet offices and fire station runs along the back of the cemetery. As a result, Albert Johnson's grave now borders on main street: the long entrance to the cemetery is right there beside the two broken tree stumps that stick like symbolic rotten columns out of the white picket fence outlining his gravesite. One stump has a large white *A* painted on it, the other an even larger *J*. Beside the grave stands a square sign with roughly painted scenes from Johnson's life; it bears the following legend:

THE MAD TRAPPER
ALBERT JOHNSON
ARRIVED IN ROSS
RIVER AUG. 21, 1927
COMPLAINTS OF
LOCAL TRAPPERS
BROUGHT THE RCMP
ON HIM HE SHOT TWO
OFFICERS AND BE-
CAME A FUGITIVE OF
THE LAW WITH HOWL
ING HUSKIES, DANGER
OUS TRAILS, FROZEN
NIGHTS. THE POSSE
FINALLY CAUGHT UP
WITH HIM. HE WAS
KILLED UP THE
EAGLE RIVER
     FEB 17, 1932

The slender white crosses, the white picket fences of the graves of the good citizens of Aklavik crowd about, spreading to the far corners of the cemetery; only this once-ostracized "fugitive of the law" whose true name is not known to this day receives so much attention. Tourists are always there, taking pictures. Why are murderers so much remembered?

I submit that Albert Johnson is simply the most obvious example of a human being in the North with a secret, and in contemplating his, some of the wider secrets of the Arctic landscape will become clearer.

In one of the most beautiful short stories ever written, "The Lady with the Pet Dog," Anton Chekhov has his protagonist recognize:

> The personal life of every individual is based on secrecy, and perhaps it is for that reason that civilized people insist so strongly that personal privacy be respected.

Chekhov's protagonist, Gurov, is thinking of the double life he personally leads. Gurov recognizes that "he had two lives, an open one" (which is the conventional life that everyone knows) "and another life that went on in secret ... that no living soul knew of ... Everything of importance ... everything about which [he] ... did not deceive himself" is in that second, secret life.

Now despite a massive manhunt and 55 years of sporadic search by police and private persons, we know nothing whatever of Albert Johnson's secret life; in fact, his public life is known only from 7 July 1931, when he arrives in Fort McPherson, N.W.T., until he is killed "up the Eagle River" on 17 February 1932, and becomes a motionless dot on the Yukon ice. His most elementary secret, that of his name, defies discovery. The legend (I use the word advisedly, in two of its possible meanings) on the grave board on Aklavik's main street which states that Albert Johnson "arrived in Ross River Aug. 21, 1927" is fact only if we identify him with a certain man who in Ross River called himself Arthur Nelson. Ross River, Yukon Territory, is as the raven flies at least 600 kilometers from Fort McPherson, Northwest Territories; it is almost twice that far by mountainous river, which is how Albert Johnson arrived there. A Whitehorse historian, Dick North, has identified Johnson with Nelson; but Nelson's past, his story, seemed untraceable before Ross River. Now, however, after 20 years of "obsession" (North himself uses that word) with Johnson/Nelson, North is at last positive he has found the man's real name, and with it all the vast revelation of human activity and personality, of family and past and birth and place which a public name must expose, that immense factual story which every human being in the retrospect of memory has lived.

Strange to say, North believes that the fugitive's name really was Johnson. Only his given name was different: instead of the relatively distinctive "Albert," North says it was, of all most ordinary names, "John." This John Johnson was born in Norway and from the age of one grew up in North Dakota; he was a convicted bank robber and horse thief by age 17 (1915), and spent several years in various U.S. prisons before apparently disappearing into Canada in 1923. After years of following every shred of evidence to build his case, all North lacked to make the last, indisputable identification between the two Johnsons was Albert's fingerprints. However, the prints taken from Albert Johnson after his death have disappeared from the RCMP's file.

How it is possible that one of the most famous police forces in the world has not kept the ultimate record of an unidentified criminal I will not try to explain here. North writes, "This left only one recourse for me, and that was to dig up Albert's body ... He was buried in permafrost and consequently his skin probably would be in good enough shape to 'lift' the prints." On 27 April 1987, the news went round the Yukon by radio and newspaper that the hamlet of Aklavik had given Dick North permission to exhume Johnson's body.

Oddly enough, on that Monday, 27 April, I was in Old Crow, Yukon. That evening I met some 20 Loucheux people of the Old Crow community who came to talk with me about my writing, and particularly what I knew about Albert Johnson. We were talking quietly, slowly comparing bits of information, when one man who had not sat down when we began suddenly asked on my left, very loudly: "Do you know who shot him first, that Albert Johnson?"

His tone was incredibly loud in the, until then, friendly room. Everyone was peering at me intently.

"I'm not sure," I said. "Do you?"

"Sure I know," he declared. "Everybody here knows that, it was Johnny Moses right from here, Old Crow, he was a special constable for the police and he had permission to shoot, he was the best shot and he fired and hit him first in the foot so he couldn't run to the bank and get away, he'd have got away, they'd of never got him, that's why he was stuck there in the middle of the Eagle River. It was Johnny Moses." And then the man was shouting. "What they say is all bullshit in all them books! Bullshit! When they got him there on the Eagle River the police shot him so full of lead they couldn't lift him into the plane, ten men couldn't lift him, he was so full of lead."

Some of the people were smiling a little. What this Old Crow man said was obviously impossible, but it was not ridiculous. Once, years before in Victoria, B.C., when I read from *The Temptations of Big Bear* the scene of the Mounted Police attack in 1885 on Big Bear's sleeping camp at Loon Lake Crossing, a Cree Indian asked me after the reading whether I knew that the

North West Mounted Police had killed over 300 of his people there and buried them so their bodies could never be found? I knew that if such had been the case more or less the whole band would have been annihilated; as it was I knew of only two men actually shot and killed there while an old woman on the retreat hanged herself for terror. But it seemed to me then, and it seemed to me also in Old Crow, that the story I was hearing was far from ridiculous. Something beyond mere facts was being told, a truth only words, not facts, could create. But before I had to say anything, the man continued even louder:

"It was Christmas, Jesus Christ, Christmas when the goddam police bang on his door, so why didn't they bring him a turkey and say 'Merry Christmas' and leave him alone? Eh?"

My mind was stumbling, but I tried to turn his rage a little. "Well, even if the police come banging on your house at Christmas and disturb you, you're *still* not supposed to shoot them through your door."

Some of the people chuckled with me, but for a few more moments he ranted almost wildly. I was stunned; could not quite believe this: but it was certainly in keeping with the whole, extraordinarily beautiful day.

It began by flying north from Dawson City, the brilliant spring sun on the snow of the Ogilvie Mountains, the sinuous bends of the Porcupine River and the tiny village set against the airstrip at the foot of Old Crow Mountain, its green spruce and streets packed in solid snow of all-skidoo traffic. That afternoon I had given a long reading and told stories at the school and then I was taken back to the airport where the band had arranged that a plane fly me to the Richardson Mountains and the Eagle River. "We're gonna show you where Albert Johnson got shot," the pilot told me. I had never been there. With us came two Old Crow high-school teachers who had read my novel *The Mad Trapper* and two band elders. One of them, the venerable old woman sitting beside me in the Cessna, introduced herself as the sister of Johnny Moses, the RCMP special constable who had been at that shootout 55 years before, though she did not then tell me her brother had shot Albert Johnson first.

So we flew east, over the widely scattered, still deserted summer fishcamps and hunting camps in the snow at the caribou crossings, along the frozen river, further east until the Richardson Mountains appeared, abruptly, like enormous unglaciated pyramids folded irregularly into each other like a white random scattering of conical shapes, and all so deadly white with their creeks outlined by black spruce. Clouds covered the Barrier River Pass which Johnson crossed in an impossible blizzard after killing Constable Edgar Millen, so we could not fly there, but the twisting loops of the Bell River, the deserted roofless walls of the three buildings of La Pierre House, the beau-

tiful circular sweep of the Bell River west around a mountain to join the
Porcupine and there, just like a map, the Eagle River entering the Bell from
the south.

We droned a little lower. We saw a moose feeding among willows and then
the pilot laughed, "Oh, what the hell," and went down to 150 feet, tilted, and
I saw tracks, mink and marten trails, looping out from the river banks, even
the tiny spoor of weasel, everything so icy sharp in the incredible air I need
not breathe, only look. And then the plane made a wide turn and I saw what
I had imagined, tried to imagine years before again and again: I saw the tight
reversed *S* turn of the narrow river outlined by the straggling black spruce,
the tight reversed *S* where Johnson, deceived at last by the twists of the river,
ran backwards in his tracks because he thought the posse was already ahead
of him and, rounding the tight bend of that betrayal, suddenly met the dogs,
the men, the rifles racing after him head on.

It was so exactly as I had imagined it, in the plane I knew I was dreaming.
It seemed I saw through that window, past the strut and the motionless wheel,
under the shadow of that wing the actualization of what I had dreamt 16 years
before and then dreamt again and again trying to snare that in the words of
a short story, of a film script, of a novel. There, on exactly such ice, between
those precise, tiny, bristled trees, 55 years ago. Though of course the river
under that ice could not be the same. But perhaps it was. Precisely every
particle how many diurnal cycles later?

The man in the Community Center at Old Crow, standing in the steady
10:30 p.m. daylight of 27 April, had stopped shouting. He was talking quietly
now, but with very great intensity.

"Men go crazy, you know," he said. "I've seen men, anybody here has seen
men go really crazy. You can't help that and you should just get out of the
way, leave them alone, they'll be okay, just leave them alone. Why do you
have to bother a man when he goes really crazy, huh?"

Such words did not seem to expect words in reply. After a while I asked
them all, "What do you think, should they dig him up now to get his
fingerprints?"

Nobody said anything. "They'd probably find out for sure who he was
then," I said.

A woman at the back said, "They should leave him alone."

Next morning a skidoo stopped beside me as I walked down the street; it
was driven by a lean, handsome man about my age in a wolverine trim parka.
We'd met at the hall the night before and now in the sunlight he wore dark
glasses so I couldn't see his eyes.

"I was gonna say something," he said, "but then that guy got going ..." He
shrugged.

"Oh, yeah," I said. "We talked after. He told me his father was a Danish
whaler who came to Herschel Island on a whaling ship, so I asked him where

were his blue eyes and blond hair."

But the skidoo driver would not laugh. He said, "Johnny Moses was my uncle. My mom lives over there, she was with you on the plane."

"Did your uncle ever talk about that manhunt?"

"Not to me."

"How come?"

He said thoughtfully, "I guess he didn't want to. He talked to my mom a lot, I know, but that's all."

"Would she talk to me about that?"

"I don't know." He was silent for a time, but made no move to go. The morning sun was almost stunning on the snow. "Once a few years before he died he was working with a construction crew near the Eagle River, they got close to that place on the river and one of the workers made a joke about it, said something like, 'Hey, Johnnie, isn't this the famous place you shot Albert Johnson?' and he just put down his tools and walked away from there. Just disappeared. The foreman got worried and radioed my mom and I went out to look for him. It took me two weeks. He was camped in the bush way up the Porcupine, just his rifle and knife. Not even a tent. He knew how to live in the bush like that."

"He came back with you?"

"Yeah. I stayed with him a few days and then we came back."

I didn't know how I could ask what I wanted so badly to ask, and finally I said something unnecessary, totally obvious. "He wasn't working for the police any more?"

"No. He never did after that," and it was clear from his tone what "that" was. "There was something about that Johnson ... something strange."

That was the same word a Hareskin man from Fort Good Hope used to describe the Mackenzie River. He said it twice, very thoughtfully, remembering perhaps his own lifetime beside its heavy brown darkness and all the people that had vanished into it: "The river is strange ... strange. It will roll a body along the bottom for six days before it lifts it up so you can see it, 40 miles away." That had happened to his best friend that very spring who with his girlfriend was late one night following him in a river boat headed for Fort Good Hope. In the morning they found the boat, its kicker still idling slowly, turning circles on the river and the girl sleeping huddled in the prow, still unaware that she was alone. "His body was way past Good Hope six days later, it come up. We only recognized him from the bits of clothes left on him. Sometimes they won't come up at all, if the water's too cold. Maybe in the spring, somewhere. By then you don't know them anyway."

One looks into a moving, dark, strange river like the Mackenzie and you will see nothing; only yourself. You follow a moving, dark strange man in linear (like a river) pursuit for six weeks along Arctic mountains and rivers and what else can you expect to see? Some who took part in that pursuit cannot bear ever to talk about it; some will talk a little; but none of them will *do* it again; they refuse to repeat that story.

There were only three Loucheux Indians in that police posse on the Eagle River on 17 February 1932: Johnny Moses, Peter Alexis, and Lazarus Sittichinli. Only Sittichinli is still alive; in fact, he is the last man left of the entire hunt.

Lazarus Sittichinli now, in his small red house two blocks from Albert Johnson's grave and across the street from the Anglican Hospital, the Anglican Church, opens the door to me whom he has never seen or heard of: a tiny dark shrunken man, a few hairs bristle on his face, oddly powerful hands still with heavy horn-like nails. He walks to the kitchen table supporting himself on a four-point walker; he gestures for me to sit down. He is 97 years old and he says he lifted Johnson up, out of his hole in the snow on the Eagle River, and turned him over so they could look at him. Peter Alexis and Karl Gardlund, who had been shooting from the same side of the river as Sittichinli, had advanced with him. Behind them came trader Frank Jackson and the police inspector.

"You know this man?" the inspector asked.

Alexis said, "I never know him."

In the warm house Mrs. Sittichinli sits dozing in a soft chair while the old man tells me that whole story again. Without prompting, as easily as if it had happened yesterday and acting out all the parts, changing voices, his brown hands shape the story in air, and I know it so well I only hear details that no one else can ever give me: "Johnson had a bullet cut all across his belly; he had no grub, he'd been eating spruce gum and whisky jack; he had a string with a rag tied to it in the barrel of his 30-30 to keep out the snow so it wouldn't clog and explode; he could jerk the string out, clean the barrel and shoot almost in the same motion." I mostly watch Lazarus' high-boned face move in his slightly off-beat English, or his ancient wife, a soft mound breathing, her moose moccasins laced up under her long cotton dress. They have been married 76 years and 12 of their 14 children have already died. But there are plenty of grandchildren and great- and great-great-grandchildren around. He's fed them hunting caribou at the river crossings and sheep, lots of Dahl sheep in the mountains. "I'm always lucky hunting," he says. "All the men from town here always follow me hunting in the Richardson mountains, sheep. All my life we live on hunting and trapping, we always live in the bush."

"Could you do that, working as special constable for the police?"

"I never did after that," he says. "I quit, then."

So then I could ask him why. He is tired now, and clearing his throat of phlegm, his toothless jaws moving sometimes as if he were eating Loucheux words which my Canadian ear could not understand anyway. The story is long, but he wants to tell it long, how he brought his dog team back then from the Eagle River over the mountains after four days, and the inspector, who had flown in with the badly wounded Hersey and Johnson's body, told him he should take a holiday after so much hard work on the two-month patrol. He was only earning $75 a month. But next morning the inspector (Lazarus never calls him Eames or Alex; he names him only by function) was at his door as usual, told him to haul in four big trees for flag poles. Several other things happened then, but now Lazarus shifts erect at the table, his black eyes suddenly fierce, bright. "I get the trees but I was mad," he says. "I tell him I'm not working no more. I quit now, you break your word, I break my word. I go home. A little later the inspector he come to my house. 'Why you quit?' 'You're asking too much.' 'No, no, you stay with us.' 'No.' 'Well, be the town police then.' 'No,' I say. 'I won't police my own people. That's no good.' So I go home and I stay quit."

Like every storyteller in the north he has acted all the parts as he speaks them, his voice changing to suit authority or obedience or anger. But at times there was something else in his tone; something like the man in Old Crow remembering his uncle Johnny Moses who had followed the twisting spiraling river of Johnson's self-mocking flight almost as far as Lazarus Sittichinli, and who had been there when Lazarus lifted that frost-blackened, starved body out of the snow. "I said I have a good place on the Husky River," this ancient man tells me in that strange, abstracted tone. "Good for trapping. And I work sometimes in the hospital. But not the police." William Nerysoo spoke the same way. He is 94 years old, living alone in a one-room house in the middle of Fort McPherson on the Peel River. He took no part in the six-week hunt; he was the man who originally reported to the police that he believed Johnson was disturbing his traps, which report started it all. When I visited him in 1983, almost the first thing he said to me was, "I won't tell you anything about that. Everybody comes here and asks me, I go to the store and the little boys yell after me, 'Hey, Madtrapper! Madtrapper!' I don't tell you anything." "Okay," I said. "Okay." What else could I say? A neighbor man came into the little house then, we talked of the spring caribou moving north to their calving grounds, and suddenly Nerysoo said, "Maybe I'll tell you one thing." After a while, he had told me his whole story, and though I will not repeat it, his tone and his gentle, gradually insistent return to that trapline telling me more than his words about that trap and the fatal report he had once made. What is it about these men? They are, in Chekhov's terms, "insisting so strongly on preserving someone's personal secret." It seems they are, for that insistence, the most civilized of people. I asked Lazarus Sittichinli about digging up that famous grave down the street.

"I don't like that," he said. "There are people who do all kinds of things to themselves—if you want some fingerprints, take theirs. But no digging. Johnson, he had enough suffering. Leave him alone."

Alone with his locked, his unlockable secret. His untold, untraceable story. The long river of his flight is as opaque as the Peel on which he first appeared, the gigantic Mackenzie whose opaqueness it somewhere, indecipherably, enters.

But those Indian men who remembered their roles in the hunt for that man who defended his aloneness with such single-minded and truly horrifying intensity, they remember their roles with no joy, no recalled heroism; those men were the farthest thing from being "loners." White people like Albert Johnson appearing somewhere from southern Canada may be that— leave them alone—but a Loucheux or Inuit "loner" seems incredible. It is a contradiction by very concept. Both Indians and Inuit have extended families that stretch beyond children in all possible directions of cousins and nieces and parents and adoptions and in-laws. It seems in the Arctic that everyone lives in a community; in any one community everyone, except for a few whites, is related to everyone else; when any community has a celebration, all the other relatives within a day's flying from all the other communities will arrive by chartered plane to help in the celebration. When they do that, they tell each other their continuing stories even as they live any number of new ones: stories here are a construct of spoken words by means of which we remember. And this oral story-telling, so refined and perfected by millennia of skilled practice, is the very affirmation of their non-aloneness: the story-teller and the poet-singer presuppose a community of listeners; otherwise nothing could be told. One may read a book alone (in fact, most of us prefer that) but one cannot tell a story alone. That is why any language changes so drastically when it moves from oral to written form. Now the most minimal word, spoken or written, about any human being is *name*, and everyone who hides even that goes beyond secret into enigma. That is, into intentional obscurity. There is then no story to tell and the original people of the Canadian Arctic living in tiny communities on the immense landscape find such a refusal of story especially strange, disturbing, puzzling as only an oral, communal people can; but they respect it. Leave him alone. There is no story to tell; or, as William Nerysoo tells me, I won't tell you the story I know is there. Yet he is too much a person of his people and his landscape to ultimately refuse it; all you have to do is wait.

Nevertheless, Nerysoo's refusal to tell me his stories until he had some confidence in me underlines their enormous power. Songs, stories are the memory of a people, the particular individual rivers of the sea of life which constitutes us all. And when you hide that, when you insist the river of your life is as opaque as the Mackenzie or Peel, you are defying the ancient assertion of that sea: you still do have a story (you cannot *not* have a story: you had a mother, you had a place and time when you were born, you have moved because you were alive) but if you persist so absolutely with silence, motionless silence even unto death, then we will respect your refusal of your own story. We will leave you alone, though we will continue to tell what little we do know because that is the only way human life continues.

Death continues to hide Albert Johnson. Experts disagreed about the permafrost at Aklavik being strong enough to preserve his body so well that fingerprints could still be taken. "Hell," one Aklavik resident told me, "I've lived here for 12 years and I've seen the Mackenzie flood the graveyard so bad there were bones floating around. There's nothing left of him." The river, hiding a secret again. Besides, the territorial governor explained to me that between 1932 and 1933 three suicides had been buried beside Johnson and now, even if the bodies were well preserved, no one would know exactly which body was whose. Ironically, the iconoclastic Johnson, who in life refused to live near anyone, in death is now protected by what he would have considered a crowd. In any case, soon after the 27 April announcement, a petition against the disinterment was signed by more people than actually live in Aklavik. It seems that Dick North with his implacable white man's obsession to know is not going to get his clinching evidence. Johnson remains an enigmatic secret. Perhaps 55 years is enough to leave him at that; to leave him *alone*.

The Spirit Weeps
STEPHEN HUME

· · · · · · · · ·

In anticipation of the high international profile Canada would achieve during the 1988 winter Olympics in Calgary, organizing officials planned a dazzling constellation of parallel events intended to showcase the richness and diversity of our national culture. Writers, poets, musicians and painters were to celebrate the Greek ideal of mind and body with demonstrations of their creative prowess to match the physical performances of athletes. As part of this program, Alberta's Glenbow Institute, backed by the major corporate sponsorship of an oil industry giant, Shell Canada Limited, began preparations for what was to be the most complex and complete display of the art of Canadian aboriginal peoples in world history.

For five years before the Olympic Games began, a committee of six distinguished scholars, each bringing specialized knowledge from one of the six cultural regions of aboriginal Canada, began planning the exhibition. The Glenbow is itself a world class museum and archive, particularly with reference to the culture and ethnology of plains Indians. But it was clear from the beginning that the scope and magnitude of the exhibition planned could not be mounted with the resources of the Glenbow alone. Starting with a commitment of $600,000 in seed money from the Olympic Organizing Committee and $1,100,000 from Shell, the curatorial scholars began taking inventory of where Canadian aboriginal artifacts might be located outside Canada and subsequently borrowed for exhibition before national and international audiences. By the time they were finished, the committee

---

"The Spirit Weeps" was Stephen Hume's comment on the controversy surrounding "The Spirit Sings," an exhibition of native artifacts that drew the ire of Indian leaders because it exposed certain sacred relics to public view. Hume (born 1947) began as a copyboy on the Edmonton Journal *in 1966 and was the paper's editor until 1987 when he became general manager; this essay appeared in the* Journal *and some other Southam newspapers between February and June 1988. Hume is also a poet, his most recent collection being* And the House Sank like a Ship in the Long Prairie Grass, *published in 1987. A collection of essays,* Ghost Camps, *will be published in 1989.*

had scoured more than 150 museums and private collections across 20 foreign countries and arranged the display of more than 600 artifacts. The show was staged in two segments. The first took place at the Glenbow itself, preceding and coinciding with the Olympic Games; the second, in association with the new National Museum of Civilization, was mounted three months later in Ottawa, using the former premises of Canada's national art gallery for the eastern venue.

The Spirit Sings proved a curator's tour de force. The committee had mounted a show of stunning power and intensity. All the displays resonated with aesthetic genius and a deep sense of spiritual place. Yet this exhibition of the artistic traditions of Canada's first people, so wonderful in the hermetic context of ethnological display, was also an act of national hypocrisy so shocking as to border on the obscene. It triggered deep anger and hurt among the very native peoples it purported to celebrate and raised profound questions regarding the integrity of Canada's social and intellectual conscience.

Art cannot be detached from the social and historical matrix in which it originates, however much museum curators might desire to do so in the interests of neat classification and compartmentalized analysis, and however much the state might seize upon it as an opportunity for shameless propagandizing and outright lying. And that was the great irony of The Spirit Sings. Mounted in celebration of our first peoples, it used their art to tell the world a fundamental lie about our national concern for their rights and well-being. The exhibits displayed in The Spirit Sings and the powerful controversy surrounding them were testimony not only to the richness and diversity of native culture, but also to the rapacious and destructive force of European settlement in North America and the continued brutality of Canadian institutions toward native social and political aspirations.

If much of the early destruction of aboriginal culture was caused by people who were not Canadians, but the worst of European adventurers—the ancestors of those who now piously seek to deprive remote and impoverished native communities of their traditional economic base in hunting and trapping—Canadians later had the opportunity to chart a different course. The Spirit Sings exhibited damning evidence of our choice not to do so.

While the relics displayed were the beautiful works of sensitive and intelligent artists, they also represented the debris that we robbed from the rubble of cultures whose traditions we first demolished, then sought to extinguish.

Indiscriminate bombardments of Indian villages by naval flotillas, massacres of women and children by punitive fur traders, tolerance of the ravages of disease and economic impoverishment, denial of universal access in the law, selective official segregation, the corporal punishment of children for speaking their own language in federal schools, the legal banning of ritual, ceremony and religion, denial of the vote—these are phenomena not of some barbarous Dark Age, but of recent Canadian history.

It was significant that while the officials and curators were congratulating themselves on the commercial success and aesthetic quality of their show, Georges Erasmus of the Assembly of First Nations was warning Canadians that a new generation of young native "warriors" may be contemplating armed violence instead of talk, having learned that negotiation in good faith with Canada's political institutions appears to be a failure. Indeed, as Alberta officials basked in the Olympic limelight, the Sioux nation was announcing the appointment of its first formal war chief since Sitting Bull crossed the Medicine Line not far from Calgary, carrying the scalps of Custer's Seventh Cavalry. The Sioux had called back Philip Stevens, the 59-year-old great grandson of Chief Standing Bear. Stevens, head of a multi-million-dollar engineering firm, was charged with responsibility for recovering the Black Hills, a sacred spiritual center for the Sioux nation which was never surrendered by treaty.

In Alberta, while The Spirit Sings talked about the importance of art, no less than a dozen outstanding aboriginal claims awaited formal adjudication in the courts. Some of them, like the question of title to the lands of the dispossessed—and now conveniently dispersed—Papaschase band, are the matters of historic and legal curiosity. The Papaschase lands, now occupied by the University of Alberta and most of the south side of Edmonton, may have been surrendered to land speculators under manipulated, defective and highly questionable procedures. But with no survivors of the band, who could legally reopen the issue? Other aboriginal claims are more immediate, from the Peigan of southern Alberta who object that the Oldman River dam constructed by the provincial government destroys their ancestral spiritual centers, to the Lubicons of the north who simply want a settlement after half a century of moral dithering, legalistic equivocating and political indecision by federal and provincial authorities.

The tiny and isolated Lubicon band, 20% of which had just tested positive for tuberculosis—a disease long banished from the general population— went so far as to attempt political action, demonstrating outside the Glenbow in Calgary and seeking public support for a boycott of The Spirit Sings during the Olympics. The 350 Lubicons were joined in protest by the Mohawks, who went to court in an unsuccessful attempt to block the showing of a sacred ceremonial mask, public display of which amounted to a religious desecration. As the simple, rural Lubicons made their small public protest outside the Glenbow, the racist and abusive remarks of Calgarians entering the exhibition shocked even the worldly correspondent from *The Chicago*

Tribune, assigned to cover the show and no stranger to racism. The attitude of the public towards the Indians, of course, marred the Olympic spirit in a far more fundamental way than the Lubicons' protest had. It also revealed the true nature of The Spirit Sings exhibition: not so much a celebration of native culture as self-congratulatory propaganda regarding the importance of such peoples to the Canadian state.

In this context, passing through the opening gallery at the Spirit Sings exhibition and gazing upon the 30 or so pathetic little artifacts that represented Canada's extinguished Beothuk nation in Newfoundland, what manner of person could not feel appalled and shamed that the memory of an exterminated nation should be so evoked in the service of our national pride? What perverted manner of pride could be taken from this? It was as though the Berlin Olympics had put on a display of Jewish religious objects to celebrate the diversity, pluralism and tolerance of Nazi culture.

Staring at the tiny pair of baby's moccasins, or near them, the little effigy taken from the grave of a four-year-old child, I could think only of the story of Demasduwit. She had given birth only two days earlier when she was seized by John Peyton's party in 1819. Her husband pleaded fruitlessly for his wife's return. When he struggled to free her, he was killed before her eyes like a troublesome cur. Demasduwit's baby was abandoned to die. The mother was taken off to be "civilized." A month later, in an act of unusual generosity, her corpse was returned to her dwindling people in a coffin—a gesture intended, no doubt, to emphasize her captor's civilized concern with appearances. Ten years later, the last of her people had died in captivity and the Beothuk nation was extinct.

Demasduwit had not even the dignity of a quiet grave. In 1827, in the interests of preserving for posterity something of the vanished Beothuk culture, William Cormack robbed the grave of the woman, her husband and the little baby, taking two skulls and the collection of burial offerings. To witness the murdered woman's modest possessions—for murder it most certainly was—displayed in honor of a sports event and Canadian self-aggrandizement, is to sense the trivialization of a tragedy of enormous proportions.

Elaborate apologies have been written regarding the fate of the Beothuk in Canadian history, dismissing as mere legend the popular accounts of bounties paid for ears and 18th Century "hunting" expeditions by European settlers. In many cases the demise of the Beothuk is blamed upon incursions by warlike neighbors from the mainland. Denial, prevarication and casting of blame upon the victims are typical of the consistent Canadian refusal to take ownership of the ugly parts of our past, although this approach fails to address the simple fact that the Beothuk were a coastal people when the European settlers arrived, then suddenly fled to a bitter and inhospitable interior that remains largely uninhabited even today. It was there, as far from the settlers as they could get, that they finally perished in poverty, starvation and disease.

The magnificent artifacts of the Beothuk's neighbors in the Maritime provinces, also displayed by The Spirit Sings, are equally poignant in forcing our attention to the brutality of European conquest and occupation. Think of their fate this way: when the most bloodthirsty Roman despots set out to terrorize dissident elements, they would order a "decimation" in which every tenth person was executed. Between 1600 and 1700, not one out of every 10, but nine out of every 10 people of the Micmac and Maliseet nations died or were killed—a number which makes Caligula seem moderate by comparison. Or one might admire the lovely decoration of deerskin dresses by Huron women. The Huron population declined by 65%, from 25,000 to 9,000 people, in little over a decade. A similar rate of decline in contemporary Canada would see the disappearance of every person living outside Quebec. The Huron's major mistake was in becoming an ally of the French, who lost to the English. By the time the winners were finished, the Huron were in diaspora, some fleeing as far as the present state of Oklahoma. This pattern is characteristic of the Canadian experience. It is estimated by some scholars that the total native population of the Canadian landmass might have been as high as 1,000,000 people at the time of first European contact. At the turn of the century it had declined to about 100,000. This is a cultural destruction that approaches genocidal proportions.

The Spirit Sings exhibition dealt with these unpleasant realities in an oblique and less than forthright way. It was, after all, an "ethnological" display rather than an expression of historical context. On reflection, it is clear, the show was actually intended to tell the world and ourselves what a generous and tolerant country we live in; how quick we are to recognize and honor the way in which the culture of native peoples has enriched our broader society. In fact, the social, ethical, political, spiritual and philosophical values of native culture have been almost universally rejected by the dominant society. On the other hand, native culture has certainly enriched museums, even if we consistently exclude it from contributing to the mainstream. And many of the museums that have been enriched are not even Canadian. Douglas Cole, a historian at Simon Fraser University in Vancouver, exhaustively documents the patterns of theft and acquisition in his important book *Captured Heritage*. An estimated 300,000 artifacts from the Northwest Pacific coastal cultures are now held by international collections—this is looting on the scale of the Visigoths.

The cataloguing and administration of such collections have made fine careers for curators, who by some extraordinary ethical gymnastics find easy praise for the value of native art while remaining strangely ineffectual regarding the social value of the human beings who produced it. But instead of debating the collective responsibility of the collectors, we might consider instead the social context of a selection of wonderful Assiniboine drawings, kindly loaned by their European owner to The Spirit Sings organizers for display in Canada.

The Assiniboines, numbering about 9,000 and among the great traders of the plains tribes, ranged across the central Canadian prairies. In 1833, the winter counts of the Teton Sioux, Kiowa and Blackfeet record unusual numbers of shooting stars, generally considered a harbinger of some natural catastrophe. Major Alexander Culbertson at Fort McKenzie confirms the sightings. The native people did not have long to wait. By 1837, horrified European travelers were reporting the whole prairie region littered with the rotting corpses of men, women and children, abandoned equipment, straying horse herds, and the encampments that brought a new term to plains Indian language—the Ghost Camp, where the lodges are occupied only by the dead.

The pestilence and infection of smallpox reduced the Assiniboines from the most powerful nation on the great plains to a pitiful, ragged remnant, begging for food. They had been, in the reports of appalled observers, virtually exterminated. While the cycle of plagues which ravaged the plains cultures in 1837 and again in 1864, 1868 and 1883 could hardly be attributed to federal policy, they did offer a convenient clearing of the landscape for unencumbered settlement by the huge influx of farmers that was deliberate policy in Ottawa.

Shortly thereafter, the strategic elimination of the plains Indians' primary food source occurred. In 1875, the Baker Company of Fort Benton, Montana, shipped 75,000 buffalo hides to the east. Most of them had been taken from the hunting grounds of Canada's Blackfeet, Blood, Peigan and Sarcee tribes, the carcasses left to rot in the summer sun, the bones later collected and shipped for fertilizer production. Four years later, the buffalo were gone forever from the southern Alberta grasslands and Canadian society marched its native people into the concentration camp.

Today we call them Indian reserves, sharing our love of the euphemism with the South Africans, who call them "homelands," but let us not deceive ourselves about their original function. The rationalization for reserves, of course, was that they were created to save the few aboriginals who managed to survive the dismantling of their economy and the wrecking of their political structure, social organization, religion and family units. Indian reserves were invented by bureaucrats to control the movements of free-ranging people and to "concentrate" them in one place and bring them under the power of the dominant society.

Indian reserves were designed with the specific purpose of destroying plains Indian culture, which was predicated upon movement and freedom, so that the land might be carved up by newcomers who could get more productive use out of it by farming. As the topsoil of Palliser's Triangle, the arid region of southeastern Alberta and southwestern Saskatchewan, blows away on the dry winds of drought, demanding more and more dams and irrigation districts, with the attendant hazards of salinization—not to mention the overall tax burden—the definitions of what constitutes productivity require a new evaluation.

The most intense element of The Spirit Sings was its remarkable and moving celebration of the deep and complex spiritual nature of Indian life. In this, too, the exhibition brings shame upon us. Consider all those missionaries, acting in the name of a compassionate Christ, whose objective was the displacement of all the spiritual beliefs the exhibition purports to celebrate. To this day the church has difficulty bringing itself to acknowledge its role as an agent of cultural destruction. Yet with all the best of intentions, missionaries representing the two mainstreams of Christian religion waged an active campaign to displace traditional religious belief and value systems among native peoples. At a time when aboriginal societies faced enormous upheaval and change, their societies threatened by the growing military, economic and commercial pressure from the European invaders, church missionaries set about sucking out the glue which held native communities together. By devaluing the moral force of traditional spiritual leaders and co-opting the belief and value systems of native people, the church served as an active agent in fomenting confusion and increasing vulnerability—always there with compassion, of course, to help pick up the pieces and shape them into a Christian and essentially European framework.

Evocative examples of the disruptive influence of Christian missionaries can be found almost everywhere. The Inuit settlement of Igloolik, high in Canada's central arctic, provides one good example. It was the site of a shameless "war for souls" which raged between Anglicans and Roman Catholics, as though the numbers of converted were pieces in a chess game. Fifty years later, a visitor from outside could still witness the scars of deep division in a community that had been homogeneous and secure. The Tsartlip Indian Reserve of Vancouver Island is another example. It had the early distinction of having all its residents formally converted by itinerant priests, first to Roman Catholicism, then Anglicanism and then Methodism—all in the same year.

The state certainly concurred with this approach, seeing the church as a powerful instrument of assimilation. Missionaries like William Duncan, who established a mission to the Tsimshian at Metlakatla, off the coast of what is now the Alaska Panhandle, saw traditional native rites as an obstacle to Christian conversion and lobbied for their prohibition. Duncan was particularly offended by the ancient puberty rites that accompanied potlatch ceremonials. By 1885, with the wholehearted backing of the various churches,

Canada's Parliament had passed legislation which prohibited the practice of native religious and spiritual ceremonies.

The Canadian state took suppression of native ceremonies seriously indeed. In 1922, following a traditional potlatch at Alert Bay, a prosperous Kwakiutl community located just off the northeast coast of Vancouver Island, a large number of men and women (the Indians say 45, the official records say 29) were arrested for the offences of making speeches, singing, dancing, arranging and distributing gifts. The police action followed complaints from the federal Indian agent, William Halliday, who, in a gross conflict of interest, conveniently doubled as magistrate for the trial. The arresting officer, an RCMP sergeant, took the role of prosecutor. In this perversion of justice, 20 of the men and women arrested were sentenced to prison terms of two and three months. Fines were levied in the form of their ancestral ceremonial regalia, which were seized by the federal government. Halliday reported more than 450 items filling 300 cubic feet of space. Some, according to Cole, he sold off to a foreign collector for $291, the rest went to the curators at the National Museum in Ottawa, the forerunner of the same Museum of Civilization which hosted The Spirit Sings.

These officials salved their conscience in the matter by assigning arbitrary commercial values to the items and sending cheques to the Indian agent for distribution. Cole points out in *Captured Heritage* that some Indians claim never to have received a penny's compensation for the priceless material—one item of which was believed by the Indians themselves to have a value of 18,250 Hudson's Bay Company blankets. Ultimately, part of the stolen property was returned after 66 years and a legal battle, but much of it has been lost to the owners and, in any event, as Cole points out: "The charges and convictions, the surrenders and imprisonments, were a severe blow even to so resilient a culture as that of the Kwakiutl ... But the forced cessation of the public potlatch, the feasts, and the dances was a more severe blow."

This essential contempt by the collectors of artifacts for the validity of traditional cultural values which the material items represent continues today. At the Calgary segment of The Spirit Sings, the curators insisted on displaying sacred objects in bald defiance of the wishes of those who consider them sacred. Sacred objects, it seems, are merely property, and in Canadian society ownership is nine-tenths of the law. Would the Pope and the Archbishop of Canterbury feel that way about the sacraments and holy relics of their faith, one wonders. At the Ottawa segment of the exhibition, at least, the authorities reportedly decided not to include the false-face mask of the Mohawk nation, public display of which the Indians had fruitlessly sought to block by court action. One wonders, however, whether this decision had more to do with the proximity of angry Iroquois to Ottawa than with real understanding or compassion for the ethical issue.

At the Glenbow exhibit in Calgary, which is surrounded by the Blood, Peigan, Sarcee, Blackfeet and Stoney reserves, cards were provided for observers to record their feelings. "Sometimes our spirit has wept," wrote one viewer. "Sadness for my people who lost so much of their spirit when their ceremonial objects were laid down or taken away"—an interesting irony considered in the context of the consistent robbing of native cultural items in order that museums might provide evidence of the "preservation" of native culture. This juxtaposition of the aboriginal view and the official view says much about Canadian values. It confirms what has long been clear—that we actually prefer our native culture in museums. We certainly do not prefer it running the Department of Indian Affairs or the Department of Fisheries. Nor do we prefer native culture announcing the news on national television or determining its own political destiny.

"Where are the natives whose heritage this is?" asked another observer in Calgary. "Couldn't you find ANY to guide us through THEIR history ... the spirits must be crying." This, too, draws attention to the wretched lie at the heart of The Spirit Sings. We prefer native culture that we may put on display when it conveniences us, called out for ceremonies that make us appear magnanimous—whether the creators of the artifacts like it or not.

"Why get upset, it's all in the past," one young white observer said to me after hearing my feelings about the show. "We didn't do it, somebody else did. Don't expect me to feel guilty for my great-grandfather." This view I did not find surprising. It is the constant bleat of Canadian society with respect to native peoples. It was somebody else's fault. It is somebody else's responsibility. This familiar refrain lies at the very heart of northern Alberta's Lubicon band dispute, still festering after 50 years of political buck-passing and evasion of moral responsibility by the federal and provincial governments.

"It's all in the past ... "

Tell that to the people of Peerless Lake, where on 10 March 1986, six young people died after drinking methyl hydrate—children erasing their futures with school duplicating fluid.

Tell it to Donald Marshall, imprisoned for 11 years for a crime he did not commit because of what is now the obviously entrenched racism of the justice system.

Tell it to the relatives of Helen Betty Osborne in The Pas, Man. She was abducted, raped, stabbed 50 times with a screwdriver and left dying in the snow by four white teenagers. For 16 years the murderers were sheltered from the law by their community. Testimony at the trial made it clear that the identities of Helen's abductors were no secret in The Pas—but then, the victim was only an Indian.

Try telling the Lubicons that the injustice is all in the past. They who struggle to defend themselves against the encroachments of the very same oil industry that so sanctimoniously sponsored The Spirit Sings exhibition in honor of native culture.

All of this adds up to the old story. Native culture is nice, but not if it gets in our way. Native culture is important, but not in terms of the people in whom it resides, only in the artifacts—the things we can collect and display in museum cases.

In the context of what The Spirit Sings claimed to say about the importance and value of native culture, Canadians need to ask some pointed questions of ourselves and our governing authorities. We need to ask why, in a province as wealthy as Alberta, we permit continuation of the conditions which lead to a death rate among Indian infants that is more than twice what it is for the general population. Why, in a country prepared to spend millions of dollars telling the world how much we value native culture, we tolerate conditions in which native people are four times as likely as the rest of us to die before reaching their life expectancy and three times as likely to die by violence.

We need to ask how we can accept the conditions under which native people are 10 times as likely to be diagnosed as alcoholics. Why it was possible, for nearly a decade, for the suicide rate for native people in northern Saskatchewan to remain 15 times greater than the national average. What landscape of sorrow and despair do such people inhabit?

Why do 75% of native students in the Northwest Territories abandon school between Grade 7 and Grade 12—is this a failure to be blamed on the victims, or is the failure in the structure of a system which can neither visualize nor address their needs? How can it be that only 2% of the Canadian population provides 10% of the prison inmates—perhaps because the unemployment rate for native people consistently runs about 800% higher than that deemed acceptable for mainstream society?

These statistics provide the reality behind the self-serving lies of exhibitions like The Spirit Sings. They reveal far more about the hypocrisy of the dominant culture than they do about the propensities of native people. They tell us, in fact, that far from honoring native culture, Canadian society dismisses it in its living forms.

Made invisible by our denial of the worth of their own cultural values; excluded from economic participation in the dominant culture and squeezed into ghettos at the least productive margins of society; cheated of their promised patrimony; cheated of an equal opportunity at life itself and fully cognizant of our hypocrisy, aboriginal Canadians are far from the honored participants in our society that The Spirit Sings would have the world believe. They remain deeply estranged from the social and political process of this nation. How long before, as Georges Erasmus warns, the sorrow and despair becomes rage and vengeance? The tragedy, unfortunately, is not all in the past. It is all in the present. It is not somebody else's responsibility. It is Canadians' responsibility. If The Spirit Sings served one purpose, it was to remind thinking Canadians that the pathetic remnants of the Beothuk should be on display all right. They should be on display in a national shrine of shame and humility. The first act of every prime minister should be to kneel before them and pray to the God that we invoke in our national anthem—both for national forgiveness and that what was done to the Beothuk, the Huron, the Assinboines, may never be done to Canada.

The Porn Patrol
MARGARET ATWOOD

• • • • • • • • • •

It is a dark and stormy night. I'm tucked under the duvet in my flannelette nightie and my fuzzy foot-warmers, reading detective fiction as is my wont after a hard day hammering out the innuendo, when an imperious knock sounds at the door. It is the dreaded Porn Patrol.

"Sorry to disturb you, Ma'm," says the first policeman—Canadian policemen are devilishly polite—"but there's been a complaint filed against you. My wife just loves your work," he adds apologetically.

"That's right, Ma'm," says the second one. "Making sleaze and filth, and having same on premises. It's all here in Bill C-54, neatly itemized so the police will know exactly what is porn and what is not. You know, menstruation and lactation in a sexual context (whatever that is), incitement to sex (any kind), acts involving persons who appear to be under 18 years of age ... No grey areas left at all."

"Kissing and hand-holding?" asks the first policemen hopefully.

"That was in the first draft," the second one says severely. "They took it out. They're against depictions of kissing and hand-holding, naturally, but you have to make allowances for the change in modern morals. They didn't want the thing to look ludicrous."

"I'm a serious author," I protest. "Why aren't you going after the real pornographers?"

"Oh, they went underground as soon as the law was passed, sort of like liquor during Prohibition, and they're hard to track down," says the first policeman. "But a serious author, now, they're sitting ducks, you can pick 'em off real easy and no big Mafia money will shoot off your kneecaps for doing it. Gets votes, too. Some people enjoy trashing a bit of art in the name of self-righteousness. Heck, I do myself."

"Who filed this complaint?" I ask indignantly. "When they were writing

Margaret Atwood (born 1939) is one of Canada's two or three best-known literary figures. This mini-essay on censorship, which appeared in The Globe and Mail *on 18 Feb., 1988, is evidence of her abiding commitment to social issues. Her most recent book is the 1988 novel* Cat's Eye.

this bill, the Conservative government promised that nothing bad would happen to me and my ilk ..."

"Your what?" asks the first policeman, frowning. This is a body part he's never heard of.

"Her ilk," says the second one, giving him the elbow. "Proceed, Ma'm."

"Me and my ilk," I continue, "because of Bill C-54. 'Honey,' they told me, 'don't you worry about a thing. It's those low-down porn peddlers we're after, we want to protect women and children.'"

"Yeah, they used to make lots of promises like that," the second policeman said with nostalgia. "The don't-worry kind. But now that it's become the law, it's not up to them, is it? Any citizen can make a complaint and the law can act on it if deemed fit. This complaint was filed by Mrs. Grundy and Mr. Bowdler, who leaf through novels in bookstores and libraries until they find the offending items. They can usually dredge up something or other."

"Page 105, *Handmaid's Tale*, hardcover edition," says the first one, producing his well-thumbed copy.

"You don't mean to tell me that's *porn*," I cry indignantly.

"Very kinky, we thought," says the first. "Incitement too. Turned *me* on. How about you, Dwayne?"

"Hubba hubba," says Dwayne. "A hot patootie."

• • • • • • • • • •

     And so I appear in court. "Told you this thing would be great for lawyers," says my lawyer. "Glad they never sent it back to the drawing board, or realized that the things they said they were really after were already covered under the Criminal Code. We haven't seen anything like this since the 17th century."

"You mean the rise of Puritanism?" I say.

"I was thinking witch-hunts. They were very lucrative too."

A special court has been set up to handle these C-54 cases, because the things are lined up around the block. One of the courtrooms is reserved for cases involving depictions of persons who appear to be under 18 years of age, and two age-guessers from county fairs are giving conflicting expert evidence. "Seventeen and a half," says one. "Eighteen and three months or I'm a monkey's uncle," says the second.

There's a whole section for Scientific and Educational Merit, and several anti-AIDs pamphlets are on trial today. There's another room for incitement, and three men in raincoats are recounting with considerable relish which deplorable acts involving shoelaces and sealing wax the mere sight of the front cover of Farley Mowat's *The Dog Who Wouldn't Be* has driven them to commit, against their wills.

I end up in the Artistic Merit room. I watch as Sylvia Fraser gets ten years in the slammer for *My Father's House* and Audrey Thomas is put on probation for *Blown Figures*, as long as she promises not to do it again. Alice Munro is heavily fined for depicting sex as enjoyable. Margaret Laurence's work is on trial for the same stuff they badgered her about when she was alive.

Then it's my turn. Under C-54 you're guilty until proven innocent, so the onus is on me to prove that my work has artistic merit. But as soon as I see the Crown-appointed Official C-54 Literary Critic I know I'm in trouble. The Conservatives have continued their policy of stuffing old party bagpeople into artistic and cultural posts, and the Court Literary Critic is a condominium developer from Pudeur-sur-Rideau, Ontario. Well, I think, I guess it's better than Czechoslovakia, where Josef Svorecky was subjected to a doorman doing the literary censorship.

"My wife just loves your work, and the literary judgment of women is worth donkey dung," he says, "so I know this is trash." He turns his thumb down and the cuffs are snapped on.

"I'll reform! I'll reform!" I cry. "I won't write anything from now on but children's books! Look, I've already begun one. 'See Dick. Dick has two balls. One ball is blue, and the other one ...'"

"That will be enough of *that*," snaps the judge, covering his ears to prevent contamination.

• • • • • • • • • •

"Do you think this is the way they intended this law to play once it became real life?" I ask my lawyer.

"Dunno," he says. "Maybe they just couldn't anticipate the implications of what they'd set down on the page."

"You mean they didn't *intend* to be totalitarian, anti-democratic, Draconian and silly? It's just that they can't read, write or think?"

"Something like that," he says. "Don't scratch any naughty words on the wall and we'll try for parole."

I have to pay the court costs and the lawyer's fees, of course. I also draw a term in the cooler. As I walk down the hall I pass a convicted rapist going the other way. "What'd you get?" he asks me. "Ten years," I say. "And you?"

"Ninety days," he says with a chuckle. "It's a lot cheaper just to do it than to read and write about it, eh? But I'm glad they're locking up scum like you. Gotta keep Canada safe for the women and children, you know."

I sit in the hoosegow, crocheting institutional doilies. I should have emigrated while the going was good. I should have written letters to my member of Parliament, before they scrapped the word *member* for being too suggestive. I recall the debates that went on while this law was being rollered through. "It has no legs," people said, meaning we didn't have to worry because this was a slug, not a centipede. "They'll never pass it. The international writing community will fall off their chairs laughing." They didn't realize that the Conservatives, by and large, did not care snuff about the international writing community.

Then a more sinister explanation comes to me. What if this bill was really passed to make obstreperous Canadian authors sit down and shrivel up, leaving the field absolutely free for sex-drenched American imports? Maybe it was sort of like the film distribution policy, or lack of it: a playing field level on one side.

Or maybe it was intended to erase from the collective Canadian mind anything resembling an idea, a challenge, an artistic experiment or a non-commercial desire, leaving it free for widgets and bottom lines and nothing but.

Canada was open for business. And closed for everything else.

The Moral Status of Pity
EAMONN CALLAN

• • • • • • • • • •

Pity is an emotion which is intimately connected with virtue. If I were impervious to anger I could still be a paragon of rectitude. My emotional peculiarity might even be explained by moral saintliness. If I had a pitiless heart my entire life would surely be an abject moral failure. The imputation of an inability to pity strikes us as a damning moral criticism; it is one we are likely to make, for example, against those who commit acts of extreme cruelty. Yet pity is hardly ever welcomed by its recipients, and for that reason it differs in a puzzling way from other emotions which are closely associated with virtue, such as gratitude or compassion. The prospect of becoming an object of pity is alarming, and not merely because we fear the misfortune that would evoke pity in others; it is alarming in part because we suspect that being on the receiving end of that emotion could seriously aggravate our plight. We also regard an aversion to being pitied as commendable, perhaps even morally commendable. There is something shameful in wanting to be pitied, just as there is in the indulgence of self-pity. The aged and the physically disabled do not want our pity, as a rule, and we think better of them for not wanting it. Finally, we know that those who give pity are frequently guilty of serious wrongdoing. A pitiless heart may be a terrible thing, but a fondness for dispensing pity is scarcely any better.

These reflections give rise to a troubling question. How can an emotion which is intimately connected with the practice of virtue be so widely and rightly despised? I shall try to answer this in a way that does not oblige us to abandon any of the seemingly divergent intuitions about pity which provoke the question in the first place.

Eamonn Callan (born 1953) teaches at the University of Alberta and has written widely on the philosophy of education. This essay appeared in March 1988 in the Canadian Journal of Philosophy. *His book* Autonomy and Schooling *was published in 1988.*

i

If I were to feel pity for someone I would have to see him as the victim of a substantial misfortune, and as a result of seeing him under that description I would have to feel sorrow in his behalf. But this does not help to distinguish pity from compassion. "I feel sorry for him" is ambiguous since it might be pity or compassion which I feel. It is the former only if I see the other as incapable of alleviating the misfortune he suffers, at least for the present. I must perceive him as someone *overwhelmed* by misfortune, even though it might be some culpable psychological weakness in him which makes even a moderate level of adversity overwhelming.

The connection between pity and helplessness is brought out by the fact that our moral qualms about the emotion scarcely apply at all when human beings in the earliest years of life are its recipients. When dealing with young children in distress we usually give a rather free rein to pity, and we do so for good reason. Young children have only the slightest capacity to cope with their own misfortunes. To suggest otherwise in the emotions we display or fail to display towards them would be cruel. Our pity is thus a comforting acknowledgement of their own dependence and our willingness to take control of their lives when difficulties arise. But as our children grow up pity becomes increasingly less appropriate as a response to their problems. The father who showers pity on a toddler with influenza may be a bit sentimental, but if the child is a teenager something rather less innocent would appear to be going on. A moderately sick teenager is not helpless, and parental conduct which denies that fact smacks of tyrannical paternalism.

The intuitively important distinction between pity and compassion can be drawn now. Imagine someone whose immediate family has been killed in an accident. He wants his friends to show that they have been moved by his loss, perhaps because that will ease the isolation of grief. But the intensity of his sorrow creates the fear that sorrow will consume him. In his darker moments he doubts that he has the psychological resources to re-create a meaningful life. For that reason he will also want others to reassure him that he is still capable of taking control of his life, and if they express their commiseration in a way that confirms his doubts he will feel degraded, angry and even more afraid. Is is surely natural to describe what this man wants from others as a desire for compassion rather than pity. That is to say, he wants others to feel some sorrow on his account, but he wants their sorrow to be accompanied by an acknowledgement that affliction has not divested him of autonomy.[1]

This goes some way towards explaining why compassion has been associated with a recognition of human equality which is absent from pity.[2] In showing compassion for another I tacitly affirm the common status we share as autonomous beings vulnerable to misfortune; in showing pity I disavow that common status. To be sure, I might express pity to another in circumstances wherein I acknowledge my own situation to be equally pathetic. But it is hardly necessary to argue that these are not typical cases. Indeed, if I came to see my own situation as pathetic then my own troubles would tend to absorb my feelings, and I would have little sorrow to spare for anyone else. In typical cases of pity the emotion is felt alongside the conviction that one is securely in control of one's own life, unlike the hapless object of one's attention.

At this stage, one can begin to understand why we are averse to being pitied and why the desire to be pitied is regarded as shameful. We deeply value being in control of our own lives. When some calamity deprives us of control we are reduced to the status of helpless children. The pity of others expresses their conviction that this degraded condition is indeed our own. It is a small wonder that decent people often want to disguise their pity and are embarrassed when they inadvertently betray its presence. They know that the contrast pity discloses between their own autonomy and the powerlessness of the other may be deeply humiliating for the other. Wanting to be pitied, on the other hand, which is not at all the same as wanting to be rescued from one's pathetic situation, suggests that one finds helplessness agreeable rather than humiliating. It suggests that one has not outgrown the childish pleasure of dependence, and for that reason it is shameful. But this is not the whole story of our misgivings about the value of pity. I believe many of these stem from our familiarity with something that might aptly be called contemptuous pity. It is this phenomenon which I now want to examine.

ii

The emotions we feel and display towards others partly depend upon what matters to us. Because of this connection between emotion and valuation the emotions we show will sometimes be evidence of whether we respect or do not respect others as persons. I shall stipulate that the display of pity is contemptuous whenever it indicates that one does not respect the personhood of another. In particular, contemptuous pity reveals that one does not sufficiently value the autonomy (or potential autonomy) of the other. I assume that autonomy is necessary if one is to flourish as a person. Given that assumption, acting towards others in a way that accords due regard for their autonomy is essential to respecting them as persons.

At first glance, it might seem puzzling that the display of pity (as opposed to expressions of merely feigned pity) could be contemptuous. For if my pity is genuine the fact that another is seen as helpless in the face of misfortune makes me feel sorrow in his behalf, and that could not occur if I believed his putative lack of autonomy involved no disvalue. It can be shown that pity is compatible with that belief. But there is no need to press that point here. For even if I believed that the other's misfortunes were an evil I could still fail to acknowledge (or acknowledge fully) the value of the autonomy currently instantiated in the other's life. Suppose I am convinced that the members of a certain racial group are unredeemably puerile. When I encounter a member of the relevant group in distress I respond with the unbridled pity I might show towards a young child in the same predicament. If the recipient of my pity prizes his autonomy as a constituent of his very personhood he will interpret my emotional display as contemptuous, and he will be right to do so.

The gravity of the wrong done in such cases is revealed, in part, by the kind of response we should expect and accept in the recipient of contemptuous pity. Outrage is certainly to be expected, and even some inclination to hate the giver of pity. These are the sorts of things a decent person can permissibly feel in such circumstances, and we will not think less of him for feeling them. Indeed, we might want him to experience these feelings because impassivity, say, would suggest that he agreed with the inaccurate appraisal of his situation or that his autonomy mattered little to him. There is a marked contrast between what we expect and accept in such cases and the sort of emotional response we would tolerate in other contexts when someone is subjected to a disparaging assessment of his abilities. If a student unjustly demeaned my teaching skills a bit of faint indignation on my part would be excusable, but outrage and suppressed hatred would only expose my own immaturity. I would be rightly chided for making such a fuss about the episode because one should not take one's skills and reputation as a teacher that seriously. Surely, the difference between the two cases is to be explained by the fact that autonomy is essential to our dignity as persons whereas our talents in more specific areas, such as teaching, are not. The giver of contemptuous pity impugns our dignity; those who belittle our talents merely wound our pride.

There are other instances of contemptuous pity in which there is no inaccuracy in the appraisal intrinsic to the emotion. I have already said that people who prize their own personhood are likely to be grieved when they find themselves on the receiving end of pity, and the grief may be especially acute when the recipient has to assent to the view that he is helpless. There can be no comforting thought that he really is in control of his own life, and only the obtuseness or prejudice of others has prevented them from seeing the truth. In a similar way, horror provoked by one's appearance will not cut as deeply if one believes that one is really quite aesthetically acceptable. A good person will obviously be vigilant against humiliating displays of pity, even (perhaps especially) when the other's situation is truly pathetic, just as he will guard against degrading displays of horror, regardless of the horribleness of the other's appearance. And, if I failed to hide my pity when the other's situation is truly pathetic, there could well be grounds for regarding my emotional indulgence as contemptuous.

This possibility needs to be fleshed out a bit. If I were confronted by another in a pathetic predicament the morally urgent feature of the situation is the other's need to be extricated from his predicament. So long as that need is not met the other cannot begin to flourish as a person. If I valued the other's personhood as I should then meeting that need would command my attention. To be sure, when I first confront someone in a pathetic situation I may be overcome with pity. But if my loyalties were in the right place my thoughts and feelings would quickly be re-directed to the task of helping the other to gain or regain control of his own life, or if that were not possible my foremost concern would be to relieve his misfortune as best I could. I would think that those who work in refugee camps have little time for the feeling, much less the display of pity, even though they are surrounded by people in the most pathetic situations; and if that were so their neglect of pity would simply reflect sound moral priorities. After all, it is far better to give one's attention to helping those who are overwhelmed by adversity than to dwell lugubriously on how unfortunate they are.

It might be inferred from this that where the appraisal it expresses is accurate the display of pity can be contemptuous only if it prevents one from helping others out of pathetic predicaments. Only then is the other seen and hence treated as a tragic spectacle rather than a person whose worth entitles him to the aid of others. But notice that seeing and treating someone under one of these descriptions does not wholly preclude seeing and treating him under the other at the same time, and so one may give aid to others which is contaminated with contemptuous pity. Suppose that a friend of mine is an alcoholic whose addiction is entirely out of control. I help him to find suitable treatment, and thereby rescue him from his pathetic plight. I could do all this while foisting my pity upon him in a intolerably derogatory manner. One might compare this sort of thing to a plastic surgeon who relieves his patients of their horrible deformities but whose conduct towards them is suffused with horror.

Displays of pity towards others are not necessarily contemptuous, though in the world as we know it they frequently are. In the case of self-pity there is a necessary connection to contempt. In order to bring the connection into focus, however, it is crucial to distinguish self-pity from the sorrow which is inevitable in the context of overwhelming adversity. It is one thing to find oneself in a pathetic situation, to know that one is and feel sorry about it; it is quite another to pity oneself. If I ascribed self-pity to an inconsolable parent who had just witnessed his child's death, I would almost certainly be making a grotesque error. The matter might be different if 10 years later we found the parent moping in the child's former bedroom, proclaiming his sorrows to all who will listen and shunning all consolation. This might be un-controllable grief, but it could well be self-pity. Perhaps, the parent's grief at the death of his child has become largely subdued while his loss has become an object of deliberate, mournful contemplation; and believing himself to be helpless in the wake of his loss, grief at his son's death becomes compounded with pity in his own behalf.

What is essential to self-pity is a distinction analogous to that between the giver and recipient of the emotion in its other-regarding variety. On the one hand, there is the self as an object of mournful contemplation; on the other, the self must be sufficiently distanced from its plight to undertake this reflexive emotional indulgence. In the throes of overwhelming grief it would be impossible to pity oneself because the requisite detachment could not be achieved. One does not *wallow* in overwhelming grief; one is simply engrossed by it, whether one wants to or not. Self-pity presupposes a situation in which autonomy already has some purchase, though perhaps only a precarious one, because it is an emotion one chooses to cultivate and one could choose otherwise. But if that is so then self-pity could never be justified. The appraisal entailed by the emotion could never fit the facts. My sorrows may be formidable, but self-pity requires that I have enough control over my thoughts and emotions to make the self-ascription of helplessness indefensible. Moreover, because self-pity always reveals a failure to acknowl-edge one's own autonomy it always involves contempt for one's own personhood.

The phenomenon of contemptuous pity explains much of our moral antipathy to pity. But what has become of the supposedly intimate connec-tion between pity and virtue? In answering this question it will not do merely to adduce cases in which the giving of pity is morally commendable. After all, it takes no ingenuity to imagine circumstances wherein the expression of virtually *any* emotion would win our moral approval. The mere fact that the expression of horror is desirable under conceivable conditions cannot justify assigning it a vital position in the moral life, and pity cannot be any different in this regard. The argument I have traced so far throws light on the evil of pity, but it would appear to leave our intuitions about pity and virtue as baffling as ever.

iii

I shall argue that if we respect the personhood of others then we are necessarily susceptible to feelings of pity when another is overwhelmed by misfortune, despite the fact that we would be disinclined to dwell on that emotion and ready to disguise its presence. To establish this conclusion I need to defend a rather different account of respect for persons than the one we have inherited from Kant.

The idea that caring for others is in some way fundamental to morality has recently received some overdue philosophical scrutiny.[3] In exploring this idea it is essential to be alert to the range of ways of seeing someone which can ground one's care since many of these are irrelevant or repugnant to the moral viewpoint. I might care very intensely about my wife but my attachment could exist only because I see her under descriptions which make it morally infantile. I could see her as a source of sexual gratification, domestic service and emotional solace, say, and be wholly indifferent or even hostile to the fulfillment of her own ambitions or the flowering of her talents. In that event, I would not care about her as a distinct person in her own right; I would not respect her as a person.

If I care about something then it matters to me in an especially pressing way; it occupies a more central position in my scheme of values than the things I merely like, say. "Caring" also has strong affective overtones. The things I care about command my emotions to a degree that the objects of many other attitudes do not. But it would be wrong to think of the affective dimension of caring as logically separable from the evaluation it implies. If I can feel no joy at the success my wife has in cultivating her talents nor any regret at her failure to accomplish some long-cherished ambition, then it follows, unless there is some special explanation for my lack of these emotions, that such successes and failures do not matter to me. (I shall have more to say presently about the possibility of "special explanations" for failure to experience the emotions to which we are susceptible by virtue of caring.) Furthermore, it would follow that my wife could only matter to me under descriptions which had little or nothing to do with her flourishing as a person. The advantage of conceiving respect for persons as a matter of caring for others as persons is that it draws our attention to a range of emotional susceptibilities which are required of someone who values the personhood of others as he should. This is no trivial advantage since Kant's conceptual dissociation of respect for persons from any emotional engagement in their lives has been profoundly misleading.

The kind of emotional engagement in the other's life which is implicit in caring for him as a person is different from that which we associate with intimacy or friendship, and it could well coincide with loathing of the particular individual who is the object of care. Gregory Vlastos's illuminating analogy between parental love and moral concern is useful in helping us to envisage this possibility.[4] Parents may abhor what their son has made of his life, but they can love him as a son for all that. Similarly, one may abhor the conduct and character of someone and yet continue to care about him as a person, and that is precisely what we expect decent people to do in the ordinary course of events. If I were wholly impervious to regret or sorrow whenever someone I detest endures a personal tragedy or suffers a grievous injustice my emotional deficiency would be a moral lapse as well. My impassivity would show that these events did not matter to me as they would if I valued the other's personhood as I should. And so my failure to care would betoken a failure to sustain the respect which is the other's due as a person.

I have suggested that the valuation of the personhood of others which is intrinsic to virtue is logically tied to a range of emotional susceptibilities. Of course, the fact that I am susceptible to a specific emotion does not guarantee that it will be experienced whenever I confront the circumstances which would justify the emotion. It might be the case that I fail to see the circumstances in the right light, perhaps through no fault of my own. I might be highly susceptible to compassion but ignorance of a colleague's recent bereavement could nonetheless prevent me from feeling it. Ignorance would explain my emotional failure in a way that is compatible with my being someone who cares enough for others as persons, and hence it is the sort of thing which can excuse failure to experience morally fitting emotions.

Ignorance is not the only source of such explanations. Kant provides one with a different source in the *Groundwork of the Metaphysic of Morals*, though he badly misconstrues it. We are asked to imagine someone so "overclouded by sorrows of his own" that he is unmoved by the sufferings of others. Nevertheless, a severe commitment to duty leads him to behave altruistically despite his "deadly insensibility." There is something morally heroic about such a man—Kant is right about that—and his impassivity towards others does not incline us to think any less of him. Why? Kant's answer is that the agent's insensibility allows fidelity to duty to determine action without any contaminating affective influence: "then for the first time his action has his genuine moral worth."[5]

There is another and more plausible account of our admiration for Kant's hero. If someone were preoccupied with travails of his own, then even if he were a virtuous person, and hence ready to feel sorrow at the distress of others, he could hardly be expected to do so as long as his own travails persist. To expect that would be to expect far too much. If he can nonetheless muster the will to help others in distress, then there is something heroic in his achievement. That this is a better interpretation than Kant's becomes apparent if we imagine a slightly different case. Suppose a man were beset with terrible sorrows of his own and he could still find it in his heart not only to help a stranger but also to feel compassion for him. Kant would have us believe that the action of this man has no "genuine moral worth" because it is not to be explained by unalloyed allegiance to duty. But surely we respond to the compassion of such a man not as a contaminating influence on virtue but as an indication of an almost miraculous level of virtue. And we have good reason to respond in that way. The ability to feel compassion for another, despite appalling misfortunes of one's own, shows that one cares about others as persons far more deeply than do ordinary, morally commendable mortals.

The point I want to stress is that it is strictly unintelligible to maintain that there could be respect for persons where there is no emotional engagement in their lives. If one does not value another's flourishing as a person, then one does not respect him as a person, but where the other's flourishing is valued there is necessarily a certain emotional investment in the object of valuation. It is noteworthy that Kant's view of moral motivation does not always seem as remote from this insight as it does in the *Groundwork*. Towards the end of the second *Critique* Kant considers the case of a virtuous man whose resolute honesty brings "extreme need and want" to his family. It is significant that Kant does not describe someone who is unmoved by the suffering he brings about. On the contrary, when his family entreats the man to relent "he may feel the pain which only a good heart can very deeply feel."[6] There is some recognition in these words that virtue is deeply connected with certain emotional susceptibilities. My only reservation is that it is misleading just to say that virtuous persons *may* feel sorrow in situations of the kinds described. It would be better to say that they *must* be susceptible to sorrow, even if they often do not feel it for reasons compatible with their being truly virtuous.

What I have said about respect for persons suggests an appealing way of explaining the intuitively close connection of pity and virtue. Given that one cares for others as persons and believes that autonomy is essential to the dignity of persons, one is necessarily prone to feel sorrow on their behalf when others are trapped in pathetic situations. The loss of autonomy undermines the victim's capacity to flourish as a person. If I am not susceptible to the morally fitting emotion when someone endures *that* loss I could hardly be susceptible in other situations, where there is less at stake from the moral viewpoint. And if I am devoid of the emotional susceptibilities implicit in valuing the personhood of others then their personhood must count for nothing to me. Thus the pitiless heart reveals a pervasive and not just an isolated failure in the moral life. We obviously expect no pity from those who have pitiless hearts but we should also expect, with as much assurance, no mercy or justice or kindness because we know that they do not value us as persons.

One might object that not every virtue presupposes caring for others as persons. Even if I possess a pitiless heart and my emotional deficiency counts as a grievous moral failure, is it not possible for me to act out of a sense of moral duty? And could a sense of duty not be sufficient for *some* virtues? It does not make sense to say that Callan is kind though he believes that the beneficiaries of his kindness are as worthless as dirt. It is less clear that more tough-minded virtues, such as honesty or justice, require anything more than persistent adherence to duty. "Callan is honest (or just) but he doesn't give a damn about people": this may describe a strange sort of person but the description is not obviously incoherent.

But it is also not obviously coherent. Imagine a situation in which someone tells the truth with the knowledge that his action will precipitate some terrible disaster for another person. It is not malice which motivates his action but rather a conviction that everyone has a duty to tell the truth. The agent views the consequences of his action with complete equanimity. He believes that persons are devoid of value and so their misfortunes are utterly without interest. This is obviously a much less prepossessing case of "honesty" than the one described in the second *Critique*. If I were to respond to this man's conduct by saying with admiration, "Now there's honesty!" I would surely be accused of crass moral naivete. In criticizing my response it would intuitively be too weak to say that I over-valued honesty and under-valued caring for persons. In this situation it seems wrong to attribute any virtue at all because there is nothing that can plausibly be regarded as a morally excellent feature of character (or as genuine adherence to moral duty) where there is callous indifference to the sufferings of others.

In order to vindicate decisively the intuitions I have appealed to concerning this alleged case of honesty I would have to explain and defend a theory of moral duty and its relationship to virtue. I cannot provide that argument here. But I would like to make two final moves which should render my position a bit more persuasive. First, I shall sketch an account of how descriptions such as "Callan is honest but he doesn't give a damn about people" could acquire a semblance of coherence despite their being incoherent. Then I shall briefly identify a major theoretical obstacle to showing that they are coherent.

There are familiar situations in which being honest or just has consequences for another which one cannot but regret if one values the other's personhood as one should. Failing an industrious but obtuse student could be the only just and honest thing for a teacher to do—and the only right thing to do, all things considered. But when a career hinges on a passing grade that action may be the cause of irreparable disappointment. If honesty and justice are to prevail in such situations it is necessary to control, and sometimes even to suppress emotions one is susceptible to by virtue of caring for others as persons. Justice and honesty go to the wall where teachers are consumed with pity or compassion whenever incompetent students appeal their failing grades. So it is tempting to infer that doing one's duty here (and hence being virtuous) presupposes no susceptibility to the tender emotions and hence that the valuation of others' personhood which entails that susceptibility is also irrelevant. But the fact that justice or honesty often requires that we contain certain emotions does not imply that we can be impervious to the latter and still be truly honest or just. It is altogether possible that any moral virtue is conceptually tied to emotions which one is obliged to regulate. Even kindness is incompatible with the indiscriminate indulgence of pity or even compassion. "I had to be cruel to be kind": that may generally be an egregious rationalization for cruelty but it is not always so.

This takes me to my final point. I take it that to act virtuously or to show genuine fidelity to moral duty means that one acts from a motive which is distinctive of moral excellence. The agent appreciates (perhaps only tacitly) the moral point of truth-telling or giving others their due, and honesty and justice can be attributed to him only because his appreciating the moral point of such actions leads him to do them. Therefore, if honesty or justice can be attributed to those who do not care about others as persons, then it must be shown that the moral point of truth-telling or giving others their due has nothing to do with the value of others flourishing as persons. It is fair to say that that is a very tall order.[7]

Notes

1. The concept of autonomy which is relevant here requires a very full elucidation, but a couple of brief remarks will be helpful. First, autonomy requires certain psychological characteristics. At least a modest level of rationality is presupposed so that one can independently evaluate the advice or commands of others, the mores of one's culture, and the like. The inner strength to act on one's judgment is also necessary. Very young children, for example, lack autonomy because they fall below the minimal standard on the psychological criterion of autonomy. But one also has to be socially situated in such a way that one can meaningfully exercise one's own judgment in shaping one's life. I might possess the psychological characteristics of autonomy but if I were on the rack I would be divested of autonomy.
2. See Lawrence Blum, "Compassion," in Amelie Rorty, ed., *Explaining Emotions* (Berkeley: U. of Calif. Press, 1980), 511-12. However, Blum's way of distinguishing these emotions is not quite the same as mine. Andreas Teuber also emphasizes the egalitarian character of compassion, though he does not attempt to distinguish it from pity in this or any other respect. See Andreas Teuber, "Simone Weil: Equality as Compassion", *Philosophy and Phenomenological Research* 43 (1982), 221-37.

3. See Rodger Beehler, *Moral Life* (Oxford: Basil Blackwell, 1978); Nell Noddings, *Caring: A Feminine Approach to Ethics and Moral Education* (Berkeley: U. of Calif. Press, 1984).

4. Gregory Vlastos, "Justice and Equality," in Richard Brandt, ed., *Social Justice* (Englewood Cliffs, N.J.: Prentice-Hall, 1962), 44-7.

5. Immanuel Kant, *Groundwork to the Metaphysic of Morals*, trans. H.J. Paton (New York: Harper & Row, 1964), 66.

6. Immanuel Kant, *Critique of Practical Reason*, trans. Lewis White Beck (Chicago: U. of Chicago Press, 1949), 253.

7. The comments of Allen Pearson and the anonymous referees for the *Canadian Journal of Philosophy* helped me to improve an earlier version of this paper.

Faith and Public Service
DAVID MACDONALD

· · · · · · · · · ·

Almost from the day that I decided that I would become an elected politician, people have constantly raised the question with me as to whether or not it is appropriate for a person who has trained himself in theology, and accepted ordination, to get involved in the considerably nasty, seamy business of politics.

When people sometimes wonder about those who take on public life, particularly those who have accepted some vocational call within a particular ministry and church, they view them with skepticism. I also find that the very question about faith and politics generates a certain kind of picture in people's minds.

I remember the first indication I had of this kind of portrait. In fact, it may have been the first time I sat in a political caucus. I was quite young and this was the first time to my knowledge that the Progressive Conservative Party had ever elected a clergyman of any faith to its national caucus. I was sitting at the back of the room (these meetings, as you may know, get to be pretty free-wheeling, people say pretty much what they want to say) and at one point one of the members swore. He stopped and looked first to the woman member of Parliament present, Jean Wadds, and said "Pardon me, Mrs. Wadds,"and then he looked at me and said, "Pardon me, Mr. MacDonald."And I suddenly realized that I was in a very unique category, at least at that point. There were few apologies in later years. The point of this is simply that there is a tendency when you put the notions of belief and commitment next to political service or public life that a lot of assumptions are made.

If we think about it for a moment, those assumptions are not as automatic as they seem. In Canadian terms, for instance, if you think about those who

David MacDonald (born 1936) is a United Church minister as well as the Progressive Conservative member for Rosedale in the House of Commons. He is the author of a number of books on Africa and served as Canada's ambassador to Ethiopia, Sudan and Djibouti: part of a long and varied career in public life that has also included the federal Communications portfolio. His essay appeared in March 1988 in Grail, an "ecumenical journal" from the University of St. Jerome's College, Waterloo, Ontario.

are committed, in a religious sense, and have been active in politics, you will almost automatically think of J.S. Woodsworth, Tommy Douglas and Stanley Knowles, as well as others from the Social Democratic movement, much of which came out of church activity and the reform movements of the 1930s.

It would be very easy to characterize faith and politics in terms of that social-democratic experience in Canada. But, before you go too far down that path, remember this wonderful story. A few years ago, when Tommy Douglas was still quite active, I was invited to introduce him at a reception. We have always been good friends and we try to play little tricks on one another. I decided to look up some of Tommy's early history, and I discovered that in 1935, when he ran and got elected federally, he quite by accident became the candidate, not only of the Co-operative Commonwealth Federation (CCF), but also of the Social Credit Party. He had a double nomination. The notion of it just astounded me because at the very same time that Woodsworth, Knowles, Douglas and all the others were becoming so active in the public life of this country, in the neighboring province of Alberta, "Bible Bill"Aberhart was launching his Social Credit movement which was also based on Christian principles. And so when we think of people in politics in Canada who are professed Christians, it is not easy to think of them as being just on the left. People like Major Douglas, Bill Aberhart, E.C. Manning and others were on the right.

What does it mean then to think about faith and public service, belief and politics? This paper is a reflection from the crucible of what I have experienced over quite a long period of time, as you will see, much beyond the 15 years that I spent as an active member of Parliament. Before we ever get to the stage of thinking about the many relationships between the two, we really have to think about the business of faith itself. And that to me is absolutely fundamental.

In the early years, when I first became a member of Parliament, I had considerable doubt as to whether or not what I was then doing as an M.P. was in concert with the vows that I had made at the time of ordination as well as the commitment that I had made in terms of my overall theological studies. I don't even remember the exact time, many years later, when I suddenly came to the realization that what I was doing as a member of Parliament was very much in concert with what fundamentally I had seen as my pathway through ministry.

The sources of faith that form the basis of that realization are what I want to focus on. One or two of my sources of faith are perhaps even a bit eccentric—there is an element of predestinarianism in them.

When I was quite young, in my early teens, I became a member of a movement that I'm not sure even exists any longer, and if it does, it likely exists only occasionally. In the late '40s and early 1950s, there was a popular movement in Protestant circles, particularly with the United church, Baptist church, Presbyterian church and, maybe, a little bit within the Anglican church, called the Older Boys' Model Parliament. It was a very simple device, but one that had a profound effect on me and a number of my close friends as we grew up in Prince Edward Island and the Maritime provinces.

What happened was that various congregations selected one or two boys in their teens to go to a regional model parliament. In fact, they took the *Robert's Rules of Order* on procedure and parliamentary decorum much more seriously than the real Parliament in which I spent 15 years. It was a bit of a shock for me to discover that when I was 14 and 15 years old I was much more disciplined and correct in my parliamentary procedures than when I was serving in the Parliament of Canada.

The centerpiece of this whole model parliamentary experience, which usually ran over a weekend, was the whole subject matter of debate. We debated very serious matters of faith and morals. Sometimes, they were the usual things of Sunday practice or capital punishment or the issue of abortion (though, actually, most of us didn't know what abortion was). But there was a tendency for us to take very seriously these topics that young people growing up had to contend with in some fashion. Then at the very end of this model parliament, we came together in a room, usually it was a room at the top of a building, a small sort of chapel, where we had what we described as a watch night service. In this service each of the boys, in his own way, tried to talk abut what this experience meant to him. It was a very emotional, very personal kind of experience for those of us who took part. That experience, without a doubt, had a profound impact on me in beginning my own faith journey.

Some of my other sources of faith were rather standard, I think, for anyone who ends up studying theology or studying for ministry: youth conferences, camps, the usual kind of Christian education programs. However, there were one or two particular experiences that for me were unique. When I became a theological student, entering my second year in what was then the Pinehill School of Theology in Halifax, there was a prison break in one of the local county jails. The break revealed the miserable conditions in the prison. When I mentioned to the principal of the institution that it would be useful to have the prison chaplain in to talk to us about what was actually happening in this prison, he looked at me in a kind of bemused manner and said, "Prison chaplain, there is no prison chaplain." I said, "Surely somebody must represent the church and go in to talk to these poor souls that have been incarcerated. "You know," he said, "why don't you do that on Thursday afternoons?" One of the highlight experiences for me was to spend every Thursday afternoon smoking cigarettes—and I don't smoke so it was a considerable effort—with some of the most intriguing characters Halifax has ever produced. But it taught me something, not only about the foibles of individual human nature, but also about the impact of structural and institutional sin.

Some other things were perhaps a bit more conventional. Certainly, being heavily involved at one period with the ecumenical movement broke me free of a kind of parochial or denominational ghetto that I might have been imprisoned in for the rest of my life. One of my friends said to me, at a certain point when I became overly active, that I had truly become an "ecumaniac."Whether that was true or not, ecumenism created for me a frame of reference for my theological formation.

I guess all of us on our own life's journey could talk about some of the influences that have been particularly important to us, a certain clergyman or adults who, in our growing-up years, seemed to stand as a kind of model to which we would return again and again. I can still think of one or two people in my home town of Charlottetown who had that kind of impact on me. Looking back on it now, they were not conventional people; they were, in one instance, a clergyman, but a clergyman who felt that the parish for him was just about every individual soul who lived in his community. Sometimes that made it rather uncomfortable for every other clergyman who believed that he had his own people to take care of.

There were also the people that I got to know, not because they were real people, but because they were brought to me in the context of their writing and historical witness. I still recall, as if it were today, discovering somebody who, I felt, was absolutely unique: Dietrich Bonhoeffer. Bonhoeffer was a German theologian who, in the late 1920s, began to wrestle with what was happening in Germany as it tried to shake off the embarrassment and the mortification of the First World War and as the Germans tried to find a kind of leader to give them the stature they felt that they had deserved.

Bonhoeffer's writings from the '20s through to the time of his imprisonment and death show a man who increasingly moved out from within the walls of the church to encounter the world in all its complexity and cruelty. For Bonhoeffer, engaging with Christ was to meet Him at the crossroads of life, which, for him, meant ultimately an assassination attempt on Adolf Hitler, imprisonment and eventual execution.

Others who remain as heroes of the faith for me were somewhat less dramatic in their own lives. One in particular is William Stringfellow, a remarkable Anglican (Episcopalian) lawyer in the United States who established a considerable reputation as a theologian. In fact, many people were shocked when Karl Barth made his last visit to the United States and came away at the end of his visit saying, "the most important theologian in North America today is William Stringfellow."Karl Barth was considered in Protestant circles a world figure as a theologian.

Not many church people were happy that he had seized upon this rather eccentric Episcopalian and New York lawyer. If you have read Bill Stringfellow's writings or know of his activity, you will know something of what I mean. In fact, if you have not read it, I would recommend as a source of background reading the book that Bill wrote just at the end of the Vietnam conflict, *An Ethic for Christians and Other Aliens in a Strange Land.* I still remember hearing about the book from a Canadian Roman Catholic, Janet Somerville. She and I were walking up Bloor Street in Toronto one day and she said to me, "I have just read one of the most disturbing books I think I have ever read. It had a very strange title, it's called *An Ethic for Christians and Other Aliens in a Strange Land,* written by a William Stringfellow." With that I was curious enough to get the book and read it. I had the good fortune later actually to meet with Bill Stringfellow and to talk to him about the experience of writing that particular book.

Bill's discovery about the prophetic nature of the church in our time, and his sharing of that discovery in the agony coming out of Vietnam, brought me closer to a sense of the substance of faith which I could only describe as a kind of holy indignation. The prophetic calling, the attempt to recapture the wholeness of the Gospel in a fragmented, contradictory, and often broken world, is the basis of faith on which my experience of public service has been constructed.

When we think of public service, we think of the total engagement of people in the political process, not just in the elected sense, not even just in the sense of being public servants, but in the sense of dealing on a regular basis with the way in which our society constantly forms and reforms itself under all of the pressures that exist. Basically, over the course of the last quarter century, I have moved back and forth among three disciplines that have been rarely brought together: religion, politics and mass media.

I have to confess that I have for a long time been fascinated by the way in which media so affects the totality of our thinking and our experiencing. It is not accidental that one of the most important people in terms of understanding media was a Canadian, Marshall McLuhan. And McLuhan's work flowed from the work of earlier Canadians, particularly people like Harold Innis. Innis, though trained as a professional economist, in the latter period of his life realized that all of his research on the great economic experiences of the cod fishery and the fur trade were really secondary to the impact of the media on the way in which society makes the fundamental decisions about itself.

Many people today, for instance, are fascinated by the fact that a person like Ronald Reagan can become president of the United States—as if it is almost contradictory that a man who has spent so much of his time as a movie star would be eligible for the top political position in the United States.

Actually, the very reverse is true. The media are the primary access now for elected public office, and as we know only too painfully—I know only too painfully, Bob Stanfield and Joe Clark know only too painfully—unacceptability in the media is the failure to achieve, or to obtain and retain high public office.

The spheres of public service, then, are first the community, later the country, and finally our own common humanity. The community is where, quite logically for me, any kind of political action was bound to begin. My involvement in politics started almost at the same time as my activity in school. Through the experience of the household in which I grew up, I found that it was natural to question the way in which things happened in a community, whether at a university I was attending or the way in which the various religious communities did or didn't deal with one another.

Many people in Prince Edward Island know that the only reason that I ever actually got elected was because of a unique relationship that developed quite by accident in a small community in the western end of the island. When I was sent to Alberton in Prince Edward Island, I was to get my basic training in serving in a small country parish made up of three little congregations.

When I arrived there, the elders of the church took me aside and said, "There are just two things that you should remember if you are going to be successful in this particular parish. First of all, since you are the clergyman it is definitely forbidden for you to attend dances or hockey games, and secondly you should stay well clear of the Catholics." During the next two years I managed to organize most of the youth dances in the community and I did this in concert with the local Roman Catholic priest. You can imagine, then, that when people finally elected me to public office, some of them were actually trying to get me out of town.

The involvement in the community was basic for me. If there is no real engagement at the level of that face-to-face continuity, everything else is merely some kind of intellectual abstraction. The experience of the brief three years that I spent in Alberton stands out as one of the most important experiences of my life. It gave me the opportunity to know that even in a community with as fixed a view and as clearly set divisions as that community had, when people began to discover that there might be some alternatives, there was not total opposition.

In 1965, partly because of the experience of that community, but also because a number of us felt that it was important to try to move the political/ social agenda beyond Alberton to the larger one that took in a good part of the western part of P.E.I., I became a member of Parliament. This was something that in a way was totally unplanned. Whereas I might have spent a number of years training to become a clergyman to exercise the normal offices of ministry, I got elected not really knowing what it all meant. What was one supposed to do in this kind of a process? I remember thinking to myself, I will have to sit in the back benches quietly for three or four years before I even open my mouth to speak.

That proved not to be the case. In fact, the experience of that whole period stretching on from 1965 was a constant discovery that I was being asked to make sometimes rather significant decisions, not about difficult questions of law, not about technical matters of regulation, but about basic questions, sometimes moral issues: questions about abortion, human rights, leadership, the imposition of the War Measures Act, and immigration. These constant series of questions seemed to come with increasing frequency and to challenge me in a way that made it almost always difficult to know whether there was any absolutely clear right and wrong that one could cling to.

That came to an end in 1980 through electoral defeat. At that point I came to the conclusion that having spent 15 challenging and sometimes difficult years as a member of Parliament, I would then resume the life that I had known before or get on with other things. It never struck me that the political life that I had known might change into another kind of public life. I guess it is easier in some ways to look back and say these were the things that were really happening even though you were not conscious of them at the time.

During the next four to five years I was involved in public policy research, an attempt to establish some new institutions in the context of the Futures Secretariat, and the establishment of the Interfaith Television Network, and I finally played a national animation role, first as logistics director with the papal visit, and then working as Canadian relief co-ordinator with the African famine.

In a way the African famine brought together almost all the experiences that I had previously learned, both in public life and in dealing with the media and in terms of the values that were ultimately at stake. Behind the immediate impact of the crisis and the challenge of trying to respond to an impossible task, there was the sense that we were being asked to discover what our fundamental relationship with the people of Africa was all about. That was not an easy task. I guess my role now, as ambassador to Ethiopia, is an attempt to follow that through in a very coherent, and I hope, complete fashion. Public life in a community or public life in a national sense has some clear boundaries and some clear definitions. Public life in an international sense, I think, is still far too new to have many real boundaries. There is no question in my mind that we are living through a time when we are exploring and exploding more institutions in an international sense than at any time in the history of humanity.

Just think of Africa itself. It is almost more than the mind can imagine. At the end of the Second World War when the United Nations was established, there were only two African nations eligible to join the U.N.—one was Ethiopia, interestingly enough, and the other was Liberia. If you look at the list of member states in the United Nations today, there are 48 more African states. That's happened in a little over 40 years—on average more than one new nation state every year since the establishment of the U.N. in 1945. What it means is that we are watching a whole restructuring of the international community.

Our relations with one another are still at a very fragile stage. It is crucial not to allow these relationships to freeze in some pre-determined pattern or pretext. If we do that, we are likely to institutionalize all the inequalities and indignities that already exist. And nowhere, I think, is that more dangerous or more potentially likely than in Africa itself.

There is a saying in the Bible, "Faith is the substance of things hoped for, the evidence of things not seen."What is this hope, this anticipation in the invisible? For me it is three things. When faith and public service are fused, there is an unrelenting search for the truth. I have been struck by this with real force in the last day or so, having read an article in a recent issue of *Reader's Digest* which I found profoundly disturbing and destructive.

Médecins sans Frontières is an organization that has provided rather outstanding medical service in a number of countries, but in late 1985 that organization was asked to leave Ethiopia because of the way it had been behaving. I am not trying to justify their being asked to leave but merely to give you an explanation for what now seems to be a concerted attack by the organization on Ethiopia itself. Unfortunately, this attack has, in my view, elements of both an ideological battle and racism. It will be very easy for people who know little, or perhaps care little, about the situation in Ethiopia to accept totally the thesis of this *Reader's Digest* article. If one wants to know the truth, one may have to spend a lot more time reading dry reports of government agencies or reports similar to the one Senator Ted Kennedy published in the summer of '86. The truth is not always obvious and easy: it is very often contradictory, quite often subtle, delicate even if unshakable, and its uncompromising nature sometimes makes the reader or the listener quite uncomfortable. But a faith that is engaged in public service cannot afford to let up on this unrelenting search for truth.

Secondly, I believe there is a need for an all-consuming passion for justice. Justice is, after all, at the center of right faith: justice for peace; justice for the full measure of humanity that surmounts the indignities of racism (whether it be in South Africa or anywhere else) and of sexism (whether it be in this community or anywhere else). A passion for justice is in profound harmony with God's total creation.

Thirdly, and perhaps in a slightly different vein, an overwhelming sense of gratitude is needed, a realization that even in spite of, if not because of, our faith there is some real justification. Such a justification surely was experienced by a Martin Luther or by a Dietrich Bonhoeffer, a justification not of arrogance, but of humor. I have two modern-day heroes who represent for me outstanding Christian gratitude and humor. One of them lives in this province and the other lives half way around the world—closer to the world in which I now live.

The one who lives half way round the world is well known now. He wasn't, just a few years ago, because he was regarded as a rather troublesome cleric who kept irritating the authorities in South Africa—that's Desmond Tutu. He has recently become known because of his Nobel Peace Prize and because of the manner in which he approaches the rights of his own people—not with arrogance, not with the sure sense of one who is committed above all else, but with a sense of his own human frailty and a profound sense of humor. I have often thought as I watch Desmond Tutu speaking that if there is anyone who could actually charm a racist right out of his last racist sentiments, it would have to be Desmond Tutu himself.

Here in Ontario, this province has at the moment a rather unusual individual who is the commissioner for human rights. His name is Borden Purcell. He also has this same kind of irascible humor and I watched him for a number of years as a parish priest. He would sympathize with the Chileans in their struggle over the dictatorship that had taken over after Salvador Allende, or sympathize with the "boat people," or he would be active in the political life of Ottawa when he was a parish priest in a downtown church there.

These people represent both a sense of integrity and a sense of humor, which in the final instance are fundamental to a Christian approach to public service that is both humble and faithful.

The Case of Ordination
MARY MALONE

· · · · · · · · · ·

The question of the ordination of women in the Roman Catholic church has been so much in the air over the past decade that the making of a case for ordination seems, at first glance, to be a relatively simple matter. The literature surrounding the topic is increasing daily and, in a delightfully paradoxical way, the refusal of the Roman Catholic church at all levels to make the ordination of woman a regular part of discussions on women is serving to keep attention directed to this one "undiscussable" topic.

As I delved into the literature it became clear that for many people no further discussion is necessary. The issue is clear. Continued refusal to ordain women is a simple matter of injustice. What is needed is strategy, first to keep the issue alive, and second to find ways to bring pressure on the institution to change its mind. What is increasingly evident is that the non-ordainability of women is no longer an abstract topic, but that the lives of many women are marked by pain and a growing alienation from their church.

On the other hand, there is another kind of "clarity" to be found. Many Roman Catholics are of the impression that the subject is closed, that the church has spoken definitively and that any further raising of the question is to be considered a mark of disloyalty or worse. To persons of this persuasion, behind any discussion of women in the Roman Catholic context there lurks the specter of ordination and a host of other not-to-be-discussed topics. All these attitudes combine to keep the topic alive, but in an often confused state. In such a highly emotional area there is a need for some clear statement, if only of the state of the question to date. That is what this article hopes to do.

Mary Malone (born 1938) teaches religious studies at the University of St. Jerome's College in Waterloo, Ontario. She is the author of Who Is My Mother: Rediscovering the Mother of Jesus *(1984) and* Women Christian: New Vision *(1985). Her report on the status of an important controversy, about whether women should be accepted as priests by the Roman Catholic church, appeared in the June 1988 issue of* Grail.

First of all, the issue of the ordination of women in the Roman Catholic church is not a closed issue. On 27 January 1977, the Sacred Congregation for the Doctrine of the Faith released the document *Inter Insigniores (Declaration on the Question of the Admission of Women to the Ministerial Priesthood)*. This document declared that, according to Catholic teaching, "the Church, in fidelity to the example of the Lord, does not consider herself authorized to admit women to priestly ordination." The declaration reaffirms existing theology and teaching in relation to new questions concerning ordination, but does not define any new and definitive teaching. In the words of the declaration, there is a new ecumenical climate; theologians, exegetes, patristic scholars, historians are raising new questions and "women have an ever more active share in the whole life of society"—it is specifically in this context that the "Catholic Church must make her thinking known."

Many have remarked that what might be considered to be the "essential" teaching of the document is stated in a vague and inconclusive way: "the Church ... does not consider herself authorized to admit women to priestly ordination." This is not a definitive statement that women cannot be ordained. There is room for discussion.

To complicate matters still further this declaration seems to contradict on several points another official document published a few months earlier. This latter, the report of the Pontifical Biblical Commission on the subject of the ordination of women, stated that the members of the commission were unanimous in their opinion that the matter could not be settled in a clear way once and for all from a study of the New Testament. Nevertheless, in what would seem to be a deliberate gesture, the declaration accepts the "attitude of Christ" and the "practice of the apostles" as clear indications of a norm that must still be observed because "it is considered to conform to God's plan for his church."

A final complication must be added. The worldwide response to the official Roman declaration was somewhat unique. Instead of silencing discussion on the ordination of women, the opposite occurred. On the one hand, opinion polls showed that support for women's ordination increased *after* the publication of the declaration. On the other, theologians all over the world, on all the continents, challenged the declaration on its insensitivity to mission countries, its lack of ecumenical awareness and sensitivity, its faulty exegesis, its novel and inaccurate use of "traditional" theological arguments, and its sexism.

It is no small wonder, then, that the case *for* ordination is not being explicitly made within the Roman Catholic community. With the possible exception of abortion, this is the most emotional discussion afloat in the church today. What this article hopes to accomplish is to pinpoint some areas where discussion may be carried on fruitfully. In fact, such a discussion is already under way by the Roman Catholic church in a public and official manner, not however with any group within the Roman Catholic community but with the Anglican church. The Vatican and Canterbury exchange of letters on the admission of women to priestly ordination, four letters in all, has appeared in a recent volume of *Origins* (17 July 1986).

Before exploring this correspondence it is necessary to point to at least two possible approaches to this discussion. One common way is to list the arguments against and then proceed to dissect them one by one. This pattern will not be followed here, because the agenda is too clearly set by those opposed to ordination. This procedure allows for no critique of the boundaries of the discussion and continues an apologetic and hostile mode of theological debate which cannot be of much help to anyone.

Another approach is to proceed along the lines of feminist theologizing based on an inclusive anthropology, and a re-reading of history, scripture and theology from the perspective of the experience of women. This approach is much more fruitful and much needed, since the experience of women has not been integrated into official Roman Catholic teaching at any level. This approach will be more helpful here, with specific attention to the integrative aspects.

The recent Anglican/Roman Catholic dialogue on the subject of women and priestly orders is particularly helpful because it pulls together some of the main arguments *for* and *against* the admission of women to priestly orders currently in use, and then brings into focus the most important and solid doctrinal reasons in support of the ordination of women (Archbishop Runcie of Canterbury) as well as ecclesial and doctrinal reasons which opposed such ordination (Jan Cardinal Willebrands of the Vatican Secretariat for the Promotion of Christian Unity). What is outstanding about the correspondence is the tone of quiet and respectful dialogue, a tone which testifies to the mutual respect and affection of the correspondents, and is a welcome change from the usual caustic nature of most discussions on such an emotional topic.

Before exploring this correspondence, it will be helpful to pinpoint some of the argumentation on this issue which is falling into disuse as a result of post-Vatican II ecclesiology, biblical theology and renewed Christian anthropology. Such argumentation would include all reference to the cultural and "natural" inferiority of women based on a supposed "order of nature." It would also exclude all narrowly based appeals to history and exegesis in the light of the rich abundance of historical and biblical research especially in the past decade. This automatically eliminates such simplistic but oft-repeated reasons as "If Jesus had wanted women priests, he would surely have ordained his own mother."

Further, the affirmation of the equality of women in all social contexts is now a commonplace of papal and official Catholic teaching. This affirmation itself raises new questions about the equality of women in the ecclesial context, as does the inclusion of women in many areas of ecclesial ministry. The Notre Dame study on parish life provides some remarkable statistics on the seriousness of women when it comes to the life and ministry of the church. The following statistics are provided from this study of 1,100 American parishes. Women comprise 55% of membership lists; 61% of Sunday mass attendance; 80% of daily mass attendance; 60% of eucharistic ministers; 50% of lectors; 85% of those active in ministry to the poor, sick and disabled; 80% of catechists; 80% of prayer group members; 75% of bible study or adult education group members and leaders; 60% of youth ministers; 52% of parish council members; and 58% of those considered to be the most influential leaders in the parishes. There is no doubt that similar statistics would appear for the Canadian church if a similar study were undertaken. It is no wonder that the question of the full admission of women to all levels of ministry will not just disappear.

The Canterbury-Rome correspondence referred to earlier was released by the Vatican on 30 June 1986. The first of the series, from John Paul II to Archbishop Runcie, is dated 20 December 1984, and specifically places the discussion in continuity with the previous correspondence between Pope Paul VI and Archbishop Donald Coggan in 1975-76.

Almost a year later, having canvassed the Anglican bishops worldwide on the subject, Archbishop Runcie replies briefly to the Pope and in much more detail to Cardinal Willebrands. Six months later, Cardinal Willebrands sent his reply to Canterbury. Both parties to the correspondence commit themselves to continue the dialogue. It is to be noted again that this is the only *official* Roman Catholic debate at the moment on the subject of the ordination of women.

Affection, respect, "brotherly frankness," and a thirst for unity mark the letter of John Paul II. The Pope's main purpose in writing is to communicate these attitudes, to renew a commitment for "a search for reconciliation" and to clarify, once again, the position of the Roman Catholic church as a basis for "frank and constructive dialogue." The Pope recalls with joy that during the past decade there has been much "progress toward reconciliation between our two communions." However, the main point of the letter is contained in the following sentence: "But in those same years the increase in the number of Anglican churches which admit or are preparing to admit women to priestly ordination constitutes, in the eyes of the Roman Catholic church, an increasingly serious obstacle to that progress."

Nevertheless, the Pope reaffirms a commitment to dialogue and to a continuation of reliance on the joint study commission whose task is to explore "all that hinders the mutual recognition of the ministries of our two communions."

As indicated, Archbishop Runcie conducted a confidential consultation with all bishops of the Anglican communion in the year prior to his response to the Pope's letter. The results of this consultation furnish the archbishop with quite specific information on the *status quaestionis* within his own communion.

The tone of Runcie's letter is as cordial as that of the Pope's. He comments on the maturity of relationships between the churches which allows for a discussion on such a controversial issue. "You may be certain that I received your letter in the same spirit of brotherly love with which it was sent and also intend this reply to reflect that `speaking the truth in love' of which your letter spoke."

Runcie goes on to affirm that there is division within the Anglican communion on this issue, but that those churches which have admitted women to priestly ministry have done so for "serious doctrinal reasons." These reasons are outlined in his letter to Cardinal Willebrands. The most important part of Runcie's letter to the Pope may well be in the proposal of a joint study commission which would deal specifically with the "question of the ordination of women to the ministerial priesthood." Runcie concludes: "I know that we are both convinced that our two communions ought to maintain the mature trust in each other which has been built up over recent years."

The other two letters of the correspondence tackle the "serious doctrinal reasons" which some churches in the Anglican communion consider to be of such a radical nature as to positively require the ordination of women. Here, for clarity, we will list these in order.

1. There is, "on the Anglican side," a growing conviction that there exist "in Scripture and tradition no fundamental objections to the ordination of women." Most Anglicans would doubt "whether the New Testament by itself alone permits a clear settlement of the issue once and for all."

2. Those Anglican churches which have ordained women are of the sincere conviction that the tradition is open to this development and that exclusion of women from orders cannot be proven to be of "divine law."

3. So much for an absence of reasons *against* ordination. Runcie now proceeds to elaborate the "most substantial doctrinal reason which ... actually requires ordination: the fundamental principle of the Christian economy of salvation—upon which there is no question of disagreement between Anglicans and Roman Catholics—is that the Eternal Word assumed our human flesh in order that through the passion, resurrection and ascension of Our Lord Jesus Christ this same humanity might be redeemed and taken up into the life of the triune Godhead."

4. "It is also common ground between us that the humanity taken by the Word, and now the risen and ascended humanity of the Lord of all creation, must be a humanity inclusive of women, if half the human race is to share in the redemption He won for us on the cross."

Runcie did not add, though he might easily have done so, that an ancient

Christian formula, dating back at least to Gregory of Nyssa, states that "what is not assumed, is not redeemed."

5. The next point proceeds to the representative nature of Christian priesthood. Anglicans would argue that "the priestly character lies precisely in the fact that the priest is commissioned by the church in ordination to represent the priestly nature of the whole body and also—especially in the presidency of the Eucharist—to stand in a special sacramental relationship with Christ as high priest in whom complete humanity is redeemed." This inclusive humanity of Jesus Christ is all the more perfectly expressed in a priesthood open to both women and men.

6. While not judging the past in an ahistorical manner, Runcie goes on to point out that most human societies have surrendered an exclusively male leadership and, as a result, "the representational nature of the ministerial priesthood is actually weakened by a solely male priesthood."

7. Runcie draws his final argument from the experience of those churches which have taken the step of ordaining women. While acknowledging "deep division" among Anglicans on this issue, he affirms that the experience of ordained women has been "generally beneficial" and that no compelling arguments have arisen which might lead to a discontinuation of the practice. On the contrary, the inclusion of woman in priestly ministry seems to be spreading among the Anglican churches.

Archbishop Runcie concludes with some of his own reflections. He is in favor of awaiting a greater ecumenical consensus and believes such ecumenical restraint to be itself a doctrinal issue. Nevertheless, he remarks, that it is through "conflict and debate that truth is often discerned."

The remainder of Runcie's letter is a passionate plea for the continuation of dialogue between two sister churches and reaffirmation of the "personal friendship" between Cardinal Willebrands and himself.

The response of Cardinal Willebrands continues in the same atmosphere of friendship and respect. It is equally significant that Willebrands confirms that the Anglican/Roman Catholic International Commission will continue to take these questions very seriously. The cardinal then proceeds to deal with some of the specific issues raised in Runcie's letter. As before, we will list these for convenience.

1. The issue of awaiting a wider consensus among the churches opens up a "profound theological dimension of this question."

2. The principal reason put forward by the Roman Catholic church is that of tradition. "The practice of the church to ordain only men embodies her fidelity under the guidance of the Holy Spirit to what was given by Christ."

3. Willebrands welcomes the theological context within which the issue was discussed in Runcie's correspondence and adds that the matter can never be solved on sociological or cultural grounds. The question of the

ordination of women can only be discussed within the context of tradition and sacramental theology. The leadership of women in "secular" society has no bearing on the question.

4. The language of the discussion between our two churches is that of priesthood and sacrament, Willebrands states. He then proceeds to his specific theological objection. The priesthood is representative, yes, but only in the sense that it represents Christ, the head of the body. And, quoting *Inter Insigniores*, "we can never forget that Christ is a man." Willebrands continues: "His male identity is an inherent feature of the economy of salvation."

5. And what of the feminine dimension? It is to be used only of the human family in God's plan of salvation. Willebrands speaks of the bridal imagery in both the Hebrew and Christian scriptures and refers also, as supportive evidence, to the role of Mary as model of church.

Willebrands concludes that the "priest does not primarily represent the priesthood of the whole people of God. However unworthy, the priest stands *in persona Christi*."

When stated in these terms, the theological issues, it seems, can be reduced to two. First, that of ecumenical consensus and the accompanying ecclesiological difficulties; secondly, the representative nature of Christian priesthood, held by the Anglican communion to be representative of the whole of humanity assumed by Jesus Christ, and held by the Roman Catholic communion to be representative *only* of Christ the head of the body. While both sides express sincere hope that the dialogue will continue, neither side seems to be aware of the deep suffering of many women in the church today. It is to the experience of women that we now turn.

It is absolutely necessary to preface this section with two comments: space allows only the briefest overview of the issues involved when the question of the ordination of women is broached from the perspective of women, and the single most important missing ingredient in this and all questions involving the role of women in the church is the experience of women. Women have not been consulted, their experience has not been integrated. Necessary though the preceding kind of argumentation and dialogue is, it is carried on as though women could not speak for themselves and were not themselves participants in the economy of salvation.

When women consult not only their own experience as Christians but when they also begin to consult the Christian tradition as exegetes, theologians, historians and canon lawyers, the parameters of the debate change radically.

What becomes immediately clear is that all argumentation is based on the assumption that there is some obvious and divinely willed affinity between maleness and divinity. And contrariwise, that when women claim godlikeness and equality of access to God and the graces of God, their claim is labeled as arrogant, untheological and sometimes quite simply as demonic.

Women and men exegetes have opened new doors for us into the scriptures, showing at one and the same time that the apostolic tradition is not as univocal as previous teaching might indicate and that the whole thrust of the mission of Jesus and the early church was toward inclusive discipleship, not dualistic and hierarchical divisions. They have called our attention to a great ministerial mosaic of enormous ecclesial and geographic diversity which makes it impossible to state that any one form of ministry or any one line of development belongs exclusively to God's design. They have reminded us that the concept of priestly ordination is not to be found within the pages of the New Testament.

Historians have traced the various elements which resulted in the exclusion of women from the church's official ministry, but are also beginning to expose for us a vast and rich tapestry of ecclesial life for women which was hitherto ignored by ecclesiastically minded historians. While there are constant condemnations of a public ministry for women, it is only for a period of about 400 years from roughly 1200 to 1600 that women are specifically excluded from ecclesiastical jurisdiction and official ministry.

During these years, the church, in its self-understanding, was specifically androcentric. Women were simply not needed for the work of the church. A good deal of current argumentation against the ordination of women and in support of an exclusively sacerdotal concept of priesthood became fixated around this time. Undoubtedly, in one sense, the argument from tradition as invoked by both Pope John Paul II and Cardinal Willebrands is true; however, the tradition is not itself univocal, as the concept and practice of priesthood was not static. One could indeed make the point that there is more evidence for women in episcopal orders than there is for women in priestly orders.

A few final points must be made about changing theological directions. The process and methodologies of theology itself are being challenged by feminist theologians when they bring to Christian theology the missing ingredient—the religious experience of women. Throughout most of our history, women have been theologized *about*; they have not done the theologizing.

One area that becomes immediately obvious to women as they approach the enormous corpus of traditional theology is the confusion of fact and symbol. This is a particularly important insight in light of the apparent deadlock in the Vatican/Canterbury dialogue on the ordination of women. The sticking point seems to be the notion of representation—does the priest represent the community or Christ or both? Is maleness a necessary predicate of priesthood and femaleness a necessary predicate of the community?

What can be perceived here is a confusion of fact and symbol in the interpretation of the mystery of Jesus and the nature of priesthood. The fact is that Jesus was a man and Mary was a woman. The statement that Jesus is the bridegroom and the church his bride is a symbolic interpretation of these facts and this interpretation cannot be used equivalently in the same process of theologizing.

The same can be said of the role of Mary. There is much more evidence in the scriptures pointing to Mary as a model of discipleship for all—women and men—than there is pointing to Mary either as a unique model for women or to Mary in a bridal role representing the church.

Another area of theology which is only beginning to be explored, but which will have enormous consequences for the question at hand, is renewed trinitarian reflection. The ancient theological principal *omnis analogia claudet* holds true in this area perhaps more than anywhere else. All our god-language limps and finally fails. We speak of God by way of human analogy and all analogies conceal as much as they reveal. Our analogies are limited by our experience. The reflection of women on their own imaging of God brings a new element of this experience and a whole new range of analogies for the trinitarian God. The question of inclusive language is obviously only the tip of the iceberg in this regard.

And so we return to the beginning and the question of the case of ordination. One of the first discoveries of anyone venturing into this area is that we do not all speak the same language. We need to ask, first of all, what ordination? what priesthood? The question of the admission of women to priestly orders opens the way way to the most radical questioning imaginable of the foundations of our faith. And, it is important to point out, even if the end result is never going to be the ordination of women, the questions themselves must be faced—questions about God, trinity, Christ, church, tradition, language, ministry, and, though we have not mentioned it before, the question of Christian marriage.

The ordination of women has become a powerful symbol in the church precisely because it is a catalyst for so many other questions. But let us not forget that the ordination of women to priestly orders is not simply a springboard to new theological discussions, or even to new inter-church relations. More than anything else, it is a life and death question for thousands of Christian women—indeed for all Christian women. For in the process of resolving the question of ordination we will, at the same time, be asking and hopefully resolving, for the first time since the early church, the question of the full ecclesial identity of women.

At A Loss For Words
ROSE BORRIS WITH PAULETTE JILES

· · · · · · · · · ·

One of my sisters, she used to pretend that she knew how to read. I didn't pretend. I said, "There's nothing I can do. I don't know how and that's it!" This was common in my parents' time, that people couldn't read or write. My father never went to school and my mother only went for a bit. My father could sign his name, but it took him 10 minutes. My mother knew a little bit more. But to them, it wasn't important. My mother said she wanted the house clean, she didn't like paper lying around. That's how it was. Your life was in the bush and when my father went there to work my mother took all the kids along. There were 14 of us altogether. Only five ever learned to read.

I was born in 1932 in a little place called Maltais, New Brunswick. My grandmother always told me I looked like a bear when I was born, I had hair all over me. And she said to my mother, "Caroline, you didn't have a kid, you just had a bear." My grandmother had a baby herself, a month after. She came to help my mother, and then my mother went to help her. This is the way it is with big families.

In Maltais the school was our neighbor. Just a one-room school. But sometimes the people couldn't pay their taxes so there was no teacher. And then somebody burned the school down so they would have some work building it again. I was five maybe, my brother and I saw a man go to the school at night with a can of gas. I remember our dog, Siffleur, barked and barked. Nobody reported the man, people were tired of the tax. Everybody was cousins anyway.

Before I was eight years old, we didn't have any money. But we had enough to eat, because of relief. It was the same with everybody in Maltais. You had a paper to go to the store and now and then people would come to your home and check your supplies to see if you had anything left over. If you

As she describes in this memoir from the June 1988 Saturday Night, *Rose Borris (born 1932) has been functionally illiterate. Paulette Jiles (born 1943), who lives in Nelson, British Columbia, has won the Governor General's Award for poetry; her most recent collection is* The Jesse James Poems, *published in 1988.*

did, then they would cut you off. My mother would hide the stuff we had under a rock out in the field—beans, brown sugar—and she would trade it to other people for the things she needed.

We had a little bit to eat from our farm—my father had a horse, a cow, and a few pigs and chickens. Every summer, we used to pick blueberries by the Northwest river. I once saw seven bears in the blueberry patch. We stayed in a black tar-paper thing, like a tent, and everybody slept on spruce boughs. I took care of the younger kids.

When I was eight I went to school, but in February I had an abscess on my knee and I couldn't go back. Anyway I didn't like it, I didn't have nice clothes and the kids would laugh. And if I hit somebody, my mother would beat me for it. The trouble was, I didn't speak very well. We had to read out loud, and I couldn't pronounce words and I was afraid and I forgot everything. Boy, I hated school. I was happy when we left for the bush.

I don't even remember the first time my family went into the bush. We would stay there five or six months, the whole winter. The camp buildings were made with logs so we had to chink them again every winter. There were always porcupine quills stuck in the bark. The buildings had only tar-paper roofs with dirt on top. My mother always had a little baby two or three months old, and sometimes the snow fell in our faces. All the children helped. We carried water and helped to cook for the men and washed dishes and put them out again, the plates upside down. We finished our work about 10 o'clock at night.

When I was 10, an Englishman took a big contract for 100 men to cut wood and work in the forest at Upsalquitch. He talked to my mother and we never came home to the farm again. This camp was big, a place where my father could make more money. But we had to work much harder.

We had three stoves, big ones. We made soup and meat and beans every day, and sometimes a roast with gravy in a big iron pot. We cooked the bread at night. Breakfast was beans and hot biscuits and bread. We made lunch for the men too—cold meat, bread, butter-molasses cookies, molasses cake, and white cake. We also had to make all the beds in the morning when the men weren't there. But it was the first time we kids had a room of our own to sleep in, even if I never had my own bed.

We never had time to play. But we talked a lot and we fought a lot, we made jokes and laughed—I miss this. I love people around me all the time. You smell food cooking, you wash the floor, and the wood smells so good, your stove is always red—this is life.

This was wartime, too. My father's cousin Emile Maltais went to war. His mother cried so much. He later said he fought and killed people. Awful thing, to kill people with a gun! And telegrams came saying people were dead, so if somebody went to be a soldier people thought he would never come back.

My uncle listened to the radio, but he didn't understand it too well. He would say: "And now the Germans are going to take that place there! Now they're going to take this place!" The way people talked, I thought the war was just behind home, maybe five miles from Maltais.

Our neighbor didn't want to be a soldier, so he hid in the bush and every day a girl went to feed him. They never caught him. In a little place like Maltais, everyone was his friend. It rained sometimes so the girl couldn't go, and once he went two days without food. He fell in love with that girl, they got married and had a big family after the war. You know, he *had* to marry her. But that's what happens when you take food to a guy in the bush, eh?

At the camps you didn't have to work so hard in the spring, and always some old people would sit down and tell stories. There's never one that's the same. Old Ouellet was a very good storyteller and he never read in his life. Sometimes a story would last two, three nights. And it was so nice when they'd say, "We ain't going to finish tonight." All the kids would listen, we loved this so much, and sometimes the small ones fell asleep. But I don't think I ever fell asleep. This was how I learned to tell stories. They'd say, "Tell us a story, Rose!" and everyone would come to listen.

There were lots of stories about Ti-Jean. He was a little man, maybe he comes from the moon. These stories have kings in them and dragons and princesses. A story like this would come over from France a long time ago, and people would repeat it and change it all the time. So beautiful!

And then there were also stories about local people. *Le vieux Joseph*, my father said, had eyes so shining that he knew when the moon was changing to full. Then this man would turn himself into the werewolf, the *loup garou*. He would take a walk into the bush and push his knife into a log. It was a magic knife, no one could touch it or he would die. Then *le vieux Joseph* would walk out on the roads and kill people in the dark.

We lived at Upsalquitch for two years. On the Upsalquitch River there were big timber rafts, and we would stand and watch them pass. The family moved when there was no more wood to cut. We moved many times, that's the way it was.

It was when we were living at Upsalquitch that my sister Stella and I took First Communion. I was 11 and we had to get on the bus, and go to the church at Kedgwick. We stayed with my grandmother Maltais. You can never get married if you are unable to pass your First Communion.

We had to learn the catechism. I had trouble because I couldn't read and my mother was not the kind of person to teach us at home. After a week of going to church I thought it was all finished. But I didn't go to confession and

I didn't know I needed to. On Sunday, the first thing I know, all the people got up and went to Communion. When I saw the little kids, five, six years, going up, I said to Stella, "It's time we go. If we don't go, we're not going to pass." Some of the women knew that you had to go to confession before you can take Communion, but they didn't stop me. And the priest didn't know and he gave us Communion.

These women told the priest after Mass. And the priest was so mad, he made us get on our knees in front of everybody and stay there for an hour. He said that God was going to come and get us, and we were never going to be saved. We were so afraid we were shaking.

He asked us, "What kind of a father do you have?" The priest didn't know we were in the bush all wintertime. He said, "We never saw people like this in our lives!" I never believed a priest again.

. . . .

After my brother Leo was born, my mother met some people who had visited Montreal. They said there was a convent where the nuns had a school for girls six to 14 years old. The people said Stella and I could go there, and work for room and board and learn to read and write. We would get $12 a month. That was good money in 1945. I was 13, Stella was 12. I thought about this and finally I said yes.

My mother and father put us on the train. You know, I was afraid. On the train we met a sailor, he was drinking liquor and he tried to catch us. I got mad and I told the conductor, but after he found us a room with a bed that opened up the conductor came in and tried to lift our blankets. After that we were so afraid we didn't sleep all night.

I had heard so many people say, "It's a very big place, Montreal!" You see, my father's cousin used to buy horses in Montreal to take them back to New Brunswick. When the train stopped, I never saw any horses so I never thought we were in Montreal. We waited a long time. The train started to move and the conductor came to find us. He said, "This is Montreal!"

I said, "What? Montreal!" I thought it was some other city, I was waiting for the horses.

The conductor told us to go up the escalator. It was the first time I was on one and I was scared. Two sisters were waiting at the top for us, they were always in pairs. They took us to the convent on a streetcar.

The convent was a big place, very beautiful. There was a curtain to close off your room, and a washroom, and water—you could take a bath. But I said to Stella, "You know, I don't like this too much." When you come from a big family, you feel so lonesome in such a place.

We had to work hard. I had to take care of seven tables in the dining room. When the kids wanted something, I had to go and get it. When they finished eating, I had to wash all the dishes and dust the tables and set them again. I also had to clean the hall and wash and wax the floor all the time. Every day I had to clean each washroom.

I learned many things there that I never knew before. Cut the sandwiches fancy, place the plates and forks very fancy. I learned how to run those huge laundry machines, and we ironed and pressed the clothes with the big ironing machines. I started to like the laundry because there was a nun there who was very nice. She wasn't yelling at me all the time, you know?

But the nuns wanted us to read and write. And I was ashamed. The way I spoke, it wasn't good French like they spoke. The little girls there, eight or nine years old, they knew how to read and write. I used to pass by the classrooms and think, "There's no way we can learn this. They're smart." Later when you're grown-up, you think: "They're smart, but they've got their problems too."

We were not allowed to talk to the kids. The only time we played outside was when the kids weren't out there. We could play outside for an hour, and after that we had to go to the chapel. We had to pray every morning and every night.

Seven months I stayed there, and the first thing I found out was who could write. You see, I had to make some of the kids write for us. I had learned to spell my name when I was smaller but I never used it, so I forgot. When you never have a book at home, you even forget how to sign your name. If a letter came, the nuns didn't read it to us right away, they had to know what was in the letter first. I was not allowed to touch it. Oh, how I hated this! My own mail.

Then the kids started leaving school for the summer and I had to do more and more. I worried about getting the rooms clean and waxing the floors. The first thing I knew, I was sick for two days and I didn't even eat. Then the eczema started. I had it for two years, I think. I was poisoned from the floor wax so I borrowed six dollars from Stella to go home on the train.

After I arrived home from the convent, we moved to a place called Squaw Cap. We had a store there. In the store, I found every box was a different color or there was something different about it so I could tell what it was. I couldn't read the labels. I don't know why, but "tomato" I could read. I guess it was because I loved tomato soup. What I hated was when they started to put the salt in bags like the sugar.

My mother was expecting another baby that fall, and my father said if she left to go in the bush with him everything was going to freeze up at the store. He said, "Rose, if you come instead, you'll be head cook at the bush camp. Five dollars a day, good money."

I wanted to bring my brother Normand with me to carry water. He was eight years old. We had to wait till the river froze, then we took all our stuff and moved in. I had to get up at four in the morning and peel 75 pounds of potatoes, cook beans, make bread and pies and cakes and cookies all morning, and then make all the lunches. I cooked for 49 men. Nobody helped me, only Normand.

Now I was 14 when I started to fall in love with a man. His name was Edmond, he was 18. He used to come to our house every night. When he went out with me, I just talked to him. When he tried to kiss me one time, I hit him in the face.

I had my fifteenth birthday when I was in the bush. I never wanted to turn 15. I wanted to stay 14 forever. I guess I was afraid that at 15 you had to get married.

Then I went to work in Campbellton. I lived in a boarding house with five other girls and I washed dishes in a restaurant. I enjoyed the job—it was hard work, but I was used to that. Campbellton was English, but I couldn't be a waitress because I couldn't read the menu anyway. You also had to buy your dinner at the restaurant. I had learned how to say "pork chops" from my brother so I ordered pork chops all the time. Sometimes I wanted something else, but what can you do?

One night a circus came to town and Edmond's cousin Albert Borris came to take me. He was a mechanic, but he used to chop wood when he was a boy for 25 cents a day. I won a doll there—I wanted one so bad. It was just a porcelain head, without any hair, but it was the first doll I'd ever had.

And then Albert asked me to meet his family. They were nice, a big family like mine. He was a good mechanic, I trusted him to have money in his pocket. Maybe that's why I kept going out with him: I cared for him, he respected me. I was afraid of the men who worked in the bush.

But Stella started to bug me about going to the convent again. She made my mother write to the nuns. They wrote back and said, "We don't need any girls to work but we know another convent where they can go." I made up my mind and said yes. Albert was coming around all the time but I wanted to be free. I was young, eh?

This time the convent was a little bit outside Montreal, on the St. Lawrence River. It was a beautiful place. But the first thing the nuns told us was, "You have to take all your clothes out of your trunk. We want to see everything you have there."

I said, "What do you mean, you? This is *our* stuff."

She said, "This is the rule."

I had a cigarette pack in there. "You're not going to make me take my stuff out!"

I got mad and cut the cord around my trunk and opened it. Then I took my cigarettes and kept them in my hand and threw everything else out. She didn't see that. I had time to put the cigarettes under the mattress.

That night I went to bed and I cried. I slept for maybe two hours. I felt like I was in prison. The walls were so high and I knew the place was strict from the way they talked.

In the morning I got up and they showed me everything. I had the same job as in the other place. All those tables to take care of, the windows to wash and the stairs and the floors—and the same wax again.

I didn't mind the work. But every night we had to go to church. And they wanted me to put my hat on, and I didn't want to put it on. And this nun I hated, Sister Vachon from the kitchen, she didn't want us to wear lipstick. The nun took a Kleenex and grabbed Stella and wiped the lipstick off. She was a big nun, almost 200 pounds.

The nuns didn't trust anyone, they only trusted themselves. I couldn't live where there's no trust. My mother trusted us, but here there was none at all. I wanted to write my mother. I tried to make a little orphan girl of 11 years write for me, and the nuns found out and punished the little girl.

Then Stella said, "We're going to say yes for the nun to write. But we're going to make all kinds of lies and we're going to laugh at them and enjoy ourselves."

That night the old nun began a letter for us. She said, "You want me to say how much you love it here?"

I said, "No, say 'I hate this place so much, if I don't get out of here I think I'm going to kill somebody. Hurry and send me money because I want to go home.'"

She wrote, "Your little girl, she likes it here very much and she's a good girl and works very hard ..."

Then Stella started. Stella had a boyfriend too.

"Tell him I miss him so much I don't know what I'm going to do."

The nun said, "Who is this?"

Stella said, "It's my brother."

She knew we came from a big family so she said, "Oh, your brother."

I told her, "Say hi to Albert. Tell him I miss him a little bit."

"Who is this Albert?"

"It's my brother, he's a baby, he's only seven months old."

She liked this. But later, we got a letter from my mother.

"Albert is fine, he still drives his truck and he stops by here and asks how you feel and misses you so much." And with Stella it was the same. Our letter stayed in the office two days, I saw it there, but there was no way I could take it. And the nun, she was so mad.

I was in that place three months. I wanted to go home right away. No way I can phone, no way I can write. To be in a jail and I couldn't even do anything!

Anyway, the nuns had to let me go. And before I left, they made me a cake.

A fruitcake, they are very expensive. "We know you want to get married soon, and this is your present." The nuns felt sorry for me because they thought I was going to get married soon.

They brought me to the train and they gave me a rosary and told me, "Sit by yourself. Make sure you don't talk to anybody. Promise us this: think about God." And they waited until the train started.

I threw the rosary away as soon as I could.

• • • • • • • • • •

Everyone was at home and I was so happy to see all the family again. But after a while my mother went to the bush camp and I had to make the food and look after the store. The baby, Aline, was 15 months old and there were four other children to take care of too.

At Christmas Albert bought me a watch. My father said, "He loves you very much, that man."

I was only 15. But around there, everybody got married at that time.

Albert came to see me. He said, "You're going to have to listen. I have something to say." It took him four hours, and he finished by asking me to marry him. I had to say yes. You know, when you get married, you always marry a stranger. You never know how it's going to work.

I got married in a big church close to Campbellton. I remember I didn't sign the marriage certificate—the priest said, "Make a cross." And my father made a cross too. Albert could sign his name, he had been to school a little bit, he knew enough to fill out a paper. But he's not fast and he hates to read.

We had a big dinner and a party, and we went back to sleep at Mrs. Borris's at Val-d'Amour, we had a room there. Albert wanted to leave at 11 o'clock. I didn't want to go, I loved to dance. If it were today I'd tell him, "Go by yourself!" He wanted to go before his parents came, to be first in the house. We went into the bedroom and I started to look at the presents, I was so embarrassed I didn't know what to do. I went to another room and put on my nightgown over my brassiere.

Then Albert's brother came home. Albert said, "Hurry up!" And he caught me and we fell to the bed.

What I found hard was to get up in the morning. Mr. Borris was there and he said, "And how did you pass the night, Rose?" If I got married again I would never stay in the same house as my in-laws.

Ten years later I had five kids: Clayton, Garry, Betty-Ann who is deaf, Shirley Ann who died as a baby, and Jerry. But one of my brothers had moved to Toronto and he said it was beautiful. Then my father got a job in construction and my parents moved to Toronto. I missed my family.

Then Albert asked me to move. When he found a job at Master Buildup we moved to Cabbagetown. I loved Toronto. It was the best of all the places that I have lived. I said, "This is where I want my life, not in a camp. In a house where you have water, hot water."

At first we stayed at my brother's place. I was 27 and Jerry was only 15 months. Albert said, "At first, Rose, it's going to be hard in the city because we're not going to make enough money." But I saw some of my relatives had rooming houses and I wanted one too. One of my cousins, he was a bootlegger on Carlton Street. He got caught and had to sell his home. I said to my mother, "I'm going to go get this." Albert was afraid. But I borrowed the money from my mother to rent the house and buy the furniture and pay my cousin's fine.

Now I had everything. A big house, 10 rooms, with my own bedroom and my own kitchen. Pretty soon my brother had two houses, then more of the family did the same, and first thing I know three were 11 rooming houses around me.

I was never afraid when my boarders drank—it made me mad. When they fought too much I'd just go and yell at them to shut up. If they didn't do that, I would hit them. Sometimes people would come in with no money. But I found I would get my way. I always have.

I didn't speak good English but I was learning it all the time. Every time I got mad, I learned some new words. I had to learn English because Betty-Ann was already in English school, the school for the deaf in Belleville, and I only knew French. Betty-Ann didn't understand French at all. I said to myself, "The time will come when she's going to be able to talk to me, I've got to be able to understand her." It was hard. We had to go up to Belleville every week. She was so lonesome, she was like me at that convent I hated so much.

It is hard to make people believe that you can't read and write. In Toronto, it's awful. You go into an office and they give you a paper to fill out and they say, "This is easy."

"All right, it's easy for you!"

"You're *sure* you don't know how to read? It's not hard."

And I say, "Well, do you speak French then?"

And they say, "Oh, but we don't know how to speak French."

"But I don't know how to read and write! Don't you understand this?"

And they say, "Oh, we're very sorry. We didn't believe you couldn't read."

When I was first in Toronto, my son Clayton wasn't old enough to fill out a cheque. I would buy a money order, and use it to pay the gas and telephone bills. The woman at the post office put on the address. And my mother, she knew all the rules for a rooming house. She said, the first thing you do is put up a sign, NO LIQUOR ALLOWED IN THE HOUSE. There's always somebody in the house who can read and write.

It's not hard to get around in the city and not be able to read. With the streetcar, I knew where I was going and you can see if it's stopping at the place where you live. But the subway, I hate this. I was afraid to go underground. The trains go so fast and I find it's not fair—they should have somebody to call out the names of the stations. If I wanted to go to a place where I've never been before, I would take a taxi. Then the second time I'd know where to go.

When Albert and I would go to a restaurant, we always asked for the special. You ask for the special and they tell you what it is. If you like it, you get it. People used to ask me, "How do you know a washroom when you stop in a restaurant?" This isn't hard—you look around and see a woman get up and leave, then you go where she goes.

I know numbers, so I always knew where to find an address. We had to learn numbers as children, my father and mother were very good on this. But when I would go in a building where they have names, I hated it. I had to ask people where to go.

I enjoyed my job. But if I had known how to read and write, you think I would have had a rooming house? No, I would have had a big restaurant on Yonge Street. The kids used to show me their report cards and they had to make sure they passed—this was very important to me. I made them so scared of not passing, they would shake.

· · · · · · · · · ·

I think when you get older, you don't like yourself as much as before. Some people hate themselves because they're getting old, or they hate the job they do, but there's no way you can stop. They're too chicken to change their lives. Then other people, they want to stay the same and there's no way you can do this. Everybody has to change.

I was thinking about my family. My sister Aline hanged herself, and my brother Ted drowned. I was at my doctor's many times. I was dizzy when I got up or when I moved. He told me it was my nerves. I didn't believe him at first. But later, I said, "I'm going to do something for myself. I'm not going to wait to have a breakdown. I'm going to make myself a road."

Now I had lots of reasons to learn how to read and write. My kids had started to leave home and I was thinking: "If I'm left on my own, what am I going to do?" I'm independent, but I knew it would be hard. Even if I wanted to phone someone, I had to wait for somebody to look up the name in the book.

When I was younger, I didn't have a phone. And in New Brunswick, when I wanted to order something from the catalogue, I would walk to my girlfriend's and she would do it for me. But now every weekend, at our cottage north of Belleville, people would come to visit and sit around on the beach, or underneath a tree, and read. And others would walk in with a newspaper. This killed me.

People would ask, "Did you read this? You know what happened here?" Oh boy, that made me mad. I would listen to the news on the radio but it was never like the paper. I said to my son Clayton: "It sure must be nice to know how to read and write."

Betty-Ann sent me a card and her little girl, Roxanne, made an X. She was only two years old. It was all that I had learned since I was small, because when somebody wrote a letter to Betty-Ann for me I always used to make many Xs, many kisses. The first thing I know, Roxanne would know how to read and write. If she can learn, what's wrong with me? But I didn't know how to start.

Just before Christmas 1977, I went up to the cottage for three months with Albert. He had a bad leg and I was stuck there, so stuck. I had to wait for somebody else just to come and read my Christmas cards. Albert wanted me to stay, he didn't want me to learn how to read. We moved back to Toronto in February and I started to watch "Sesame Street." But all the letters went by so fast. I'd try this and I'd try that but later I'd forget.

Then it was Clayton's birthday, the thirty-first of March. Clayton's the one who has made the movies about our family. He did *Paper Boy* and *Alligator Shoes* and *One Hand Clapping*, and he made *Rose's House* about my boarding house in Cabbagetown. Now he's making movies in Hollywood. I said to my son Jerry, "I want you to write, 'Happy Birthday Clayton, it's going to be a beautiful party.'" He wrote it and it took me over half an hour to copy the message down on the card. I would look at the letters and then forget what they looked like. It's hard, you know. They were not very nice letters.

Clayton found this beautiful that I wanted to read and write. He went and put my name down at Jones Avenue School in Toronto. I started there in October 1978.

It's hard to get out of home when the man doesn't want you to do this. You're lucky if you can get out the door. That's why I didn't start in September—I had to fight with Albert all the time because he wanted me at home. He said I was never going to learn. Maybe he was afraid. But one day he said, "It's no use, Rose, I can see what you want. I can't stop you." I said, "No, you can't stop me."

But when I was first at school, I was so depressed. After two months I phoned my mother. I was crying and I said, "I made a mistake, I should never have said, 'Rose is going to school.' I was crazy to think I could learn."

And she said, "Rose, you got nothing to lose. You did the best thing." I was 46 years old. I had always helped other people, but now I had to ask for help. This was hard to do.

At first I hated all the teachers. I didn't understand how they could go so fast, and I was just a little thing in the corner. But then I understood why I hated them. It's because I was thinking about the nuns in Montreal. You couldn't trust those people.

I went to school five days a week for three years. Once I started to trust people, I was okay. It was strange, I had always bought school supplies for the children, and now I had to buy them for myself. The other people in the class were from all over the place—China, Vietnam, Quebec. It was so hard! I remember sitting in the library, trying to read a book for an hour and I understood six words. Maybe it would have been easier if I'd been learning in French. But I don't speak French the way they do in books.

I didn't understand so many things. *That apple is red—that apple is not red* —it's funny when you're not used to it. "Why do you say it's red when I know it's red? If it's red, then why do you say it's not red? Why do you change your mind?" I thought that probably my eyes were different. It's hard on the eyes. The first thing you know, I had to change my glasses.

But I kept on going to school. And after I was there seven months, I wrote a letter to my principal. This is what I wrote:

Jones School, Tuesday, June 12, 1979.

The first day I came at school, I was lost and nervous. I saw all around. The principal gave me a paper. I forgot the room and my names for one week. I was always thinking about my house and I felt stupid and crazy. I hated the teacher, the principal, and myself so much. Not now. I was thirty years at home. It was strange, when my teacher Susan talked to me I jumped. Here it is nice, because we have a private teacher every day in the library. Today I'm happy because I didn't stop my school. I read and I write today, I like my two teachers very much.

Rose Maltais Borris

And at the bottom of my letter, the principal wrote: "This is an excellent piece of work."

Albert used to say to me: "You're crazy!" But now, I read in front of him. And the first thing I know, he was trying to read too, a Bible. I laughed at this: he's trying to find out what happened to his wife and he hasn't found out yet and he's probably never going to find out. Not in there!

I Moved
ELAINE JOHNSTON

• • • • • • • • • •

"Put your foot back in or I'll smash your ankle," he said. I pulled my leg back inside the car and he shut the door and locked it.

Oh, no, I had thought when he had driven behind a two-storey mound of gravel and turned off the car, he wants to neck and I'm going to have to refuse him.

• • • • • • • • • •

I had been looking for a place to live, in the country. For years I had told my friends that was where I was headed. A little cabin in the woods, homemade strawberry jam on freshly baked bread, a cat with warm fur curled in an over-stuffed chair on the front porch; that was where I would invite my friends and family to visit me. I'd be a real success.

But the opportunity never arose. I couldn't find that easy transition. How would I support myself? Without someone to live with I'd be afraid in the woods all alone.

Finally I came up with a possible compromise. White Rock. It would be close to the city, I could commute and make a living and I'd sort of be in the country.

That February morning, I boarded a bus at the Greyhound depot in Vancouver. The bus looped out through New Westminster, Cloverdale, Surrey and stopped at every intersection with a 7-Eleven cemented to it. Hours later I stepped off the bus at White Rock onto the main street running parallel to the ocean. The boardwalk. It was wintertime, the town was deserted, the fish-and-chip stands closed.

The best way to find a place was through other people. Maybe I'd meet someone. Everyone on the bus had scattered and disappeared, sure of their destinations. I bought a local paper and went into a pleasant greasy spoon.

Elaine Johnston was born in Alberta, studied creative writing at the University of British Columbia, and works in the social services field in Vancouver. This essay was originally published as I Moved: A Memoir of Rape *in* This Magazine, *May 1988.*

Over a hamburger and french fries I checked every ad in the "For Rent" column and circled two possibilities. Then I had a piece of blueberry pie and coffee.

• • • • • • • • • •

"I'm gonna fuck ya, conscious or not," he said, his arm squeezing my throat. I struggled. My brain accelerated wildly searching for an escape.

"No. Please, don't," I said, "Please." Tears flowed down my cheeks. "Oh, God, no. Please." He can't. He won't. There was nothing in his eyes to beseech. I appealed to his dog in the back seat.

He pushed me against the passenger window with his hand pressing into my throat. "I can knock ya out as easy as look at ya, so you better make up your mind."

• • • • • • • • • •

After making two unsuccessful calls at the pay phone in the café, I wandered along the street. Three hours until the bus back to Vancouver. An occasional car murmured past. It felt like a Sunday. On my second circuit I again noticed the large wood-frame hotel.

I know. I'll go inside and have a beer. Maybe two. I'll get a little drunk and then the trip back to town won't be so boring. What a good idea.

I opened the door and stepped into a darkened hallway with dirty, damp indoor-outdoor carpeting and headed towards the next set of heavy, wooden doors which opened into the bar. I had never been in a beer parlor by myself. It was lit dully and had terry-towel-covered tables, a shuffleboard, some game with blinking purple lights and the bar at the far end of the room. I sat down against the wall at the table closest to the door.

"What'll it be?" the waiter asked before I had arranged my purse, newspaper and gloves around me on the bench. "Um. I'll have a beer."

"What kind?"

"A draft." I had been to the Cecil in Vancouver with my friends and knew that was the cheapest.

An older man, probably in his late 30s, walked in. He had a raincoat on, greasy dark hair and a deep knife wound down one cheek with black blood crusted on it.

I watched him over the top of the book I had taken from my purse, *The Four Chambered Heart* by Anäis Nin.

"Can I buy you a beer?" he asked.

"No, thank you," I said, politely.

He sat down one table away.

There was a group around a large circular table in the middle of the room. They looked about my age (early 20s) and from their long hair, flared jeans and woolly clothing, I knew they were my kind of people. Now if I could just get up with my beer and walk over, they might be friendly. If I got to know them maybe they would know of a place to rent. In Vancouver I lived in a large communal house with people just like them. But what if they ignored me or just stared at me and I'd end up standing there looking stupid.

"Can I join you?" a man asked as he leaned towards me, his knuckles braced on the table.

"No thank you," I said. "I'm reading." I raised my book a little to demonstrate and fixed my eyes on the page.

A moment later he came back, put two beers down on my table and swung down to sit beside me.

"Didn't you hear me?" I asked. "Did you misunderstand?"

* * * * * * * * * *

There wasn't enough air inside the car to breathe. My mouth was dry. My tongue, like a dehydrated and shrunken leaf, felt as though it were going to disappear. I couldn't swallow. Pressure built in my head. I was going to suffocate. My breath came in short gulps into the top of my lungs.

"Please, let's get out of the car."

"You'll just try and run away," he said.

"No, please. I can't breathe."

He pushed a switch on the dashboard and the seat rolled slowly backwards.

"Lie down," he said, "and take off your pants." His eyes were dead, smoky.

* * * * * * * * * *

"Are you looking for a place to live?" he asked in the pub and picked up the paper with the circles drawn in the "For Rent" column.

"Yes, I am." It would be rude not to answer.

"You'll never find anything in this crummy paper," he said.

He had Appaloosa horses, he told me, a nice little place over in Surrey. Boy, I thought, if I get to know him and move out here maybe he'll let me ride them, but there was something about him that I didn't like. He had curly, dry, dirty-blond hair, a mustache and beard. A bit of a redneck. I immediately censored myself. I was a flower child learning not to stereotype or judge people by their appearance. That's narrow-minded, like distrusting people because of the color of their skin.

"Look," he said. "I'm just doing my laundry down the street. I could drive you over to Surrey, get a paper there, maybe even drive around and look for rent signs. I have to be back in half an hour to put my stuff in the dryer. You'll be back in lots of time to catch your bus."

Sounded good. The dark man looked up from his beer and watched me go. I must be hurting his feelings, I thought. I wouldn't have a beer with him and here I am now leaving with this guy.

His car was parked across the street. A beat-up Oldsmobile with wide strips of masking tape holding the driver's window together. I paused. An adolescent black mongrel jumped up and wagged his tail from the back seat, pacing and spinning in his excitement. There were pop cans and rags on the floor. A faint inner voice said, I don't want to get in this car. Another louder, liberated voice said, you're just being a snob, you're judging again. And he had a dog.

He told Sparky to get down. The shocks were gone; we floated like a clumsy boat out onto the highway and drove to a small shopping center. I bought a paper and he sat in the car while I made calls in the phone booth in the parking lot. No luck.

"Let's drive around and look for signs," he said.

We began going down streets where houses were far back from the road. This is the country I thought, but how would I get around out here?

He stopped the car. "This is Zero Road," he said. "On one side's Canada, the other's the States." He looked around as if he were searching for something. The sun was getting lower and I wanted to start back to White Rock but was too timid to say anything.

He started driving again. "Better head back," he said and set off in what I knew was the right direction.

We began the long ascent up a narrow road and I noticed a yellow-and-black sign that read, "No Through Road." "I don't know why they don't take that sign down," he said. "You've been able to drive through here for years." A flutter of apprehension moved in my stomach. He drove into a fenced-off area and around a large pile of gravel. Behind that were other piles and machinery. Didn't look like you could drive through here. Maybe he was lost.

He turned off the motor. Oh no, I thought, he wants to neck and I'm going to have to turn him down. I was used to Red Deer boys from my four years in Alberta.

That was when he grabbed me around the neck and yanked me towards him. That was when I opened the door and got one foot out before he grabbed the door handle.

• • • • • • • • • •

He made me take my pants off, myself. Powder-blue corduroys. I left one pant leg on shoved down to my ankle.

My father had told me that if I was ever raped to go along with it or I might get myself killed. I knew without reason that this man was very close to murder.

He penetrated me. "You aren't a virgin," he said and leered. "You've done this before." I pictured myself with a gun shooting him in the knees first to see him suffer. To make sure he knew what he was doing to me.

"Get outta the car," he said. I pulled my pants up quickly and got out. I stood with my back against the passenger's door. "Now undo your blouse." I stared at him. Now's the time I thought. My chance. I can gouge his eyeballs out. But I was afraid. He'll kill me if I don't succeed. He took my right hand, laced his fingers into mine and bent my wrist back until my knees buckled to ease away from the pain.

"I'm gonna kill you now," he said, slowly undoing the first button. "See that equipment over there?" A long steel grid chute angled down from the top of a hill of gravel, joined to a large piece of incomprehensible machinery. "I'm gonna put you in the gravel crusher," he said, "and start it up. And when you get to the bottom it's going to smash all your bones." He stared avidly into my eyes. He watched the look of fear. He was smiling. This was what he wanted. I looked away over my left shoulder, far, far away into an infinity of darkness. I searched for God there but there was only black. Like when they flash you through a time warp in a space movie. You speed towards it till you disappear and you're somewhere else. But the black would never end.

I looked back at him. I'll die fighting. He will probably overpower me in the end but—I'll move as fast as possible and kick and punch and ... The next time my parents hear about me they'll be told I was found dead in a gravel pit.

"Walk over there," he said and indicated a grassy area away from the machine.

He made me strip completely. I considered running across the ploughed fields to the nearest house a quarter of a mile away down the hill, but I knew he could soon catch and kill me because I had angered him. If I tried for the road he might run me down with the car.

He took my glasses and slipped them into his pocket. I stood shivering in the chill.

"You just laid there like you were dead," he said. "Now I want you to move. Show me a good time."

I lay staring at the dusky blue sky looking for God. Please help me I prayed. I imagined a miracle, my friends running around the hill and tearing him to pieces. I moved.

"Put your clothes on and get back in the car," he said when he finished. "You want me to drive you back to the hotel?" he asked and turned on the motor.

"Yes." Was this a trick?

He backed up and drove out of the pit. It was dark now.

"I'd give you a ride back to Vancouver but I can't," he said. "You should give me your phone number and I'll come in some time and visit you."

We arrived at an intersection, a four-way stop, grassy fields and fences. One corner had a store on it. Should I go for the door? What if he drove away with me half out of the car? Hurry up. No. It's too late. I threw myself at the door and heard him make a surprised sound behind me. I ran along the road behind the car and then crossed in case he backed up to hit me. The rear end of his car dropped down and the tires shrieked as he sped away.

A heavy man was behind the store in a garden.

"Please, help me," I cried. "I've been raped." He looked at me stupidly. "Help me." He continued to stare at me as if he hoped I might disappear. "Do you have a phone?" I asked.

"Yeah. In the store."

He met me at the counter inside.

I held the receiver in my hand and tried not to cry. "Do you have a phone book?"

The policeman who answered the phone asked me my location.

"Can you tell me the address?" I asked the shopkeeper. I relayed it to the desk sergeant through clenched sobs.

"You've got the wrong station for your area," he said. "You want ..." He began to give me a difficult-to-remember number. I felt a scream starting from my stomach.

"Uh, never mind," he said. "Just put the phone down, stay right there. I'll call them and get a detective over as soon as possible." When he arrived half an hour later I had already been to the bathroom in the back. "That's bad," he told me. "Don't pee again until you've seen a doctor."

"He was about your height," I told him during the interrogation at the kitchen table in the back of the store. "Taller than me."

"Stand up and show me," he said.

We stood up and looked directly into each other's eyes. He was almost shorter.

After taking my statement we got into his unmarked car and went looking for the gravel pit. I kept directing him up roads that didn't get us there. Finally we drove past the "No Through Road" sign. Intermittently I sobbed and strained to stop myself. He pulled into the pit and stopped the car.

Oh no. Oh no. It's going to happen again. Now he's going to rape me. The inside of the car was warm, the police radio rasped out blurred messages. Some girl had just been raped in Coquitlam. The detective was writing in a small pad. He closed it and placed it back in his inside breast pocket.

"There's mud on my shoes," I said and pointed at them. "You can use them for evidence." He put the car into gear and moved out onto the road.

At the police station I waited by myself for half an hour in a tiny coffee room. Several young cops came in and stared.

"What happened to you?" one of them asked.

"I was raped," I said.

"Can I do anything to help?" he asked.

"Ya. Find him and kill him."

"Now that wouldn't solve anything, would it?" he replied.

"No," I lied. "I guess not."

Another older policeman came into the room and asked me to follow him. In his office he took my statement. I sat, wanting to go to the bathroom while he wrote down every word in long hand. I could have typed it much faster. He was kind.

"I've talked to a lot of females that have come in here saying they've been raped," he said, "and I know you're telling the truth "

I waited back in the coffee room for over an hour. Occasionally someone appeared at the door and said, "We're trying to get the doctor to go to the hospital. It won't be long now." I stared at the table and shivered. The small of my back and my bladder ached.

Much later a constable took me to the Langley Memorial Hospital. I sat in the hall waiting. A man in a suit and tie and topcoat rushed past cursing. "I was at a party and they expect me to come in. Where is she?"

A nurse showed me into an examining area, a large, cold room with shrill lights reflecting off stainless steel and green tiles. The doctor, without his topcoat, locked my ankles into two long canvas straps hanging from the ceiling. I felt trapped. He pushed instruments inside me taking samples and made impatient noises. The assisting nurse said to a colleague off to the side, "Christ, this means I'll have to testify and lose a day's pay."

I stared at the ceiling, tears running down both sides of my face.

What's the Matter with Claude?
ANN CHARNEY

• • • • • • • • • •

In late April, when the icy grip of winter had relented, the body floated down the river. It came to rest on the banks of the St. Lawrence, near the village of Cap-Santé, some 30 miles upstream from Quebec City. There, at low tide, it was sighted by a local resident, Pierre Frenette, who was walking along the shore. "It was the large boots, sticking up in the air, that caught my eye," he told reporters. Frenette alerted local police. Six months after his disappearance, the Sûreté du Québec announced that the body of Claude Jutra had been found.

Jutra had been a special and central figure in Canadian filmmaking for decades, with a following both at home and abroad. He was 56 years old when he vanished on 5 November 1986, from his downtown Montreal home. Just a few blocks away, on Ste.-Famille Street, stands the comfortable house where he grew up, the adored oldest son of a cultivated medical family. He came under the spell of the cinema at the age of 13, when he saw his first film, *Young Tom Edison*, starring Mickey Rooney. It was the beginning of a lifelong passion. To please his parents, Jutra studied medicine, but his prize possession was not the stethoscope his physician father gave him but a three-line response from his idol, Charlie Chaplin. By the time he was 19, he had already won a Canadian Film Award for his experimental short, *Mouvement perpétuel*, and his knowledge of filmmaking surpassed that of men twice his age.

After a lengthy stay in Paris, where he worked with Jean Cocteau and New Wave directors François Truffaut and Jean Rouch, Jutra returned to Quebec to write, direct, and star in his first major full-length feature, *A tout prendre*.

Ann Charney (born 1940) is a Montreal writer of fiction as well as nonfiction, whose stories and articles have appeared in leading Canadian and foreign magazines. The following piece on the Quebec filmmaker Claude Jutra was in the May 1988 issue of Saturday Night *and won a Canadian Authors' Award for magazine writing; it later appeared in French in* L'Actualité.

Released in 1963, this frank, autobiographical account of his liaison with a black woman and his emerging homosexual preference burst upon the complacent and derivative Canadian film scene with the force of revelation. "Here was a film that was light years ahead of what was being done locally," recalls Arnie Gelbart, a Montreal writer-director. "It inspired a whole generation of Canadian filmmakers."

Eight years later *Mon Oncle Antoine*, a funny, astute portrait of life in a small Quebec mining town as seen through the eyes of a young boy, was hailed as a classic. Pauline Kael, the film critic for *The New Yorker*, called it an "international masterpiece," and Russell Baker described it in his *New York Times* column as "the most extraordinary movie ... like walking into one of Wren's small London churches just when you have come to believe that the entire world looks like the Pentagon." In 1984, a panel of international critics selected it as "the best Canadian film of all time."

In between and around these milestones, Jutra was always involved in some aspect of filmmaking. "Claude lived, breathed, and dreamt films," a friend recalls. He wrote scripts, directed, and acted—in Norman McLaren's animated classic *A Chairy Tale* among other films. During his years at the National Film Board he won so many awards for his shorts and documentaries that he told a reporter, "You forget about them. Every once in a while someone hands you a note that says you have won something somewhere." His productivity was interrupted only once: in September 1966, he was crossing Jacques Cartier Bridge on his motor scooter when he swerved to avoid a stone and suffered a skull fracture. But he recovered quickly and was soon back at work.

He took a detailed, meticulous approach to filmmaking. In the cutting room, recalls Claire Boyer, a film editor and close friend over more than two decades, "pencils were always returned to the same place, the machinery had to be in perfect working order, film reels clearly labelled and neatly stacked."

He knew more about films than anyone else around. Colleagues got in the habit of bringing him scripts that were in trouble and projects that had gone awry. "Whether the problem lay in the writing, the shooting, or the editing room," explains director and cinematographer Michel Brault, "Claude would come along and work his magic."

In a generally self-serving business, his willingness to give help set him apart. So did his charm and antic humor. His work dealt recurrently with tragedy and death—often, significantly, death by drowning—but his comic sense always surfaced. His puckish features and Harpo Marx aureole of curls stood out in any gathering, and his quirky sensibility—"a mixture of Truffaut and Tati," according to Pauline Kael—led him to odd turns of merriment. "Once he found a mirror he liked," a friend remembers. "He carried it home holding it in front of him all the way, making funny faces." Jutra was fond of dressing up, improvising games, playing bizarre characters. In his forties, resembling an aging cherub, he told a reporter, "I identify with childhood." He was sitting under a poster of Jackie Coogan, the child star, at the time.

Promising beginners could always count on a hearing—though the experience was sometimes more intense than they'd bargained for. After months of pursuing Jutra with film proposals, a writer named Clément Perron was finally invited to his home to explore ideas. He arrived to find the house illuminated by candles, rock music pulsing in the background, and Jutra himself dressed in the robes of a high priest. As Perron stood dumbfounded, Jutra explained that he was prepared to place Perron, for a week, at the center of his life. By the end of the week, Perron was thoroughly unstrung. "I hated him then," he recalls. "I had only one desire left: to distance myself from him and the week he had put me through with his cursed Doors [the rock group Jutra had discovered during a recent stay in California], his damned high-priest disguise, and this sophisticated atmosphere that made it difficult for me to breathe. And so, in order to define myself, so that he would understand I didn't belong to his world, I started to tell him about my childhood." Jutra was finally satisfied. Perron's stories of growing up in a Quebec asbestos town, where his uncle had run both the general stores and the only undertaking parlor, became the substance of *Mon Oncle Antoine.*

The film's success in 1971 marked the end of Jutra's golden period. In 1973, *Kamouraska,* an ambitious big-budget adaptation of Anne Hébert's historical novel, fared poorly at the box office. Though he'd had to spend months scrounging for funds, his whimsical 1975 domestic comedy, *For Better, For Worse,* vanished after a three-week commercial run. Jutra's preoccupation with intimate subjects struck a dissonant note in the politically turbulent Quebec of the mid-'70s. "What interests me is the human element behind the social and political context," Jutra explained to his critics. With a certain wryness, he told a reporter during this period, "At the beginning of my career I was an unknown, unemployed director. Now I am a famous director, but still unemployed."

Unable to find work in Quebec, Jutra resigned himself to working in a foreign language and started accepting offers from English Canada. To those who accused him of "selling out," Jutra patiently explained that filmmaking was "a drug, a passion," and that he had to make movies "at any cost." His English TV dramas—*Ada, Dreamspeaker, Seer Was Here, The Wordsmith*—were warmly received. His films in English fared less well. In 1980, *Surfacing,* an adaptation of Margaret Atwood's novel and his first feature film in five years, was universally ridiculed. In 1981, *By Design,* a sly offhand farce about a lesbian couple, got lukewarm reviews—though Pauline Kael, by now a friend, praised it and suggested: "Jutra isn't as well known as he deserves to be because he's trying to get past most of what impresses people."

There were a few new friends to help ease Jutra's exile in what he called that "friendly foreign country." The actor Saul Rubinek became a particularly close companion. Jutra's charm and high spirits had always drawn people to him but normally he kept a comfortable emotional distance. In any case, intimacy on film sets usually ends when shooting is over. With Rubinek, however, the friendship endured until the end of Jutra's life and was marked by an unusual degree of candor and trust. They met in 1977, when Jutra directed Rubinek in *Seer Was Here*. "Claude was wonderful with actors: he brought me out of myself as a performer in a way that no one else had ever done," says Rubinek. "Off the set, we found we were like two kids together who shared a similar sense of humor and a certain taste for eccentricity." One of Jutra's eccentricities, Rubinek noticed, was a trick of wearing his script slung like a bandoleer across his body so he wouldn't mislay it.

• • • • • • • • • •

Friends from his days at the Film Board in the 1960s remember that Jutra could describe in detail a dress worn by Lillian Gish in the D.W. Griffith film *Intolerance* while forgetting where he had parked his car an hour earlier. In fact, where he had parked his car was the kind of thing Jutra quite often forgot. His little lapses were a subject of amusement. He himself made fun of them.

But somewhere towards the end of the '70s, Jutra began to experience his unreliable memory as a significant impairment. He gave up alcohol and tobacco. He tried yoga and meditation. He consulted a hypnotist.

About the same time, friends began to note a change in Jutra. His coworkers on the set of *By Design* couldn't help noticing that he was more absent-minded than ever, and more subdued. They asked each other, "What's wrong with Claude?" but put it down to a low period. On his periodic visits to New York, Pauline Kael saw the same change; she attributed it to his quitting drinking. Jutra, for his part, sought medical help. But the physicians he consulted could find nothing wrong with him. Nor did a brain scan performed at the Montreal Neurological Institute show anything of significance. In a conversation with Rubinek in Toronto, during the winter of 1981, Jutra confessed he was feeling increasingly depressed and anxious despite the doctors' reassurances. Rubinek suggested the problem might simply be the loneliness of being away from home, compounded by Jutra's solitary nature. He urged Jutra to see a psychiatrist.

That same year, Jutra returned to live permanently in Montreal. He moved into a house on Laval Street, which he had purchased some years earlier in partnership with a young media artist, Luc Courchesne. Courchesne found his friend altered: "The edges of his personality seemed to have dissolved. The sharp wit, the biting sarcasm had vanished." Although Jutra joked as always, Courchesne sensed anxiety behind the humor. He remembers an evening when Bernardo Bertolucci came to visit, and Jutra entertained the Italian director with all his usual grace and wit. He remembers all too many other evenings when Jutra was withdrawn and silent.

Jutra's passionate attachment to movies remained the same, and when he wasn't watching movies he was trying to get back to making them. To support himself, he directed a few short publicity films for General Motors and accepted small acting parts. He tried working on scripts with other writers though none of the collaborations came to much. Then, in 1982, a young actress and writer, Louise Rinfret, asked him to act as script adviser on a story that she and another woman were writing. Jutra agreed to help. When that project was finished, Jutra and Rinfret began to collaborate on their own script. Eventually it became *La Dame en couleurs*—a whimsical tale set during the '40s in a Quebec insane asylum where homeless orphans help the nuns care for the patients. To escape from their harsh lives, the children create their own fantasy world in the hospital's subterranean corridors. Jutra wrote in a part for himself: an artist nicknamed "Barbouilleux" (the muddled one) who befriends them.

Rinfret found him a delightful teacher. "I always had the impression after a day with Claude that I had discovered something." She developed little tricks to accommodate his faulty memory, such as speaking very fast when they were reviewing scenes from the previous day so he wouldn't forget the beginning by the time she'd brought him up to date. Jutra had his own tricks. With the help of a tape recorder, notebooks, and memo pads, he recorded conversations, ideas, and errands to be run. Reminders were pinned up throughout the house.

In 1983, Luc Courchesne left and Michèle Cournoyer took over the vacated quarters. An animation artist with a talent for fantasy, she responded warmly to Jutra and became an enthusiastic ally in the games he created. Whenever Cournoyer took out a camera, Jutra ran to dress in the odd costumes he liked to pick up at flea markets. He would mug and grimace outrageously for the lens—imitations, funny songs, pantomimes. When they grew tired of the house, Jutra would take them off to a movie, or to hunt down the gadgets and second-hand bargains he loved.

That summer shooting began on *La Dame en couleurs*. Jutra was elated to be directing his first French-language film in years. When it came to working with actors, his skills were as impressive as ever. But if it had not been for an assistant who walked him through each scene before it was shot, the film would never have been realized. Claire Boyer recalls his struggles. "Claude tried hard to cover up, but we all saw that he was in deep trouble."

When Boyer and Jutra began editing the film, she found herself a participant in a strange daily ritual. Every morning she came to Jutra's house to pick him up for the drive to the studio. At the end of the day, she would drop him off and say, "I'll pick you up in the morning, Claude." Invariably, he would call the next morning and ask, "Claire, are you coming?" In the editing room, his concentration became so fragile that she had to restrain herself from extraneous questions while they worked.

The embarrassing moments were glossed over with bravura: Jutra would seize a book on cats he kept close at hand and distract Boyer by reading aloud amusing passages. If that failed, he resorted to his talent as a comedian to turn the situation to laughter.

In the fall of 1984, Jutra began to work with Michèle Cournoyer on an idea she had for an animated film about the deliriums experienced by an alcoholic. He had a hard time keeping the story sequence in his head. His exits and returns were inevitably followed by the question, "What did I go for?"

During this period Jutra spent a great deal of time arranging his papers and sorting them into boxes which he would then carry over to the nearby Université de Québec archives. Cournoyer assumed the boxes were part of his ingrained need for order. "I realize now that I didn't take any of this— the forgetting, the obsession with tying up loose ends—as seriously as I should have. Claude appeared to make light of his situation and I took my cue from him."

La Dame en couleurs was released in 1984. Reviews were mixed and even Jutra's admirers admitted the film was "imperfectly realized." The actor Gilles Renaud had been chosen to play "Barbouilleux," the part Jutra had written for himself. So it was Renaud who, as the muddled one, dipped his brush into a pot of yellow paint and stood there wondering what the yellow was intended for. It was Renaud who complained that no one came to see him any more and worried about what he could do to keep himself from forgetting. *La Dame en couleurs* was Jutra's last feature film.

Offers of work still came Jutra's way. Early in 1985, he directed *My Father, My Rival*, a TV drama for Scholastic Productions, and that summer he was offered a small part in an NFB film called *Sonia*. *Sonia* tells the story of a woman artist afflicted with a progressive degenerative brain disorder. Jutra was to play the doctor who gives her the diagnosis. Jutra's scene was scheduled for the first day of shooting. The Royal Victoria Hospital where they were filming wanted the film crew off the premises in an hour. Everyone on the set was tense and harassed. Because Jutra found it impossible to remember his lines he asked that they be written out and held up for him to see, but the letters were too big and the results unsatisfactory. Later, when the director saw the rushes, she realized the scene would have to be reshot.

"Claude wasn't acting, he was reading." In the end, it's a computer printing out the diagnosis that breaks the news to Sonia: "... we believe that you have Alzheimer's disease."

Alzheimer's disease was first identified in 1906 by a German neurologist, Alois Alzheimer. His discovery was based on his experience with a 51-year-old female patient who suffered loss of memory, disorientation, and, later, severe dementia. After her death, Alzheimer conducted an autopsy on her brain and found the two distinctive characteristics of the disease: tangled clumps of nerve fibers and patches of disintegrating nerve-cell branches. The only sure way to diagnose it remains the postmortem brain examination. Otherwise, identification requires the meticulous elimination of all other possible causes of dementia. Alzheimer's is then diagnosed by default. The disease becomes more common with age, but it may strike people in their 40s or 50s.

The early symptoms are as trivial as an inability to remember whether the stove has been turned off or the front door locked. From such an onset, the disease can take anywhere from five to 20 years to run its course. Death comes from the complications that afflict the bedridden.

Current estimates indicate that more than three million North Americans suffer from Alzheimer's disease. In Canada, at least 10,000 deaths a year are attributable to it, and as many as 300,000 victims may be in earlier stages. After cancer, heart disease, and stroke, it is the fourth most common cause of death among the old.

In the 1950s, when Jutra received his medical training, Alzheimer's was barely mentioned in the medical curriculum. It is only in the last decade that medical and public attention has focused on the disease. The cause remains unknown—though recent studies by the U.S. National Institute of Health have found that severe head injuries, such as those suffered by Jutra in his motor-scooter accident in 1966, can be correlated with the onset of Alzheimer's disease more than 20 years later. There is no known method of prevention and there is no cure.

La Dame en couleurs was nominated for a César award in 1985 and Jutra was invited to attend the ceremony in Paris. When he went to renew his passport on the eve of the trip to France, he couldn't answer any of the routine questions.

Jutra had drifted into a world that was increasingly solitary and silent. He now avoided interviews and large gatherings. Only three or four people still saw him regularly. Others, when they ran into him in the street, were put off by his disconcerting silences, and his new habit of contorting his mouth as he searched for a word. By the end of 1985, work offers had dwindled to nothing. Jutra began to take drawing lessons. His former colleagues, and close neighbors such as Luc Courchesne, worried about him, and shared their apprehension with each other, but ultimately carried on with their own lives. When his younger sister, Mimi, came to live with him, they all breathed a sigh of relief.

A beautician, Mimi Jutras (Jutra had dropped the *s* years earlier) had been living alone in another part of the city since her divorce from her husband, a physician. Her brother's condition was one reason that, in the summer of 1985, she moved into the upstairs flat that Courchesne and Cournoyer had earlier occupied in turn. Although she had been aware of Claude's problems, living with him brought a shocking discovery. "I had no idea how ill and isolated Claude had become. I saw at once that his condition was far more serious than he had led us to believe. I saw the humiliation he suffered. It made him avoid people and they in turn stayed away from him." She saw all this but said nothing to him. "I was afraid of hurting his feelings." The daughter of one physician and the ex-wife of another, she was mindful of Alzheimer's disease, but kept the dread to herself. Neither then, nor later, was the word mentioned between sister and brother.

The uneasy impasse was shattered by a visit from Saul Rubinek in the fall. The deterioration in Jutra's condition since they had last met nine months earlier was notable. Jutra couldn't remember whether he owned his own house; he couldn't form the figure *8* in writing a cheque for his groceries. Under Rubinek's probing, Jutra confessed that he was desperate about his condition. Rubinek raised the possibility of Alzheimer's disease, and Jutra admitted he was terrified. But, he said, none of the doctors would offer a diagnosis. Frustrated, Rubinek remembers screaming at Jutra: "What do you mean you can't get help? Tell Mimi to call the minister of culture if necessary. After all, you're Claude Jutra."

Mimi Jutras was on a visit to her daughter in France at the time, but Rubinek implored Jutra to speak frankly to her when she returned. Jutra was afraid he would forget what to tell her and so they recorded the conversation. "I will always be grateful to Saul," Mimi says now. "Claude and I finally talked about his illness. It was a great relief to both of us to admit openly he needed help." Jutra had already seen doctors on his own, but he agreed to try again.

At the beginning of 1986, Jutra and his sister started on a round of specialists. First they saw an internist who specialized in memory problems. Jutra couldn't think of the word for Scotch tape. He couldn't name the first film he had ever made, or the last. At the end of the visit, the doctor told them that Jutra's symptoms were too contradictory for a diagnosis, asked for the results of the brain scan Jutra had been given five years earlier at the Montreal Neurological Institute and, after two months, told Mimi a new brain scan was needed for comparison. Then she was told that the second scan was inconclusive as well. When, in desperation, she called the doctor to tell him how unhappy and lost her brother was, he said that Claude should avoid stress and stay calm. "He advised me not to overprotect him," she recalls bitterly. "That was it."

She took her brother to see a neurologist. Jutra was asked only a few cursory questions. Could he feed himself? Could he tie his shoelaces? The doctor promised that he would call when he'd had a chance to examine Jutra's medical records. But two months later, when Mimi telephoned him, he could not really say anything definite about her brother's case. Nor did he feel it would be useful for him to see Jutra again.

In midsummer, Rubinek came to Montreal for a film project and paid a visit. "The man I came to see was no longer Claude. It was impossible to keep a conversation going." Rubinek was appalled to see Mimi in despair and to learn how fruitless her search for medical help had proved. After making some inquiries, he came up with another name: a psychiatrist who specialized in memory problems.

Jutra now spent most of his time wandering aimlessly through his neighborhood, stopping occasionally to feed stray cats and pigeons, or to greet acquaintances, often twice in the space of a few minutes, as if days had passed between the encounters. Courchesne frequently ran into Jutra during these walks. "He reminded me of a sad, lonely child."

Courchesne had been trying to get Jutra to sit for one of his video portraits. Jutra kept promising to come but always forgot. Finally, running into him in June, Courchesne took him by the arm and brought him to his house. On the tape Jutra speaks in a slow, hesitant voice about his cats, his drawings, and other pastimes. His mobile features twitch almost automatically into the ingratiating grimaces of a clown. Then, suddenly looking without any expression straight into the camera, he says, "I live in a no-man's-land. I don't always know where I am."

• • • • • • • • • •

The psychiatrist Rubinek had suggested could see Jutra and Mimi in July. He proved to have a warm and sympathetic manner, and arranged for Jutra to undergo a three-hour examination. He promised Mimi a prompt assessment.

That same month, Jutra and his sister attended a family party in Buffalo, New York. Throughout the visit, Jutra "cowered like a frightened child." Mimi had never seen him like this before—panic-stricken—and she was so upset that she called the psychiatrist as soon as they returned. The news wasn't very good, he told her. Was it ... Alzheimer's? she asked. The answer was yes.

At the beginning of August, Mimi Jutras, her ex-husband, and their daughter, who was also a doctor, met the psychiatrist and listened while he described the disease's three stages. During the first stage, the forgetting stage, he told them, times, dates, appointments, names, intentions, and events become confused, particularly in situations of stress. The memory lapses and language problems are accompanied by mood swings, depressions, and insomnia. The victim becomes embarrassed and tends to withdraw from social contact.

In the second stage, the stage into which Jutra had moved, the lapses become more pronounced, and in addition the victim grows increasingly frustrated, restless, hyperactive, and panicky. Ahead lay the third and final stage, dementia. All memory is gone, all learned abilities forgotten. Reflexes turn abnormal and the victim becomes prey to infections and physical disorders as the mindless body deteriorates. Death follows.

At the end of his explanation, the doctor advised the family to obtain power of attorney and take control of Jutra's affairs.

"I sat there listening to him in an absolute state of shock," Mimi recalls. "Finally, I forced myself to ask what we could do to make Claude's life easier." Nothing, she was told. Jutra's depression would pass as the disease advanced. There was no point to the mental exercises he asked for. They were useless and they would only add to his sense of frustration.

Several months after Jutra's death, clinical trials began in the U.S. and Canada of an experimental drug that has shown promise in reducing memory loss in Alzheimer victims. The drug, tetrahydroaminoacridine (THA), is not expected to stop or reverse the underlying brain deterioration, but it may temporarily alleviate the symptoms of the disease in its first and second stages, thus extending the period when the victim is still independent and able to work.

Although the family was advised to inform Jutra of his condition, they decided against it, wanting to spare him the hopelessness of the prognosis. Whenever he asked Mimi if she had heard anything, she said the doctor was still away on holiday. By night, Jutra's insomnia grew worse. By day, he was still working with Louise Rinfret, but it was mostly her patience that kept them going. He also drew, but the drawings were becoming more and more childlike. He continued to arrange his papers: whenever he filled up a new box, he took it over to the archives. He made entries in the small notebooks that he kept about him, writing down bits of dialogue in preparation for telephone conversations, noting routes to follow between his house and a desired destination, listing words that evaded him when he needed them. Only the pleasure he derived from watching films remained unchanged.

Occasionally, there were evenings spent in the company of the few friends who remained. Rubinek, in town for some film work, came to see him. One evening, when they had gone to the movies together—they had seen *The Color of Money*—Jutra seemed particularly anxious to communicate something. Back at the house, he pulled out his diary and some drawings he had made during his travels in Africa and seemed to want Rubinek to take care of them. Rubinek reminded him that he was in the process of donating his papers to the archives. "That seemed to calm him," he recalls, "but he still wanted me to know where he kept his diary."

Claire Boyer was another of the rare visitors. Each time they met, Boyer noticed that Jutra's fears were multiplying. The last time, in October, he appeared beset by demons wherever they went. During dinner, he complained about the decor of the restaurant and begged Boyer to leave. Later, they walked out of a screening of *Blue Velvet* because Jutra found its violence unbearable. On the way home, Boyer made a detour to pick up her mail at the National Film Board. The familiar streets were deserted and dark and Jutra clung to her in terror all the way.

"Our conversation that night seemed to me as bizarre as his reactions," she recalls. " 'I've been thinking of getting married,' he said to me, 'and I thought of you, Claire. We've always gotten along so well; you're free, you're amusing, and you have great inner strength. I need someone like you.' I understood that he was looking for someone to take care of him. I tried to console him. I offered him the names of a couple of psychiatrists I knew." She adds bleakly, "I really didn't know what else to do."

Jutra made a similar appeal to his friend Don Chan, who lived in Toronto. "Claude wanted me to move in with him. I explained to him I doubted I could learn French and, in any case, I had a life in Toronto that would be hard to abandon." During October, Jutra's biweekly long-distance calls to Chan became daily. "He telephoned every night even though he really didn't have anything to say. Towards the end of the month, he asked me to come and see him, but I couldn't just then. I promised to visit him in a few weeks and Claude replied in a rather uncharacteristic, brusque way that he would be too busy then." At the end of October, Mimi Jutras organized a visit to Amos, the town in northern Quebec where the Jutras' parents had resettled and where Michel Jutras, the younger brother, practiced medicine. The purpose of the trip was twofold: Claude Jutra was running out of money and the family had decided to sell off some inherited property; at the same time they wanted to consult the family notary in Amos about obtaining power of attorney on Jutra's behalf.

The trip appeared to aggravate Jutra's symptoms. As soon as they arrived, he pleaded with Mimi to return to Montreal. "We got there on Saturday morning after an eight-hour overnight bus trip. I couldn't face the return trip so soon, and I asked Claude to wait until Tuesday." Originally, they had planned to spend a week with their younger brother and his family. Jutra agreed to wait, but the noise and the activity in the house seemed to make him cringe. At the end of the first day, he took his sister aside and said, "Mimi, I feel very anxious. I have to leave." Again she persuaded him to wait.

"Every moment of that visit I was struck by how changed he was. When we were indoors, he just paced the rooms. Whenever he saw me, at least 10 times a day, he asked, 'When are we leaving?' The only time he seemed more like himself was when we went to buy a winter coat. He examined all the coats with a great deal of interest, but complained they were all too expensive. We finally found one he liked and bought it. Then he selected a scarf, and a hat. I was surprised because Claude never wore a hat—he was always proud of his thick, curly hair. With his hair hidden inside his hat, his appearance was entirely changed." Jutra also picked out for himself a pair of heavy winter boots.

They left for home on Tuesday night. The bus was quite empty and Mimi, still irritated with her brother for cutting short their trip, suggested they take separate seats so that they could sleep better. "Now, when I think back to those hours on the bus, I feel just dreadful. Claude must have sensed that I was put off with him, because he came over several times to sit beside me. He made some overtures of affection, but I pretended to be asleep. At Val d'Or, we changed buses. This time we had to sit together because the bus was crowded. I suggested he take off his new overcoat because of the heat. He refused. There was a stop for refreshments along the way. Claude became quite animated in the restaurant and made amusing comments about the other passengers, comparing them cleverly to various animals. As you can see, I have become quite obsessive about these details of his last hours."

They got back to Montreal on the morning of Wednesday, 5 November. Mimi went up to her apartment on the top floor while her brother stayed downstairs to play with his cats. Several times that morning he came up to her flat. She asked him if he had anything on his mind. He replied that he just wanted to see how she was. "I'm sure he did want to say something, but I was stupidly preoccupied by all the silly things you feel you have to do when you just get back. Around noon, he came up again to tell me he was going for a walk. That was the last time I saw him."

As the hours passed with no sign of Jutra, his sister grew uneasy. It was not like him to stay away without calling. She telephoned her brother's friends including Saul Rubinek, who was still in town, but no one had seen him. Then she and her daughter set out to search the neighborhood. Jutra hadn't been seen in any of his usual haunts. They returned and began telephoning all the hospitals. Finally, they combed the house for clues. In her brother's bedroom, Mimi Jutras found his credit cards, his address book, and all the cash in his possession. At first, she thought he might have forgotten to take them, but when she saw that he hadn't changed his clothes since the bus she understood he had left them behind deliberately. Then she found a note: "Love my cats and give them to those who will love them."

Saul Rubinek arrived. Together, they found further evidence of Jutra's carefully prepared departure. He had bought food for his cats and provided a drawing to go with it which depicted each cat's preferences and the treats it liked. They found a tool box, converted into a padlocked strongbox to hold Jutra's passport and some signed traveler's cheques. There were other notes explaining what he wanted done with his old clothes and the papers he still hadn't deposited. Rubinek, remembering Jutra's instructions on their last evening together, looked for his diary but found instead a small notebook in which Jutra had written some last messages for his family and friends. It proved to contain, as well, an astonishingly lucid record of the progress of his disease and the growing apprehension that had led to his final decision. Here are some excerpts. The first was written only a few months after he moved back to Montreal, the second two years later during the summer when he was directing *La Dame en couleurs*. The last three entries were made within 11 days of his death.

"August, 1981. I'm losing my memory. At work, I'm constantly repeating myself. I have to transcribe everything that's said. Otherwise, it's as if I've never heard it. I must check constantly what I've written. When I open my notebook, I find only surprises. In the name of memory, of love, and of survival, I must write things down. Everything."

"June, 1983. I believe it's all over. The angel of death floats around me. Or else, I'm going mad. If that is the case, I prefer to die. It's strange knowing one's going to die. I say this while still hoping I'm wrong. I don't know if I'm afraid of death. No, that's false. I'm afraid. First of suffering and then of nothingness. Like everybody else."

"October 26, 1986. Early morning in the park. I'm certain now that I suffer from Alzheimer's disease. There's nothing I can do. It's set in motion and there is no stopping it.

"Some of those who are close to me know the truth. But I don't know if they suspect that I know.

"Mimi is the closest to me. She is the one who takes care of it. Poor girl, in the beginning, when she understood it was Alzheimer's, she must have been afraid of me.

"I don't know how quickly the symptoms evolve. Last night I wanted to use my answering machine. I couldn't remember how it worked. I called Mimi to help me. Seeing her struggle with the machine, I realized to what extend I had mangled it. That kind of thing happens all the time now. She acts as if nothing is wrong, and I pretend as well!!"

"October 27, 1986. Now it begins for real. My hand trembles as I try and write."

"October 29, 1986. For a very long time now I suffer horribly from anxiety.

Waves of panic engulf me at any time and without reason. These attacks last several minutes and leave me shaking.

"An aura of evil surrounds me, suffocating me, then someone comes in the room and it retreats.

"This morning I got up at dawn, as I have for some time now. The insomnia is atrocious, but with the first ray of light, I feel better.

"My cats ... if only I didn't have them! I must depend on all the good people in the house to take care of them and love them.

"I have always been loved, since my birth until now. I've often felt that I didn't deserve it. Now I will make all my loved ones cry. I separate myself from you not by choice, but I'm content to leave with the knowledge that I know what I'm doing. You will understand that I'm doing this for you. There will be a horrible moment ... but none of us can escape it. Now it's my turn. Will we see each other again? I've lived on this planet where I've loved a great deal ... as to what follows, we will either see or we won't."

"October 30, 1986. I'm pretty sure now that Alzheimer's begins in one's youth, but is not detected until much later. Too late.

"I read things that I have written at different moments of my life, and I realize the difference in quality, in vitality. I amaze myself that I can even understand what I'm writing right now. If I'm not careful, I will fall into a horrible trap. I must act before it is too late."

"My sister Mimi, without knowing it, has dressed me for my final agony. I thank her for it. I no longer have the words to express myself.

"Perhaps darkness is another kind of light. I hope so."

Jutra's ordeal ended on 5 November 1986, when, apparently, he jumped from the railing of the Jacques Cartier Bridge into the St. Lawrence. A line in his notebook suggests the route from his house to the bridge and the pedestrian entry point onto the bridge. Despite a lifelong fear of heights, Jutra had forced himself, in the weeks before his death, to climb to the roof of his house, as if rehearsing his final climb and descent.

His departure was dramatic and filled with mystery. In the months before his body was found, fantastic rumors circulated about his whereabouts: he had taken shelter in a monastery; he was hidden near by, following the search with mischievous delight; he had left the country to assume a new life elsewhere. These speculations, Jutra's long disappearance, and that fatal leap would not have been out of place in one of his own films. In fact, in *A tout prendre* Jutra walks off a dock into the water and vanishes. His friends are left to keep asking each other, where is Claude? His final dramatic act, executed with an irony, a precision, and an attention to detail that characterized his finest moments in filmmaking, was his flouting of fate. Unwilling to accept the ending life imposed, he created his own.

In Defence of Simone Weil
GEORGE GRANT

· · · · · · · · · ·

The *Republic* is, at the least, a drama about how Socrates cures
Plato's brother of righteous anger. I need to remember the benefits of that
cure in reviewing this book. Dr. Robert Coles has written a book about
Simone Weil in the Radcliffe Biography series (*Simone Weil: A Modern
Pilgrimage*). He is a professor of psychiatry at the Harvard Medical School. His
book is in a biography series but is in fact a commentary on her personality
and life, accompanied throughout by an *obbligato* of quotations from his conversations about her with Dr. Anna Freud, the daughter of the founder of
psychoanalysis. I have the temptation to anger because the two writers
patronize a great saint and thinker. By "saint," I mean those rare people who
give themselves away. By "great thinker," I mean somebody who is remarkably open to the whole. Simone Weil wrote with genius about the two most
important Western matters, Christ and Plato. It is hard to avoid anger when
one's chief modern teacher is patronized in the sweetie-pie accents of
Cambridge, Mass., and Hampstead, U.K.

Coles' and Freud's commentary reminds me of the following: "Shakespeare
was really quite a good poet. Some of his verses are to be commended. He
obviously did not have our advantages, but he wrote pretty well. His writing
shows how neurotic he was, but he can't be blamed for that. He did not do
too badly, considering that he did not have the benefit of our help."

To take two examples where Coles' words lead away from what Simone
Weil was:

1. Coles writes: "She had no sexual life." Simone Weil's closest friend told

---

*The philosopher and teacher George Grant (1918-88) was the very essence of Red
Toryism, and had a profound influence on a generation of Canadian writers. His
best-known books are* Lament for a Nation *(1965) and* Technology and Justice
(1986). This essay on the French philosopher Simone Weil (1903-43) from The Idler,
January-February 1988, is one of the last pieces he published before his death.

me in the Gare du Nord in Paris: "I can tell you that Simon Weil knew human love in its most complete form." Clearly the friend thought I was some kind of American and would therefore judge sexual life as the decisive matter in the discussion of another human being. She cared that I write properly of Simon Weil, and knew that as a North American intellectual I was unlikely to understand the Mediterranean tradition of chastity. But she certainly would not have told me this if it were not the case. Simone Weil wrote: "The desire to love another human being as the expression of the beauty of the world is the desire for the Incarnation." Does that sentence suggest that "she had no sexual life"?

As Coles and Freud are doing the psychoanalytical bit on Weil, it is well to mention the account written for herself,[1] just as she is preparing to go to work in the Renault factory, at the age of 25. In this account she writes of what she must overcome in herself if she is to be what she wants to be. It is extremely detailed about the particularities of her body and soul. Because it is written for herself it is very intimate, and therefore I have some hesitation in writing of it. But Mlle. Pétrement is certainly a wiser human being than I am, and has published it. It is probably true that concerning the saints all evidence must be made public. It is not written in terms of the "id" psychology that Freud got from Nietzsche. It is, rather, a fine example of Socrates' "Know thyself."

2. It is now necessary to discuss the much more serious question of Coles' account of Simone Weil's relation to the Judaism of her ancestors. Obviously this must be written about with the greatest care because of the terrible events in Europe and the Middle East in this century. I think Coles does badly here for a reason of decency. He wants to open her thought to the students at Harvard, and knows that he must explain her refusal of Judaism if he is to succeed. But in this process he makes bad errors about her and her family, and about what can best be called the history of religions. It is therefore necessary to pursue this second subject in some detail.

· · · · · · · · · ·

Coles rightly calls Weil a Christian, but then makes the error of identifying that Christianity with modern Western Christianity.[2] To put it religiously, one might say that Christianity on one side has turned towards Judaism and on the other towards the Vedanta. To put it philosophically, one might say that Christianity in its meeting with philosophy for the purposes of self-understanding has had Aristotelian and Platonic wings. Weil is clearly with the Platonists. Weil's writings therefore contain a clear and sustained rejection of Roman Catholicism—that is, a refusal of the most important tradition of the West. She criticized it more often than Judaism, though often on the same grounds.

The impression that Coles has gathered of Weil's flirting with Catholicism has some justification, but in essence misses the point. Weil did clearly long to take part in the sacrament of the Eucharist, because that sacrament concerns the suffering of God. She was a Christian in that she accepted the suffering of God. We should remember that some of the classical philosophers, such as Proclus, rejected Christianity because they did not believe that God could suffer. Although Weil accepted the suffering of God, nevertheless she could not fulfill her hunger for the bread of eternal life because she could not accept Roman Catholicism on other grounds.

Categorizing great thinkers is always a dangerous task. It may, however, be possible to cautiously call Weil a gnostic. Yet there must be immediate qualifications. As a follower of Plato, Weil holds within her thought that measured blending of "gnosticism" and "agnosticism" that characterizes her intellectual master. Moreover, "gnosticism," as a recurring historical fact, has had within it excesses and follies, as have all forms of Christianity. (It would be impertinent to speak of other great religions.) In our time, as good a thinker about politics as Voegelin has wrongly used "gnosticism" as a term of abuse in his fine book, *The New Science of Politics.* Therefore it is with hesitation that I categorize Weil as a "gnostic," in order to make clear that it was more than accident that held her from becoming a Catholic.

Nevertheless it is not without significance that Simone Pétrement, who has written the definitive biography of Simone Weil, is also a leading scholar of agnosticism. (Her biography is so clear and so complete that it must be ranked among the great biographies.) Coles recognizes in a short paragraph Weil's closeness to Marcion. What he does not seem to recognize is that gnosticism has returned again and again within Christianity, and Weil's writings are filled with references to these recurrences. To take one example: she wrote frequently of the gnosticism of medieval France, which produced the civilization of Languedoc. The sympathetic have described this movement as the religion of the Cathars (from the Greek work for "pure"); its members are also known by the geographic name of Albigeois. Their civilization was extirpated by northern knights under Simon de Montfort, encouraged by the papacy. This extirpation goes by the title of the "Albigensian crusade." The Inquisition was first founded for the purposes of that crusade, and its ecclesiastical leadership was in the hands of the Dominican order. As Stalin said, history is written by the winners, and therefore we have few authentic records of this movement. Most of what we have is the testimony of its adherents under torture. In this century in France there has been a partially successful effort to find out what Catharism was. [3] Two of Weil's noblest writings are about the Cathars.

• • • • • • • • • •

The reason it is important to mention these historical matters in the present connection is that Coles' lack of interest or knowledge of them is, I think, determinative of the worst chapter of his book, "Her Jewishness." Weil was essentially a gnostic saint, and her criticisms of Judaism are similar to those which have appeared through the centuries in gnostic writings: namely, her rejection of the Hebrew Bible and its account of God. Catholics quickly recognized this after her death. Cardinal Daniélou edited a book of essays in which she is indicted for her rejection of the Old Testament. Indeed this book goes much farther than Coles' and Freud's patronizing psychoanalysis. It directly accuses her of "penis envy," and her "misinterpretation" of the Hebrew Bible is laid at that door. Unlike Coles, the Catholics have had no doubt that her Christianity was not at one with Western Christianity, but rather with what had been continually rejected by official Western Christianity.

Apart from these comments about the history of religions, it is necessary to touch upon the particular details of "her Jewishness." I am hesitant to do so, because the details of the lives of thinkers are unimportant compared to the universal truths in which they participate. But sanctity is not the same thing as philosophy, and in describing sanctity, details matter. Coles writes of these details in such a way as to impugn that sanctity. Also, the relation between Weil and her parents is one of the tender parts of her greatness, and it is discussed by Coles with a singular lack of feeling. He writes of the hurt to her family when she left Judaism. I talked to Mme. Weil at length about this matter. I cannot speak about Dr. Weil because I did not meet him, but Mme. Weil had obviously been very attached to her husband, and therefore had some right to speak of his opinions. Mme. Weil came from a family which had moved west from Russia under the influence of the Enlightenment. Paris was after all the center of that movement, and of the revolution that had attempted to realize its ends politically. She belonged to the France that believed that human freedom required putting away the superstitions of religion, whether those of Christianity or of Judaism. She early recognized that she had produced two remarkable children. (Her son, André Weil, is considered in many quarters to be the greatest mathematician of this century.) She loved the greatness in her daughter, and devoted herself to protecting Simone from its consequences. It was not always easy. When Simone Weil had Trotsky to stay with her family, her mother accepted this because her daughter's "left-wing" opinions seemed only an extension of her particular brand of modern French rationalism. Like many of her generation, Mme. Weil had learned to loathe war between 1914 and 1918, particularly from her connection with the wounded patients of her husband, who served the French army as a doctor during the first great massacre. Being a decent rationalist, she had thought of herself as French without any religion.

It was almost inconceivable to her to find suddenly that the racism of the gutter had come to power in Germany in 1933. This was a common experience of many progressive Western Europeans. Gershom Scholem has described it well in his autobiography. Something had come to be in their midst which they did not identify with a Western country such as Germany, but with the superstitions of a pre-progressive age. Never having thought of herself as in essence Jewish, she now had to realize that she was being forced to consider herself a Jew, because of this modern craziness.

At the end of Simone Weil's life, she indeed used a greeting from Krishna in her letters to her parents. Her parents knew little of her movement to Christianity, and at this difficult time of her dying far away from them, she knew that they might be disturbed or surprised by what had happened to her. But after all, the Bhagavadgita is an inspired text, and for Simone Weil Krishna and Christ were perhaps the same being.

After her daughter's death, Mme. Weil spent her life holding together Simone's manuscripts, before Camus and Pétrement saw that they were placed in the Bibliothèque Nationale. When I talked to her, she had pondered every line of these manuscripts and thought they were of high truth. Once when I was leaving her flat, she stopped me and repeated Herbert's great poem "Love," which had been central in her daughter's life:

> Love bade me welcome: yet my soul drew back,
>   Guiltie of dust and sinne.
> But quick-ey'd Love, observing me grow slack
>   From my first entrance in,
> Drew nearer to me, sweetly questioning,
>   If I lack'd any thing.
> A guest, I answer'd, worthy to be here:
>   Love said, You shall be he.
> I the unkinde, ungratefull? Ah my deare,
>   I cannot look on thee.
> Love took my hand, and smiling did reply,
>   Who made the eyes but I?
> Truth Lord, but I have marr'd them: let my shame
>   Go where it doth deserve.
> And know you not, sayes Love, who bore the blame?
>   My deare, then I will serve.
> You must sit down, sayes Love, and taste my meat:
>   So I did sit and eat.

That was not the act of somebody who had been wounded by her daughter's acceptance of Christ. I have before me Mme. Weil's account, in her own handwriting, of when and where her daughter wrote the "Prologue," in which she describes how Christ came to her. Mme. Weil wrote it out for me, because there had been some historical confusion as to when the event had occurred. It cuts across what Coles has written about Simone Weil having wounded her parents. It is a document of lucidity and joy. Any confusion she may have experienced by having brought into the world this eagle was utterly subordinated to her acceptance that her daughter had been visited in the flesh directly by Christ.

The silliest thing in Coles' book is what he writes about her letter to Xavier Vallat, [4] who had the appalling title of Commissioner of Jewish Affairs in the Vichy government. Weil wrote that she could not get a teaching job in Vichy because she was considered Jewish. She says that it is irrational to consider her as Jewish because her intellectual traditions are entirely classical and French. Coles maintains that this was a weaseling letter of a coward denying her Judaism at a time when Jews were being persecuted. It is a long letter of ironic contempt from a well-known French woman to a powerful man in a position that Weil knew should not exist in any constitutional government. Of course, such an extreme difference of interpretation could only be decided by a long *"explication du texte,"* which is not possible in a short review. Two things can be said. 1. Could Weil possibly have expected to get a job after writing such a letter? 2. Does Coles imply that Judaism is a given that one cannot leave?

Pétrement describes accurately the content of this letter: "If in this letter Simone boldly affirms that she doesn't consider herself a Jew, it is not in order to disassociate herself in practice from the Jews—she would not disassociate herself from anyone, above all not from people being persecuted, and in Marseilles she did much to help Jews—nor in any way to deny her origins; nor is it to affirm a religious conviction that would have no interest for the Commissioner of Jewish Affairs. Instead, she did this in order to emphasize again the difficulty of defining the word 'Jew,' and to show quite clearly that she does not understand its significance and considers the statute concerning the Jews absurd and incomprehensible."

Of course, the high style of irony is hardly the forte of Americans. The public spirits of the United States are capitalism, imperialism, and a certain form of democracy. Irony is too high a style to be consonant with any of these spirits. The mordant wit that suggests contradiction requires too great an attention for that swift-moving society. American-popularized Freudianism has not added to the capacity for irony. This book is indeed a warning to those who write about any *"kalos kagathos"* from the position of superiority. One is apt to expose oneself.

Of course, Coles has the right and perhaps the duty to defend Judaism. (I use "perhaps" because I do not know whether he is a Jew. If he is, he obviously has the duty to defend Judaism.) Catholics have the right and the duty to defend Western Christianity against Weil's criticism of it. But the combination of the defence of Judaism with the patronizing tones of the Harvard Medical School is repellent. I am sure that the theologians of Judaism (for example, the Roth brothers in England) have a lot to say about where Judaism is correct and Simone Weil is wrong. Theological debate does not sit well with psychiatric imputation as to motive. Beyond matters of debate, it is absurd to impugn the courage of this undaunted woman.

• • • • • • • • • •

Enough about this book. As Simone Weil's writings are largely in the form of notebooks and essays, it is hard to find one's way into them. Therefore I hope it will not seem impertinent to mention means of doing so. Simone Pétrement's biography is much the best. Before sanctity one can either be silent or matter-of-fact. Pétrement's *Life* is astringent French scholarship at its best. Theoretical comprehension is of course easier than writing about sanctity. For such comprehension, M. Veto's *La métaphysique religieuse de Simone Weil* is the most careful among many good books. As Professor Veto is now at Yale, it is to be hoped that his book will be translated into English.

The center of what Simone Weil writes is something that human beings must learn for themselves in the terror of thought and prayer. To read her sentence "matter is our infallible judge" is to understand what Christ meant when He said, "I come not with peace but with a sword." At a more theoretical and exoteric level, at a less immediate and therefore more palatable level, she is saying something about what is happening in the Western world. She returns continually to Plato's statement: "How great is the real difference between necessity and the good" (*Republic*, 493c).

What is given in that sentence cannot but touch what is given in Christian teaching. Weil wrote that she was ceaselessly torn by the contradiction between the perfection of God and affliction of human beings. How is it possible that human beings are given over to the afflictions of necessity? What is it to contemplate Goodness itself in the light of the afflictions of necessity? She waited upon that contradiction with ceaseless attention. In that waiting she restated the idea of creation, not in a new way in terms of what is given in the Gospels, but in a new way in the sense that her idea has not been primary in modern Western Christianity. The idea of creation is obviously an abyss in which our minds are swallowed up. Despite the absurd contemporary use of the word "creativity," we cannot think of something coming to be out of nothing. Nevertheless, quite rightly, people have tried to find analogies which can lead us to see as in a glass darkly.

For Western Christians—let us say, loosely, since Hildebrand—creation came to be thought of as an act of self-expansion. For Weil, creation is a withdrawal, an act of love, involved with all the suffering, renunciation, and willingness to let the other be, that are given in the idea of love. For her the passion of God is at one with the creation. In this sense it is one with the teaching about Trinity. It is not possible here to work out how this is so consummately developed in her writings. (To repeat, outside her own writings this has been best done by Veto.) Nor is it possible to discuss what is thought in the idea of God as love in relation to what is thought in the idea of God as power. It can be said, however, that the two leading forms of Western Christianity are in intellectual chaos. Can one imagine that large elements of Roman Catholicism took and take Teilhard de Chardin seriously as a Christian theologian? It is clear that civilizational identity depends on primal religious affirmations, in this case the post-Augustinian self-understanding of Christianity. It is clear that the descent of Western civilizational identity into wild technological scrambling goes with the self-confusions of organized Western Christianity. Moreover Nietzsche's formulation that Christianity produced its own gravediggers in the modern technological rationalists has some historical sense to it, but perhaps in a different way than Nietzsche's positive affirmations would suggest. One must remember that modern technological rationalism was itself more penetrated by Western Christianity than Nietzsche would allow. The self-expansion of the modern technologists attacked certain aspects of Christianity, but took from that which it was attacking the self-expanding power that came forth from the "*Rex tremendum majestatis,*" in which creation is utterly defined as power. At a time such as this when on the one hand the Gospels stand in their indubitable perfection, while on the other hand the civilization of the West has become mainly technology, it is well to read carefully a thinker of consummate intelligence and love who understood that Christianity becomes meaningless if the creating of God is detached from the passion of God. Simone Weil often speaks of "the lamb that was slain from the beginning of the world."

When in admiration and love I look for a description of Simone Weil, some lines from Crashaw's invocation to Saint Theresa of Avila come to mind:

O thou undaunted daughter of desires!
By all thy dow'r of Lights and Fires;
By all the eagle in thee, all the dove;
By all thy lives and deaths of love,
By thy large draughts of intellectual day,
And by thy thirsts of love more large than they —

Notes

1. This is published in Simone Pétrement's *La Vie de Simone Weil (Simone Weil: A Life)*; in the French, Volume II, pp. 11-14, in the American translation, pp. 219 to 222. It must be said that the American translation is often poor. In this passage, "*jouissance*" is translated as "pleasure." If possible, it is well to read it in French, especially when it comes to Weil's own words. She wrote the most luminous of Western languages with a clarity that is breathtaking. Nothing seems to stand between the words and what they are about.

2. Weil had no knowledge of or interest in Protestantism. So far as I can discover, her only knowledge of it was of a Baptist church in Harlem which she admired. Of mainline or fundamentalist white Protestantism, she had no knowledge or interest. As matters of ecclesiastical persuasion influence judgment, let me mention that I am an Anglican Protestant.

3. We are lucky to have a fine historical novel in which the Cathars appear, Zoé Oldenbourg's *The Cornerstone*. Her later novel about the Albigensian crusade, *Testament of Fire*, is such a literal account of the horrors of that extirpation that I can only recommend it to people of strong stomachs.

4. For the letter in full, see Pétrement's *Life*, in the French, Volume II, pp. 377 to 379; in the English translation, pp. 443 to 444.

The Future of Our Past
RICK SALUTIN

. . . .

I wish I had written this before the Tories signed their free-trade deal with the U.S. It would have been easier, far more ... straightforward. I'd have started:

Let us begin with a trenchant formulation, written almost a century ago, of the problem that Canadian history poses for Canadian literature: "Could Count Tolstoi write *War and Peace*, or Ivan Turgenieff hold you as firmly as the Ancient Mariner did the wedding guest if they lived in Canada? How could they? They could not learn war here, they could not be fired by the daily, hourly human agonies, worse than those pictured in Dante's *Inferno*, which a Russian sees. The follies and cruelties of the great, the meannesses and sufferings of the poor; violent love, equally violent hate; jealousy, cruel as the grave, treachery—are on all sides of the 'unspeakable Russ.' The Slavonic race is scattering tragedies broadcast. We sit in the broad sunlight by day, in the glare of electric light by night; we are nice and warm in summer, and thanks to self-feeders, and hot air, and steam, equally nice and warm in winter; we love conveniently and properly, we have mild dislikes during which we riddle the character of our pet aversion with a pea-shooter. We are even equal to triolets. We must have something strong and great within us before we can produce anything strong and great. Canada must be born again."

I'd have gone on, commenting on the above passage:

Those lucky Russians. Their blood has flowed. They've endured mass slaughter and catastrophic natural disasters. *They can write novels!* This is the view of the essayist and critic, L. O'Loane, writing in the Toronto magazine, *The Week*, "An Independent Journal of Literature, Politics, and Criticism," in 1890.

Coming as it did in the January-February issue of Books in Canada, *Rick Salutin's essay was one of the first salvos of 1988 against free trade, the issue that dominated public discussion throughout the year. Salutin (born 1942) is a Toronto playwright and journalist. He is also the author of a novel,* A Man of Little Faith *(1988), and is one of the editors of* This Magazine.

It's true the statements seem dated; the quest for Great Literature of our own, for instance. We may feel that, since 1890, Canadian literature *has* arrived; or alternately that the discussion about why it hasn't is fruitless, self-indulgent, and/or neurotic. The formulations are certainly quaint (a triolet is a verse form); yet the issue remains with us. In fact its current versions are, I'd say, far less incisive than O'Loane's.

Today we're more likely to hear the flat complaint, "Canadian history is boring." Probable answer: "Canadian history is *not* boring." Followed by " 'Tis." " 'Tisn't." And so on. And we may well wonder, "So what?"

What is interesting for us about O'Loane is that he pins many of the problems—or, to be non-judgmental, many of the *characteristics*—of Canadian literature (and, let us extrapolate a hundred years later, other cultural forms like film and television drama) on *our history*. It seems to me the passion of his argument, and at least to some extent its pertinence, abides.

How might one deal with O'Loane's contention? There are a number of routes.

The first is by way of what we might call the colorization of Canadian history. It seems to me that Pierre Berton has pushed this approach as far as it can go—qualitatively if not quantitatively. One does up the fact that there was a *pirate* who operated on the Great Lakes, or that one of our prime ministers communicated with his dead mother through *mediums*, or that as an NFB film about Norman Bethune shows us, the man *drank* and *womanized*. Compare the current CBC Radio drama series *A Different Drummer* : a new Canadian eccentric from our past every week. It seems to me this route concentrates on the charge that our history is dull; it sets out to refute the claim by discovering color in our past; and, at least for me, it doesn't work. Colorful people can be awfully boring—once you get used to them. It protests too much: desperate to reclaim the bored Canadian reader (or viewer), it assumes the dullness it strives so earnestly to negate. It thereby confirms what it aims to deny. Besides, the strength of O'Loane's formulation is that he does not trivialize the issue by making boredom the problem of our history. What he says, in effect, is that our history is not historic. Not momentous, not significant. Those dedicated to the colorization of Canadian history do not deal with this critique. They more or less accept the outline of our history as given, and color it in: they do not question its basic themes, or lack thereof; they seek to present what is there in a better way, but our history's importance to us surely resides in more than its entertainment value.

Another approach is to attack the assumption that other peoples have more *historic* histories than our own. How many actual Russian peasants, for example, participated in the grand battles of Russian history? Didn't the majority of them, like most human beings through all time and space, live and die according to the normal rhythms of birth, work, love, and death? How many of us are really touched by the grand and historic? Are Canadians really much different from others in this respect? Perhaps not, but that doesn't alter the fact that history—however few or many it touches—does differ in its character from nation to nation; and ours, such as it is, does seem peculiarly, maybe even uniquely, placid.

Or one could argue that it is not a grand and gory history that makes for memorable literature but the reverse: well-executed literature *creates* a momentous history. What was the outbreak of the American Revolution, for example? A skirmish near a colonial town—until it became, in Longfellow's hands, the place "where once th' embattled farmer stood, /And fired the shot heard round the world." What could be more provincial and uninteresting to later generations in other lands than Britain's Wars of the Roses—except that Shakespeare took them on? For that matter, what would we know about Napoleon's Russian campaign (just another disastrous military miscalculation) without *War and Peace?* In this light, it is not Canada's history that has failed our writers, but our writers who have failed to create for us a worthy history. In this view it is the responsibility of writers to take whatever raw historical material is at hand, and shape it into something that stirs their compatriots. I think there is a lot to be said for this argument; it takes the roles of culture very seriously, but it makes a rather large claim for the power of the writer to create out of virtually anything at hand; and it ignores the question: what is it in the history of a society that predisposes its writers to *play* this role in creating a sense of history?

There is one final way in which one might respond to O'Loane's challenge. One might, with qualifications, agree with him. I find myself in that position. I don't endorse the formulation, but I think we do have a problem between our history and our literature, and I lean towards O'Loane when he says the problem lies in our history.

• • • • • • • • • •

Now (I would have continued, had there been no Canada-U.S. free-trade agreement), let us turn the question somewhat, and ask not how our history affects our literature, but how literature treats our history. I write here not with detachment, but as someone who has tried to make the connection, primarily in theater, but also in film and television drama: for example, in 1973 with the play *1837*, created collectively with Theater Passe-Muraille, and in 1977 with another play, *Les Canadiens*, which covered all of Quebec's history in act one and the momentous provincial election of 1976 in act two. I worked on two collective plays in Newfoundland, one based on the woodworkers' strike of 1959, and the other on the life of Joey Smallwood, which is exactly coincident with the history of Newfoundland in this century.

At a certain point I became suspicious of the effects of history on drama and began trying avoid it, but I return to it compulsively. My last television script, for example, *Grierson and Gouzenko*, dealt with the end of the Second World War and the rise of the Cold War; and a recent radio play, *The Reluctant Patriot*, returned, like a dog to its vomit, to 1837.

I think it is interesting that many of my colleagues feel a similar attraction to historical material—even those who seemed very far from it early in their careers. Take, for instance, Montreal playwright David Fennario, whose earlier plays all dealt with contemporary working-class anglophone Montrealers. His most recent play, *Joe Beef*, is a recapitulation of the entire history of Canada from Fennario's own political standpoint. The play's engine is the fury of bartender Joe Beef that his patrons have failed to learn the lessons of their own history, that they're hopelessly uninformed about their past; he flings this anger desperately in their faces in an attempt to liberate them from their ignorance.

Or take Martin Kinch, one of the outstanding directors and playwrights of the theater renaissance of the early 1970s. Kinch's field then was almost exclusively contemporary; his 1973 play *Me?* was a superb delineation of the urban bourgeois Canadian sensibility. After the usual horrors of a Canadian theater career, Kinch found himself spending five years in CBC-TV drama—doing a series of dramas covering Canadian history since Confederation. If you don't go through an obligatory attempt to deal with history early in your career, then it seems you must do it late.

What are we all looking for when we turn to history? It seems to me we are *not* wondering about our Canadian identity; we are not asking who we are. On the contrary, we have arrived at an answer, or a partial answer to that question. What we want to know is, How did we get this way? Martin Kinch must have wondered what accounted for the peculiarly earnest and moral (or artistic) quality of the middle-class Canadians he'd brought alive in his plays. Fennario, on the other hand, wondered why his workers, so noble and justified in their needs, were so ineffective in pressing their demands. Speaking for myself, I wondered what accounted for the apparent placidity of Canadian society, the absence of any serious strife—social, national, or political.

I should add that one is unlikely to ask the question "How did I (we) get this way?" unless one is dissatisfied to some degree with how one is, and desirous of changing.

Is there any trait that characterizes and unifies these literary interrogations of the Canadian past? I'd like to point to one element: something somewhere on the scale between humor and irony. The number of Canadian literary treatments of history that fall within these categories is striking. Kinch's series of TV dramas took an eccentric and ironic, if also serious tack.

Fennario's play is a good-hearted series of songs and vignettes. *1837* wanted to be a history in the Shakespearian sense, more than a docudrama, but the elements of humor and irony emerged very strongly. I'm thinking also of poetry like Dennis Lee's "1838" or Margaret Atwood's "Ten Little Fathers of Confederation." I don't mean there aren't humorless treatments of history in our literature; there are. Nor do other nations lack a humorous approach to their own pasts. But *1066 And All That* is a spoof on the vast body of solemn and momentous treatments of English history. In the Canadian cast, a large number of the treatments are humorous already.

Why do we laugh, or smile wryly, when we travel back? For the usual reasons: the unexpected. We don't find what we had expected would be there; and what we find was unanticipated.

Let us take a basic starting point. We know we exist as a nation. How did we come to exist as a nation? Confederation. So we backtrack and interrogate Confederation. We expect some yearning for national expression, some need akin to, say, Italy's or Mozambique's. What do we find? A business deal. We laugh in surprise. What of our founding father, John A.? We anticipate: a statesman with a vision; stirring words from the first Canadian, such as, "When in the course of human events ..." What do we hear? "British subject I was born; a British subject I will die." We smile our wry Canadian smiles.

We find answers, but not the kind of answers we had expected. What do we not find? In a word, a national project. What does a project mean for a nation?

The project of the United States is independence. Or perhaps even revolution. Everything that happens in the United States must answer in the light of such a national project or projects. It doesn't matter a damn that the United States does not fulfill such projects, that it may even contradict and abhor them in practice. They are still the standards by which national behavior is judged; they are distorted but never denied.

The project of France is liberty, or equality, or fraternity. It doesn't really matter. But there is a sense that the nation is embarked in the name of some project, and will hold itself to account in terms of that project. Without a project a nation might exist, but only in the sense a tree, or a species, exists; it wouldn't quite exist historically.

What is the Canadian project? Are there any contenders? To build a nation on this vast northern half of the continent? Tautological: you are a nation in order to be a nation. What about survival? Survival is not a project. The point about a project is not to succeed in it, but to provide a worthy standard against which to measure the degree of one's failures. A project too readily achieved might well be an unworthy project. But survival is no project at all.

At this point we rejoin O'Loane's critique of 1890. Canadian history is lacking, but not bloody battles or *Weltschmerz*. Canadian history lacks a project, or projects. What is it all *for*, this nation Canada?

Because our history seems to lack a project, much of our literature, rooted in our history, also feels lacking. We often tell tales that seem to have subjects but no point. Such-and-such from our past would make a great play/novel/epic poem/film/mini-series, say our writers. Why? Because it's full of color/heroes/episodic detail. So they write the story. Their works may well contain colorful and even heroic content, and end in some notable achievement like the building of the CPR. But they are feeble as literature because they enunciate no project, they represent no historically inspiring commitment.

It seems to me the existence of a historical project may be even more important for the literature of a country than for its actual history. After all, there is something mythic in this notion: a national project. If not mythic, at least Hegelian. Life is complex, and so is history as it actually exists and moves. Our discovery of national projects may be mere (pardon) projections; or at best bits embedded in a generally incoherent mass. But the discovery of such projects, of at least partial believability, does seem essential to construct a literature based in one's history. We need them; if they didn't exist, authors would have to invent them.

Canada, it seems, lacks a believable project. Without a project we don't have a history, as O'Loane suggests. Now this need not be quite fatal for our literature. There is a way out. We could explore the many ways we do not quite exist as a nation, the ways we don't, or don't yet, make it as a real nation. This could be fascinating; it could be unique; it could be of great interest to readers and writers form other nations. What a remarkable perspective to hold on what it is to exist as a nation in the world today.

We are, we might say, echoing Marx's phrase about humanity, still in our prehistory as a nation. Might there even be a historical project for a nation still in its prehistory? Yes: the project is—to find a project. This is not as vacuous as it sounds. What it means in plain terms is conducting a conscious rational discourse among all our fellow citizens about what kind of a society we choose to attempt to become. It means bypassing the irrational and mythic stage, which is irrational and mythic anyway; there is something invigorating and even pathbreaking about this route ...

• • • • • • • • • •

That, and more, is what I would have written before the free-trade deal. Now though, things seem different, and those thoughts too ... harsh?

Suddenly, Canadian history has lost its distance. We are in the middle of it, it is too much with us. It is not "back there somewhere," behind us in space; something we can glance back towards and contemplate with dispassion in its relation to our fiction and drama. History never really has this distance, but most of the time we feel it does. History isn't really anywhere, it's in no place, except as it exists in us, in the present. In truth, there is *only* the present, and whatever history "exists," does so embedded in us.

But we only very rarely feel this is the case, and never in my lifetime as we do at this very moment. I feel as though we Canadians have discovered a kind of genetic or archetypal memory—and its token is Free Trade. The issue has been with us before, and always in crucial moments: in 1854, when reciprocity was negotiated; in 1865, when it was abolished by the Americans; then in 1911, when Laurier fought a bitter election on the deal he had negotiated, and lost. Now it is with us again, as if it never left, as if it's one of those matters, like one's relationship to one's parents or to death, that is never fully resolved, that lingers, and requires continual attention and adjustment. The free-trade deal has pulled Canadian history into the present, has made the past itself present. The distance between our Now and our History has simply vanished.

But there is more than a kind of racial memory evoked by the deal. What we face is not just a moment of the Canadian past made suddenly present; instead, we face what is potentially the final moment in Canadian history, or at least the moment that makes the final wind-up inevitable, and just a matter of time. I don't want to argue about this, I am simply stating it; I accept Ronald Reagan's straightforward interpretation that the natural effect of the free-trade deal will be similar to the economic union among the 13 independent American colonies, which paved the way to full union. I am not insisting that this *will* happen, but it is the most likely outcome. That prospect makes a detached examination of the relations between Canadian history and Canadian literature less plausible that it would have been before the deal. The whole cargo—our history, our literature—appears differently in the light of the fact that we may be living the last moments of that history.

What has changed? Well, the achievements of that history seem less paltry, and the lack of a project less persuasive. The theme of Survival—*mere* survival—I want to think about again. As a friend of mine, a non-writer, said, "What it means is that the little character Canadians had will disappear." It is an awfully sad thought, put that way. And that little character we have attained suddenly appears quite an achievement.

Perhaps a national project has been there after all, and only now, in the light of our potential disappearance, can we see it: the illogical, unlikely project of existing on this continent in the face of and separate from the United States. A non-imperialistic, non-mighty, non-ideological nation. As a country we were always improbable: why didn't the Americans just take us over? Now that they might, and we can imagine it happening in our lifetime, the fact that they were prevented before now starts to loom as a considerable feat. Once Canada is gone, won't we look back and feel, *It's rather impressive that they kept it from happening for as long as they did.*

• • • • • • • • • •

And what of the specific question with which we started—the relation between our history and our literature—now that we may be living the final moments of that history? Does something change in that relation? I think it does.

It becomes clearer than ever that a people's literature, art, and culture have almost nothing to do with literature, art, or culture. That a people's literature is about nothing *but* its history, as included in its lived present. The government claims to have kept our culture "off the table." This is a devious statement and does not stand up to scrutiny, but let us pretend, for the sake of argument, that it is true. So what? What have we saved our culture for, when we have given up everything that makes us a country: our ability to control our destiny economically, socially, politically, and in the councils of nations? What will we write our books about and sing our songs about and play our plays about, when there is no substantially distinct Canadian society? Literature is not about literature; it is about human life, which takes place in socially and nationally organized groups. When you give up your right to a history of your own, what does it mean to have a culture? This seems to have suddenly become clear to the writers I know; they feel deep despair in the aftermath of the deal; pointing to vague "protections" for culture does not comfort them at all. It seems so obvious—now. The fight should never have been to protect Canadian culture; it could only have been to protect Canada.

So what happens to our literature? Does it simply disappear? Paradoxically, maybe not. The prospect of national obliteration concentrates the literary mind marvelously. We appreciate those we love most as they die. We seek as writers to enshrine them in words at their funerals and in biographies after their deaths. It works for countries too. National catastrophe can do wonders for literature. Think of Ireland. Think of Scotland. Think of Poland. If that's the kind of literature we want for Canada—laments for a nation that might have been—Canadian history may do a great deal for Canadian literature by, as it were, committing suicide. This however is a misleading metaphor. Canadian history is not about to do itself in; it is the victim of attempted murder.

I am speculating in all this. I do not mean to say the free-trade deal is an inevitable *fait accompli.* I believe our national fate still hangs in the balance. If all of us—writers, readers and everyone else—strive as best we can, perhaps we can force an election. Then the future is open, then the Canadian people will decide.

Alternatively, if a deal is forced through, or even for the sake of argument, if it triumphed in an election, I still do not mean to say Canada would inevitably disappear. I think this is the logic of economic union of the sort contemplated by the deal-makers on both sides. But history itself is often wilier than those who try to control it. It is possible that Canada could survive despite the worst efforts of the United States and Mulroney's Tories, along with their business masters and their sycophants (with rare exceptions) in the press and media. In part, the outcome would depend on vagaries of global history, such as the evident decline of the United States. There is no doubt our Tories have hitched their wagon to a falling star; but mostly it will depend on the grit, vision, and need of the Canadian people for this nation to survive, or even, as I speculated in the part of this piece that would have been written had there been no deal, for this nation to become.

Off the Road: Journeys in the Past, Present and Future of Canadian Literature
ROBERT BRINGHURST

• • • • • • • • • •

I must apologize, first of all, for speaking to you in English. I might, to excuse myself, say that what little German I know, I have learned entirely in silence, from books. But the truth is, I have learned almost everything I know in silence, and there is some doubt in my own country, especially among journalists and reviewers, that I can speak any language at all.

Through some additional fault in my education, though I have visited Europe several times, I had never before yesterday set foot in a German-speaking country. I have been here now for 24 hours, but I have spent most of that time sleeping, to recover from what in English would be called a *trip* instead of a *journey*. In an earlier time, a traveler crossing the Atlantic trespassed on the sea as climbers trespass in the mountains, or as worshipers risk attracting the gods' attention through their prayers. The sea sulked or spoke, and the seafarer listened. Now we spend part of a day and a shortened night in a sort of movie theater and restaurant disguised as a very large bird. We relinquish all informative contact with air, land and sea—but at the same time, we avoid the informative darkness and solitude that Jonah encoun-

This bold rethinking of Canadian literary tradition was read as a lecture at Universität Wien in Vienna in April 1988 and printed as an essay in the winter issue of Margin, *a British little-magazine. Robert Bringhurst (born 1946) is a poet and designer who lives on Bowen Island, British Columbia. His best-known book is* The Beauty of the Weapons: Selected Poems 1972-82.

tered in the belly of the whale. This is not what was meant by a journey to people living in Canada in precolonial days. Travel in any useful sense is not sightseeing or voyeurism; nor is it the transport of human cargo—tourists or noblemen or politicians, pampered and cabined to prevent their being changed. A journey is a kind of carnal knowledge; it costs us our virginity. And like other kinds of carnal knowledge, it has its spiritual aspects as well: it always involves an episode of darkness, a time of looking in instead of outward. A journey, in short, is not a daytrip, not an excursion from which the traveler returns untransformed. One must touch the world and be touched by it in turn if one is ever to leave home. The *jour* in *journey* means 24 hours, a full rotation of the earth. To go on a journey, you must spend the night with the world, which is hard to do in an armchair.

One must touch the world all over again, of course, in order to speak of what one has learned. And that is a reason why one sometimes speaks most clearly without words: using instead the gestures of the dancer, the shapes and colors of the painter or the tones of the musician. Language, because we use it to disguise and cushion meaning as often as to reach meaning and touch it, frequently seems to come loose from the world, to float in a meaningless space in which nothing is true because everything is seen in the recycled light of the human.

In my own country, we have a special way of anesthetizing language in public life. There we say and print everything twice, or speak alternate sentences in English and in French, for we pretend, in public life, to be bilingual. Two languages are four times better than one, and the insistence on two official languages has done Canada enormous good. But in real life, it is a country not of two languages but of a hundred—and no one is fluent, and no one has ever been fluent, in them all.

Very little is being written, or has ever been written, in Canada except in the two official languages, English and French—and these as you know are both recent imports. But a rich oral literature existed in the older tongues, and traces of it still exist in some of them. At the end of the 19th century, some of that oral literature was transcribed by the German anthropologist Franz Boas and a group of linguists working under his direction. Those transcriptions constitute nearly everything that remains of the real, ancestral Canadian literature, and they are a rich gift, but the barriers of language between them and us are difficult to cross. Translation is not good enough. If I could send a generation of young Canadian writers off now on a grand tour, it would not be a tour of European capitals; it would be a journey through time, mind and landscape involving the serious study of these ancestral North American languages and literatures. This may sound like a romantic project, but I mean it as a very classical one indeed. I would expect results as valuable as those produced in Europe five centuries ago by Erasmus and his colleagues, through the secular study of Latin and Greek.

The essential features of literature seem to me, if not beyond the reach of time, at least beyond the reach of history. Indeed, one might define literary history as the study of literary inessentials. (It is a fascinating subject, of course, but that is usual with inessentials.) The ancient stories collected in northern Europe by Jakob and Wilhelm Grimm, Peter Asbøjrnsen and Jørgen Moe, for example, though they had passed through many filters, and were pressed again through a fine mesh of 19th-century patriarchal sensibility when these gentlemen wrote them down, often seem immune to human time, impervious to history. One may say the same for the *Metamorphoses* of Ovid, the *Eventyr* of Hans Andersen or the stories of Lewis Carroll.

When we look at the literary canon, however, it seems that the earliest European literature we possess belongs to the late bronze age, and most of it exhibits what Northrop Frye once called, in another context, a garrison mentality. That is to say, quite simply, it is obsessed with military life. Aboriginal Canadian literature is not without its references to warfare, but it is free of any references to the military profession, and to military and political institutions, including warfare, on any major scale. It speaks from a deeper layer in the phylogeny of human culture, and from a more intimate and habitual confrontation with the world beyond the limits of human technology, craft and control.

The remnants of paleolithic oral literature that have been salvaged in Canada are an artistic and spiritual link with that earlier world—one whose value and relevance to us has not expired, and in my opinion *cannot* expire. It is even a world to which, in a practical sense, we may soon return. When our profiteering culture has finally eaten itself out of house and home, when its ever-increasing mortgages on the future finally fall due, when the last river is dammed and the forests and fossil fuels are exhausted, and when the idea of perpetual growth has become once again an innocent joke, like the idea of perpetual youth or perpetual motion, then whatever creatures remain on the earth may have to learn to walk again, and to do their flying in their dreams. The stories and songs of the paleolithic will make fresh and vivid sense to them.

I have no reason to think anyone in that world will learn to read books, still less to think that anyone then will memorize my unharmonious verses. I have no reason, in fact, to suppose that the inhabitants of that future will be other than prokaryotes, dinoflagellates and rhizopods, or cockroaches and feral laboratory rats. Yet it pleases me sometimes to ask whether our paleolithic descendants could make sense of some of my own poems if they heard them. That seems to me a test of poetry more to be trusted than the judgments of current reviewers. But the test I value most depends not at all on the prospect of human survivors. I like merely to ask whether a poem dishonors or honors the world. I like to ask whether it is fit to be thought about next to a glacier-scarred stone or the limb of a mountain larch or a grassblade, or fit to be listened to with kingfishers and finches. It is not that I confuse, or wish to confuse, culture and nature. They are as different one from another as herbs from herbivores—and as intimately linked. But the works of art that matter most to me are bridges between us and the world we live in: a means of making that difficult crossing. The hardest journey of all, and one we can never make too often, is the journey to where we are.

In my own part of the world there is, as you know, a long tradition of monumental sculpture. Large trees of the species *Thuja plicata*, western red cedar, are felled, trimmed and carved with figures from myth, dream and history. The finished product is called, rather inaccurately, a totem pole. These poles are carved by the Haida, the Tlingit, the Tsimshian and the Kwakiutl people, each in their own visual language, and in many different dialects, difficult to copy but easy to learn to recognize. And as there are many different manners of carving the figures, so there are differing conceptions of the kind of ceremony required for raising the poles. It is a custom, for instance, among the Nass River Tsimshian that while the newly carved pole is still prone on the ground, a squirrel must come to inspect it. The squirrel decides whether it is as good, after all that work, as it was before the carving began—and whether it is fit, therefore, to be raised up again.

"Matter is our judge," says the poet Dennis Lee. He is quoting the philosopher George Grant of Halifax, who is quoting Simone Weil. We have here, as it were, the same sentence in various languages: enacted in ritual by a native Canadian community, spoken in abstract nouns and verbs by a European mystic, and repeated in English translation by two of the most eloquent and taciturn of my countrymen, caught in the wide expanse between. It is doubtful that the sentence means exactly the same in each case—it is doubtful that *any* sentence means the same thing whenever it is spoken—but I think it points nonetheless toward the nearly forgotten common ground. In native Canadian thought, the world is a dangerous place through which to travel; it is potent and terrible, but it is intricate, fecund and good at the same time. So it is never manmade items—codes of law or tools or weapons or totem poles—nor lifeless objects such as those with which we have recently peopled the heavens, but always *living* matter—numinous, undomesticated nature—that does the judging in native Canadian literature.

There is not just one such literature, of course; there are many, as there are many native languages. That is why no scholarly and nationalistic poet has come along, as Elias Lönnrot did in Finland more than a century ago, to weave the remains into a North American *Kalevala*. The materials are so varied that, despite the urgent and unhealthy craving for a continental epic, no one may ever undertake the task. But there are a few North American poets who approach literary composition in something like the way Béla Bartók approached the composition of music. They know the difference between the present and the past, and they know that only the two together add up to a future. In their work, we sometimes find strong links between the aboriginal oral literature and contemporary writing. I say here North American because this phenomenon is not restricted to either Canada or the U.S.A., and it routinely involves ignoring the border between them. Gary Snyder, for example, has studied the oral literature of the Haida, who live off the coast of British Columbia, since his days as a college student in Oregon. Howard Norman of Oklahoma has worked extensively among the Cree of Manitoba and Ontario. I have crossed the borders the other way myself, to study with the Tlingit in Alaska and with the Hopi and Navajo in Arizona and Utah. Besides that, many of us—Canadians especially—are political transvestites, born in the United States or elsewhere, making ourselves up as we go along. In this too, Erasmus has set us an excellent example.

North Americans of my generation were born into what was still proudly and wishfully called the New World. Beautiful and peaceful as it was, I must tell you that *culturally and racially* it would be fairer to compare it to central Europe at the close of the Thirty Years' War, or on Armistice Day in 1945, than to the Garden of Eden. It was a very old world, and it was in ruins. It was a continent in which the indigenous human cultures, like the buffalo, had been knowingly and deliberately hunted nearly to extinction. To accountants and industrialists, it was the healthiest economy on earth at the end of the Second World War, but culturally speaking it was in desperate need of foreign aid. It lay poised midway between two culturally rich Old Worlds, Europe and Asia, and it harbored immigrant communities from both. To some of us who were young writers or students in the 1950s and '60s and '70s—and especially to those of us who lived near the Pacific—it was obvious that the cultural aid should come from both sides—not only because we needed whatever we could get, but because we were keenly suspicious of the dominant immigrant strain, which of course was European. Asia looked like a promising moral and intellectual counterweight—just as it does now to many Third World states in the market for foreign aid of other kinds.

The pioneer in striking this cultural and literary balance between East and West was a rather unbalanced man himself, but a great poet nonetheless. He made Europe his home, and never visited the Orient, but he did take up the study of Chinese, and his work rests in the end on a skewed but stable set of four classical languages and cultures: Greek and Latin, with their romance descendants, on the one side; Chinese and Japanese on the other. His name was Ezra Pound.

He was a prewar man and an American to boot—two facts that may help to explain why, until late in his life, he remained convinced of the virtues of empire. We who were raised in the postwar world have been instinctively more distrustful, instinctively less interested in the imperial traditions both east and west, and more in the archaic, the nonconformist, the Buddhist, the Taoist, the unmissionary and meditative strains. I revere Pound like a father, though his totalitarian persuasions and his racist bigotry have no value to me at all except the cautionary value of a bad example. Neither do the profiteering instincts and ethnocentric biases of my own father, for that matter. But relationships in art are much like love and blood relationships. They represent genetic bonds, which no amount of good sense can reverse or deny.

You may believe, with the anthropologists, that the native peoples of North America came from Asia over the Bering Land Bridge during the Wisconsin glaciation, 40,000 years ago; you may believe with the Haida, that they were born *in situ*, at the Raven's instigation, from freefloating human genitalia disguised as chitons and clams; or you may believe with the Hopi, that they clambered up out of the ground. The Haida and the Hopi stories seem to me irrefutable, while the version of the anthropologists is at best incomplete as well as unproven. But the thesis of the two streams, one from Europe, one from Asia, does, I admit, exert a powerful attraction. In one way or another, many of us who think about the shape of North America have tried to find in that continent, or to make of it, what Columbus first mistook it for: a juncture of Orient and Occident: a closing of the circle: journey's end. Mixed, as it often is, with the overt or residual dream of empire, this is one more recipe for disaster. Seen in individual terms, as a vision of human reintegration, it may not be quite so bad.

Where one journey ends, another, on different principles, must begin. That is the prophecy of Teiresías at the conclusion of the *Odyssey*, confirmed by other sages everywhere. By Simone Weil in Paris in the 20th century, and in the 8th by the poet Hán Shan, singing from the modest little peak in the Tiantai mountains of eastern China which gave him his name. At the conclusion of Odysseus' circuitous wandering at sea comes a linear pilgrimage into the mountains. It is counterbalanced in the poem by Hermes' journey, guiding the dead souls into the ground. And at the conclusion of Hán Shan's pilgrimage into the mountains comes an end to death and rebirth, a dispersal of words and perceptions like ashes on the wind. At the end of a migration over sea or land comes a vertical journey shaped like a tree, reaching into earth and sky: a journey into other worlds layered next to this one. And at the end of the vertical journey comes a reconciliation, realignment or reconfirmation of things, a kind of pollination or blossoming. (You may think of Freud when I say this in Vienna. I think of maple trees and evergreens. There is plenty of sexual symbolism in native North American literature, but there is no point looking for phallic and vaginal symbols. The question to ask is, What do these phalluses and vaginas themselves symbolize?)

In the old stories, these vertical journeys often take a supernatural form. After walking into the forest, the hero may climb a ladder of arrows into the sky, or pass through fire and become invisible, or descend through water or ice or earth to another world on the seafloor or under the ground. Anthropologists sometimes call these stories vision quests. But for many native Canadian narratives, this term is inadequate. Often they are more like the Greek myths than the gospels: often the hero does the work, suffers the pain and makes the journey, but only the teller and his audience are permitted to see what it means.

In a world where almost everything we make and do now keeps us away from the earth, or bends the earth to our will, and where machinery has made our daily travels supernatural, these vertical journeys sound more surreal and less dangerous than they once did. The medicine we need is somewhat different. Vertical journeys in recent Canadian literature usually take what in English we would call a *pedestrian* form—like the vertical journey that comes at the end of the *Odyssey*. Alighting at last from the airplane, the railroad, the automobile, as from the ship, one must touch the earth, one must travel on foot. In some of the best recent North American literature, poetry especially, you will find this theme. *Das Denken ein Handwerk ist*, Martin Heidegger used to say. But in poetry, both archaic and contemporary, thinking is frequently footwork. In German you have perhaps an even better word for it: bonework, *Beinarbeit*. And in Rilke's poem *"Wendung,"* it is called heartwork:

Werk des Gesichts ist getan,
tue nun Herz-Werk
an den Bildern in dir, jenen gefangenen; denn du
überwältigtest sie: aber nun kennst du sie nicht.
Siehe, innerer Mann, dein inneres Mädchen,
dieses errungene aus
tausend Naturen, dieses
erst nur errungene, nie
noch geliebte Geschöpf.

Work of the eyes is done.
Do the heartwork now
on the images in you, imprisoned there. You
overcame them, but still you don't know them.
Look, inner man, on your innermost woman:
attained from a thousand true natures, but only

attained: a creature
you haven't yet learned how to love.

There is a great deal to be learned, from that poem of Rilke's, about the condition of recent Canadian literature. More perhaps than from any Canadian poem that has yet been written.

Perhaps there is also something to be learned from the novels of Jack Kerouac, an American of French Canadian extraction, who was a great but temporary literary hero in Western North America among people of my generation. If, at the end of the migration, one does not dig in, if one does not learn love, as Rilke says—and if a new journey of another sort does not begin—the habit of persistent motion may continue anyway, so that the end of the journey becomes a journey without end. Many of us, back there, back then, found ourselves in just such a relationship, or lack of relationship, with the world, and Kerouac, more than any other writer we knew of, articulated these themes. In Kerouac's work we recognized our distinctly American appetites for traveling endlessly across the continent by automobile, and for traveling through the mind by means of drugs—which are the spiritual equivalent of the automobile: an effortless, exciting, but restrictive, indeed imprisoning, means of transportation. The people in Kerouac's novels seldom own and maintain cars, just as they seldom *buy* drugs; they are hitchhikers for the most part; which is to say, they *can* travel on foot, and they do so some of the time. But they are imprisoned by the roads and dependent on the society that built them. They are what most of us in North America are born as: parasites of the journey, with no world to dwell in and no direction of our own.

In retrospect, I can tell you that there was a Canadian who wrote very perceptively of that experience and who, unlike Kerouac, sensed a way through it. Moreover, unlike Kerouac, he is still alive and writing wonderful poems. His name is John Newlove. No one I know of has spoken more eloquently of the problem of the endless journey in Canada. And no one has thought more eloquently about the possible solutions than Dennis Lee, another Canadian poet of the same age. Newlove's voice is rural and Western; Lee's is urban and what we in the West call Eastern—that is to say, he lives in Toronto, which Torontonians call the center. If we had more time, I would like to spend several hours reading you some of John Newlove's poems, and some of Dennis Lee's, as well as telling you some native North American stories. But neither the poetry nor the stories are meant to be heard in snippets. This is not an art of the moment, nor of the momentary. It is an art of large spaces, and it requires, therefore, a certain investment of time.

It remains to be seen how long we can inhabit those spaces without an empire to protect them—which is probably to say, without destroying them, as a man often suffocates the woman, or a politician the freedom, that he has sworn himself to honor and defend.

The turn, the *Wendung* from one journey to another—horizontal to vertical, natural to supernatural, or motorized to human—involves a rebirth or renewal, whether dark and slow or luminous and swift. This language, however, is subject to some suspicion. Many of the most outspokenly self-righteous North Americans now claim to have been born again into the conviction that a strict vertical ascent awaits them. The change of heart to which the old North American stories encourage us is considerably more modest. It involves rebirth into the world with a sense that we belong to it and not the other way around. The war between these views is still fought on many fronts and fiercely in the Americas, but not perhaps widely and fiercely enough. In Western Canada, as in Central America and Brazil, there are, for example, frequent confrontations between logging corporations, whose plan is to clearcut the timber and move on, and Indians whose plan was to live beneath those trees forever. It is a story that began with the conquistadors, whose hunger was only for gold. Now any commodity will do—wood, water, minerals, metals, oil, coal, the ground itself. Anything that pumps the drug of money up the highways of the veins.

There is a little fragment of Herakleitos, 13 words, over which I have puzzled for 15 years but which seems almost lucid to me now. *Athánatoi thnetoì, thnetoì athánatoi, zôntes tòn ekeínon thánaton, tòn dè ekeínon bíon tethneôtes,* says the Greek text: The gods can die, and men can live forever— *but not both at the same time.*

Canada is a large and primarily anglophone country, but it may have escaped to some significant degree both the imperial nostalgia that afflicts Great Britain and the imperial presumption and ambition that distemper the United States. New Zealand and Australia have to some degree escaped them as well. What this may mean for the art and literature of these countries we have yet to see, but I confess I have certain hopes. I like to think that political sanity and artistic sanity—in other words, political humility and spiritual attentiveness—encourage one another, though patently we do not always find them hand in hand. At the present moment my countrymen are toying with a kind of *Anschluss*, which goes under the name of the Canada/ U.S. Free Trade Agreement, and we will see what damage that does to the terms of my thesis. It is, as you may know, a proposal to institute something like the Common Market in North America—with the difference that there will be only two partners, one with ten times the power and population of the other but only half the combined natural treasury to prey on. It promises to be more like the forced marriage of a brass band and a clavichord than like a sonata for piano and violin.

The human music I myself would like to hear in those vast spaces is not the homophonic rhetoric of military bands, but the polyphonic thinking of string quartets, jazz trios and other small groups, and of solo musicians. That is the scale with which I am comfortable. The marching band, like the railroad, terrifies the animals, and goes uphill too heavily for my purposes, and takes far too long to turn. Worst of all, it leaves no room for the silences on which music, like learning, depends.

Inuit women on Baffin Island and in a few adjacent areas of eastern Arctic Canada sing short, two-part polyphonic songs, apparently derived from hunters' imitations of birdcalls. This Inuit throat singing, as it is called, sounds to me like nothing else I have ever heard except the Arctic birds themselves and some of the compositions of Clément Janequin. Apart from this throat singing, the occurrence of polyphonic music in precolonial North America has not, so far as I know, been proven. Its presence is beyond dispute in aboriginal Australia and Polynesia, as in subsaharan Africa, Indonesia, the Caucasus, and among the folk cultures of Europe. And given the clear connection in the visual arts between Polynesia and coastal British Columbia, I would be surprised if no musical connection existed as well. But we have not yet learned to uncover songs and poems, as we have stone sculpture, from the silent village sites and middens.

I mentioned earlier the example of Erasmus, perhaps the most articulate European pacifist after Euripides. I find myself obliged to mention also a very articulate militarist, Georges Clemenceau. Years ago, during an interlude when I often found myself in military courtrooms, a phrase of Clemenceau's lodged in my head, where it remains. "*La justice militaire,*" he said, "*est à la justice comme la musique militaire est à la musique.*" The logic is pure, and one may, I think, turn the assertion around. In the welter of cultures which my country has become, polyphony and cacophony seem the alternatives which remain. On the whole, plainsong is lost to us. Our music, like our journeys, must carry us in more than one direction. And that is a fate against which I can find no reason to complain.

But here in Vienna, surely someone can answer a question I have asked in vain before: is there any country on earth with a polyphonic national anthem?

Fashions in Feminist Film Theory
KAY ARMATAGE

· · · · · · · · · ·

1.

Black Lace Slips and Other Accessories

I was looking for a quotation. It's the way all the best pieces start these days. A delicious quotation, a juicy descriptive paragraph from popular culture, sets absolutely the right tone for a piece. Witty, preferably humorous, the perfect quotation displays an imaginative eclecticism in use of sources, a confident light-heartedness in relation to scholarly material, and a post-modern savoir-faire with respect to readers. Such a quotation can be returned to again and again, phrases plucked from sentences to be re-read in new contexts, teased and played with to elicit new meanings, new ironies, new insights. I have in mind Jane Gallop's wonderful work with prefaces, cover blurbs, textual asides, misprints, and translators' disclaimers in *Reading Lacan*, Patricia Mellencamp's hilarious use of *National Enquirer* stories, Kaja Silverman's delightful and insightful choices of exemplary scenes from movies, and Teresa de Lauretis's fresh and useful re-plays of political slogans. Beginning a piece with the transparent text is as de rigeur as natural shoulders.

But I couldn't find it. I found the trashy exploitational novel, a vile confection called *The Feminists* by one Parley J. Cooper (New York: Pinnacle Books, 1971), a dystopia set in 1992, when "to be a man is a sin; to take a woman is a crime," when the feminists "rule the world, and top dog is a bitch!" I tracked its pages from beginning to end, following that "small band

---

Kay Armatage (born 1943) is a writer and filmmaker and teaches cinema studies and women's studies at Innis College and New College, University of Toronto. This essay was published in the Spring 1988 number of the literary quarterly Descant.

of men and their women [who] go underground to fight the final battle of the sexes!" But those succinct little two or three lines just weren't there. Oh yes, there are suggestive phrases: the flash of "a blood-red dress and high, black boots" on a woman rebel, the one-line impression of the double agent, "impeccably dressed in a severe grey suit and hat," the sneer at her "drab clothes" and "sexless appearance" and the repeated emphasis on "the same severe suit," once embellished with a note that "her hair was still pulled back from her face and twisted into an unattractive bun." And there is the perfumey vision of the rebel's mother, one of the founders of the apocalyptic movement: "Her mother, as usual, was propped up against the pillows, coiffured hair spilling in ringlets about the shoulders of her expensive gown. Her face was heavily made up and she wore the necklace of rubies and emeralds given to her by the Feminists; she wore it as a medal, a constant reminder of her past successes." We can discern the transgressive sexuality of the "subterranean" woman, the hint of flesh and hormones in her "blood-red" dress, the suggestion of kinkiness in the "high, black boots," so different from the "severe" and "sexless" garb of the coopted or semi-coopted women above ground. We can infer the hypocrisy of the Feminists, who bedeck their heroines with jewels, allowing them to luxuriate in traditional femininity as a reward for their service to the monstrous Feminist cause. But there's no description of the Feminist Fashions of the future.

So my slip is showing. To cover up, I've had to resort to another fashion truism: if one aspect of the outfit/body is deficient, try to draw attention away from it. Hemline a bit ripply and no time to fix it? Try a large brooch at the throat, or the always-effective bit of decolletage. My ploy here is exactly that baring of neck and chest, the coquettish first person, the charm of the colloquial. Yvonne Rainer shines at it, Meaghan Morris is terrific, but Jane Gallop is ravishing in personal revelation. And almost everyone—at least the most popular girls—emblazon their texts with their own sexuality and/or anxiety. The personal narrativization as accessory.

I wonder if it would be overdressing to add just one more detail to the ensemble. Accessories make the outfit, as we all know. Just a touch of the visual, perhaps. The Feminists are represented on the front cover of the book. Long straight hair, not too clean-looking, a manly shirt and tie (but without the insouciance of the lesbian cross-dressing of the '20s—I'm thinking of Djuna Barnes's cravat and pork-pie hat) and the inevitable military jacket. The face features the angry glare and the finger points in accusation. The feet, we know, are in aviator boots. Feminist fashions from 1971.

2.

Cross-Dressing or the Thrill of Negation

In an early formulation of the notion of masquerade, Claire Johnston proposed an alternative to the notions of the classic realist text which had dominated film theory of the early '70s. The classic realist text was theorized as a closed, over-determined discourse which constructed a spectator position fixed in an essentially masculine structure with the aim of denying the possibility of radical heterogeneity, reducing all questions of difference to the straight opposition masculine/feminine. Johnston countered with the notion of difference as simply male/non-male, a radical repression of femininity altogether ("Femininity and the Masquerade: *Anne of the Indies,*" *Jacques Tourneur*, eds. Claire Johnston & Paul Willemen, Edinburgh: Edinburgh Film Festival, 1975).

Johnston explored Joan Riviere's now famous "Womanliness as Masquerade" (*Psychoanalysis and Female Sexuality*, ed. Henrick M. Ruitenbeck, New Haven, 1966), in which Riviere discussed those women whose desires are "masculine" in terms of definitions imposed by patriarchal culture, and who fulfill those desires not through a homosexual object choice, but by assuming a mask of "femininity" in order to avert their own anxiety and the imagined retribution from Patriarchal Law. In Riviere's argument, the "feminine" was assumed as a mask to hide the "masculine" in the female subject. Riviere's target was the homosexual woman (defined through her "masculine" desires) who, by assuming the mask of excessive femininity and asserting her masculine characteristics as a game, could avoid the reality of castration and the impoverished human heritage of "femininity" in our culture, and thus continue to pursue her "masculine" desires without being "found out."

Johnston shaped her argument around Jacques Tourneur's *Anne of the Indies*, in which Jean Peters assumes the persona and dress of a *male* pirate captain, a form of disguise we now call transvestism. Transvestism as a metaphor has been useful in discussions of the gendered spectator position which the classic realist text constructs, notably in the possibility of female spectatorship. The hypothesis is that the classic realist text insists on a transvestial spectatorship for women, who must identify themselves with the mastering male gaze in order to "read" the text. Johnston compares George Cukor's *Sylvia Scarlett* with *Anne of the Indies*, suggesting that in the former, Sylvia/Katharine Hepburn, must suspend her feminine desires in her "performance" of masculinity—Sylvia becomes Sylvester to become the central protagonist. With Pascal Kane (*Cahiers du Cinema*, May-June 1972),

Johnston argues that Sylvia's masquerade effectively excludes her feminine self from the social order, and, in her consistent *mimicking* of "masculinity," the phallus is confirmed as primary signifier. With *Anne of the Indies*, however, there is a radical refusal of the reality of castration, for in the presentation of the conventional, fetishized image of masquerade—the female star in male attire—and in the distinct foregrounding of the process of fetishization throughout the film, the masquerade indicates the absence of the phallus and a refusal to recognize the masculine/feminine contradiction. Johnston argues that the masquerade here dramatizes the possibility of a radical heterogeneity, and that the film is concerned essentially with the "problematic nature of the fundamental fact of bi-sexuality." The masquerade/transvestism becomes a pivot for radical heterogeneity, opening up, therefore, the possibility of sexual difference and a bi-sexuality beyond the determinations imposed by culture and the classic text.

Johnston backs off from her conclusion, however, finally emphasizing the repression of the feminine—the heroine's scorn and loathing for femininity and her inevitable death: "The point is not simply to assert a fundamental bisexuality, blurring the effects in culture of sexual difference, because under patriarchy we are condemned to live by our sexed identities, the ideological definitions of the 'masculine' and the 'feminine' ... Perhaps [femininity] can only be fully understood in its symptoms, as in the case of hysteria ... which embodies both the representation of desire and its prohibition. It would seem to me that within patriarchal culture ... female sexuality is indeed repressed, its full nature only fully knowable with the overthrow of patriarchal culture itself." Johnston finally asserts the reduction of difference into the dichotomy male/non-male (the absolute repression of femininity within the text), as a more (bleakly) salutary construction.

3.

Vicissitudes of Feminist Fashion

As I read through Johnston's article again, I shiver at its severe grey tone. I remember well those military uniforms and aviator boots, and the prohibitions on feminine sexual display which were their internal representations. Paradoxically, I also remember a coincident theorizing around bi-sexuality which was part of that season's fashion cluster, albeit on the North American runway. Separatist lesbianism was quickly becoming a staple of the feminist wardrobe, but separatist heterosexuality was definitely consigned to the back of the closet. Heterosexual women were encouraged to explore our "fundamental bisexuality." The rhetoric was either straightforwardly political—"smash heterosexual monogamy" was the phrase that rang through many of the 1971-72 collective meetings that I participated in —or psychoanalytic, the re-discovery of a true female sexuality (repressed in patriarchy through the Oedipal trajectory), to be effected through a return to the original love object, the mother's body. Naive and idealist formulations perhaps, but they led us into personal adventure at least, and spoke to an ebullient optimism which I now recall with the fondest nostalgia. That moment came at a transitional point in feminist theory. A few of us were still decorating our military uniforms with hippyish accessories, hanging onto the hedonistic notions of the sexual revolution which remained only as a trace of sexual adventurism on our new, more tailored militancy. I wore my army surplus shirt with waist-length hair and an antique red silk fringed shawl.

Feminist fashions in Europe, it must be noted, did not take up the army surplus look, nor its prohibitions on feminine sexual display. This is a vividly remembered period for me, because I lost my red silk shawl to "Psych et Po." It was the summer of 1971, and I had spent the winter with a collective which was formulating the first women's studies course at the University of Toronto. I had been a fashion delinquent in that group, for although I had long ago, as a hippy, eschewed lipstick, I continued to decorate myself with eye make-up, and although high-heeled shoes, so blatantly emblematic of the patriarchal conspiracy to immobilize women both figuratively and physically, were not part of my wardrobe, neither did I ever appear in workboots. Thus my vestimentary system—to use Kaja Silverman's term—was retrogressive and sartorially delinquent.

In France that summer, I was invited, through an acquaintance, to spend a country weekend with "Psych et Po," the group of women studying psychoanalysis and politics to whom Juliet Mitchell would dedicate *Psychoanalysis and Feminism*. You can imagine my shock, that weekend, when I found them not only in the latest fashions, but with dyed, permed hair, lipstick and even nail polish. I was further mystified to find, in their midst, a naked woman who was immobilized in full paralysis. She was carried from house to garden throughout the weekend, anointed with sweet oils, and offered gifts of richly embroidered cloths, beads and talismans. Their leader was a lay psychoanalyst who, I was told, had cured herself of paralysis by auto-analysis, and was now in the process of treating the naked woman, the second in the group who had fallen into hysteria. It was she, the leader, who carried off my red silk shawl.

This was my first encounter with the vicissitudes of feminist fashion.

4.

The Body Beneath the Clothes

In *The Power of the Image* (London: Routledge & Kegan Paul, 1985), Annette Kuhn returns to the question of sexual disguise opened by Claire Johnston. Using a broadly semiotic approach, she examines the cultural meanings surrounding cross-dressing as a social practice. At the cultural level, cross-dressing may be understood as a mode of performance which plays on the disjunction between clothes and the body. Thus the socially constructed nature of sexual difference is foregrounded, subjected to comment; what appears natural is revealed as artifice. As cultural meaning, cross-dressing intersects two discourses: the constructs of gender identity and sexual difference, as well as performance. In effecting a distance between persona and the real self, performance constructs a subject both fixed in the distinction between role and self, and, simultaneously, paradoxically, calls that fixed subjectivity into question in the very act of performance. Performance thus poses the possibility of the mutable self, a fluidity of subjectivity and gender.

Clothing as a signifier, the outward mark of difference, pivots specifically on gender. In cross-dressing the contradictions are rampant. Far from the fixed signifier of fixed gender identity, clothing can disguise, alter, reconstruct and thereby undercut the ideological fixity of human subjectivity, at the heart of which lies gendered identity. Cross-dressing thus constructs sexual disguise as a play upon the fixity and fluidity of gender identity, commenting ironically on the conflation in ideology of body, gender, gender identity and subjectivity.

In her detailed and insightful study, Kuhn uses the methodologies of genre studies, spectator identification and address, cinematic codes around the feminine, theories of the classic realist text and specifically the question of narrative closure or textual openness, to investigate the limits of the cross-dressing problematic. Although fictional narratives involving cross-dressing are always *about* the ideological construction of sex differences, they do not always challenge patriarchal truths. With Sandra Gilbert ("Costumes of the mind: transvestism as metaphor in modern literature," *Critical Inquiry*, vol. 7 no. 2, 1980), Kuhn argues that the "visionary multiplicity" of gender relations (as found for example in Virginia Woolf's *Orlando*, which suggests an androgynous subversion of gender fixity) depends on the openness of the text. In other forms of narrativity, the quest to uncover the truth of the concealed body beneath may be the desire that activates the narrative of sexual disguise, only to offer as the pleasure of resolution the body confirmed as the location of absolute difference. If cross-dressing problematizes sexual difference, it may do so only to confirm the absoluteness of both fixed gender and unitary subjectivity by reasserting the "natural" order of the body (Kuhn, 57).

Kuhn ends with an emphasis on those films in which male characters are disguised as women (e.g. *Tootsie, No Way to Treat a Lady, Some Like It Hot*). Through the construction of the disguised male characters as objects of pleasurable looking, attention is drawn to the conventions of cinematic representation which are usually invisible, emphasizing especially the processes of fetishization (Kuhn here echoing Johnston). But since—in the comedies at least—the spectator knows that these "women" really are phallic, the reassurance offered by the fetishized image is redundant. She raises the possibility that such spectacle also fulfills the primal fantasy of the fetishistic look, banishing the castration threat by gratifying the masculine desire for the woman to be like a man. She concludes—bleakly—that thus the cinema asserts firmly that the body beneath the clothes *is* the ultimate site of sexual difference, and that this difference is absolute (Kuhn, 73).

5.

Haircuts and Other Transformations

The question which Kuhn touches on only in passing is that raised by films in which the woman character adopts transvestism. In films such as *Queen Christina, Sylvia Scarlett, Calamity Jane, Victor/Victoria, Anne of the Indies, National Velvet, The Bad Sister, Yentl* and probably many more, the transformation that is effected through female sexual disguise is almost invariably revealed to the spectator at the outset. We see the woman in the process of transformation, usually in the traumatic scene of the haircut. In an elaborate play on castration, often involving inappropriately large shears, the marks of her femininity are brutally cast off.

In cinema, literature, legend and contemporary social history, we find one principal model—castration—for the construction of meaning of male haircuts, whether it's the Samson story, the boy child's first bob, the movement away from hippiedom of the mid-'70s, or the other historical movement towards male "sartorial sobriety" (Kaja Silverman, "Fragments of a Fashionable Discourse," *Studies in Entertainment*, ed. Tania Modleski, Bloomington: Indiana University Press, 1986, p. 140) that came in the 18th century, when aristocratic men put aside their wigs, frills and luxurious fabrics in what J.C. Flugel calls "The Great Masculine Renunciation." Silverman comments on this moment as an "avowal of castration," and produces an intriguing reading of the resultant fascination of men with female dress. What is striking to me in her account and in the dominant reading of male haircuts as castration is the fact that there are indeed two very separate models being subsumed into one. In the case of Samson, his long tresses were the mark of his masculine strength, which could not return until they grew again—true "symbolic" castration. In the case of the boy child, the hippy, and The Great Masculine Renunciation, however, that "castration" is the mark of the repression of the feminine which prefaces their entry into patriarchy and the discourse of the phallus.

It is the latter model which always pertains in the case of the female haircut. Whether in F. Scott Fitzgerald's "Bernice Bobs Her Hair," Louisa May Alcott's *Little Women*, or in those films in which the women cut their hair in order to effect a masculine disguise, the common construction is of release from the social position of castration, represented through ironic reversal in the wielding of the parodically oversized castrating shears. Jo in *Little Women* proclaims, "Now my brains can breathe"; Bernice is freed from the constraints of the Victorian ideals of womanhood to become "the new woman" of the '20s; and in *Sylvia Scarlett, The Bad Sister*, and *Yentl* (to cite just three) the woman escapes from a social order which prohibits women from—respectively—professional mobility, transgressively violent revenge, or the acquisition of knowledge. As opposed to the fetishized phallic woman (Johnston's Mae West), we find the woman released from spectacle and the concomitant cinematic codes which genderize both the feminine character and the processes of spectator identification. While I would agree with Kuhn that the body itself as site of sexual difference is returned as the inevitable "always already," there is also an opening out of both the social order represented in the narrative and of the structure, trajectory and viewpoint of the narrative, a "space of self-referentiality" (Kuhn, 54) which is put into play through this radical marking (or unmarking) of the feminine body.

Kuhn argues that in comedy, as in film noir, as opposed to the "view with" (equivalent to the point of view of the character) the spectator is placed in the "view behind" (i.e. the superior position of knowledge—in the case of the transvestite comedy, knowledge of the truth of gender), and that therefore comedy is incapable of denaturalizing sex differences (Kuhn, 62). Janey Place argues for a different kind of reading of the women of film noir, a reading based less upon the narrative trajectory towards closure and containment of the transgressive woman. She emphasizes instead other forms of visual signification: mise-en-scene, lighting, camera and character movement, and a re-reading of the circulation of looks within the text. "[Film noir's] special significance lies in the combination of sensuality with activity and ambition which characterizes the *femme fatale*, and in the mode of control that must be exerted to dominate her ... Even more significant is the form in which the "spider woman's" strength and power is expressed: the visual style gives her such freedom of movement and dominance that it is her strength and sensual visual texture that is inevitably printed in our memory, not her ultimate destruction ... [Thus] despite their regressive ideological function on a strictly narrative level, a fuller explanation for the current surge of interest in film noir must acknowledge its uniquely sensual visual style which often overwhelms (or at least acts upon) the narrative so compellingly that it stands as the only period in American film in which women are deadly but sexy, exciting, and strong" (*Women and Film Noir*, ed. E. Ann Kaplan, BFI, 1978, p. 54).

At any rate, in 1974 I cut my waist-length hair to a Sassoon above-the-ears sculpture reminiscent of a '20s bob, and in 1977 went to a punkish brush-cut.

6.

Satin Slippers and Fur-Lined Shoes

The British cine-feminist intervention took as its first target the naively realist prescriptions of the North American radical feminist attack on stereotypes and its demand for their replacement by positive role models. The North American movement, which called for an end to the distorted, damaging Hollywood representations of women and their replacement with images of "real women," had been stunningly effective in encouraging a feminist cinema by women which populated the screens of the 16mm distribution circuit with working class, militant, "artistic" or "alternative" women. From *The Women's Film* (1968) to the feminist portrait films of the '70s (e.g. *Chris and Bernie* [1973], *Antonia* [1975], *Nana, Mom and Me* [1974], *Jill Johnston* [1977]), and the remarkable grass-roots success of the NFB's Studio D with its early series on working mothers and its self-mandated emphasis on the problems of "ordinary, garden-variety women" (Kathleen Shannon), the screens were filled with women wearing sweaters, skirts and down-at-the-heels sling-backs (for the working class or newly emerging women) or jeans, mannish shirts, army surplus parkas or jackets, and work-boots (for those who had already broken into a militant or "alternative" lifestyle).

Although the British attack was clearly directed to the field of "images of women" in order to shift the site of the confrontation to the territory of the signifier itself, the metaphorical uniform of that discourse was, paradoxi-cally, like the language I am using right now, not only identical in source to the apparel of the North American militant women, but even more extreme in the rigor of its fashionable vision. Like the aesthetic avant-garde before it—a term which comes from the military strategy of sending out as the front ranks the peasant or working-class foot-soldiers, the avant-garde, as opposed to the cavalry and officers, the derriere-garde—the semiotic and post-structural discourse took its determining metaphors from the military. "Intervention," "site," "deployment," "territory," "opposition," "interrogation," "occupation of positions," "strategy" and countless phrases taken over from the revolutionary discourse of the Russians and Brecht became the terms of this new discourse. The military metaphor is further located in a discourse increasingly dominated by the economic ("exchange," "circulation," and the incessant repetition of the word "economy" itself—libidinal, narrative, of difference, of desire, of the signifier, etc.) and the medical-psychoanalytical—a conjunction inherited from Freud's structural model of psychic economy. I don't mean to denigrate in any way this language or its intent. I merely point to the curiousness of this new metaphorical structure (which early on was proclaimed as "scientific"—cf. the *Cahiers du Cinema* editorial on "Cinema/Ideology/Criticism," 1969), and the striking parallel with the material/sartorial expression of the North American discourse, whose metaphoric structures on the contrary played on feelings, experience, empathy, emotional identification, authenticity, a transparently available subjectivity and its arch enemy, objectification.

In this climate, the entry of the French feminist psychoanalysts and *l'ecriture feminine*, with their emphasis on the body at its most sensationally feminine, seemed like the arrival at the party of the femme fatale, sweeping across the room in a rustle of silk and a waft of warm, exotic perfume. Their language—of the body, on the body—was poetic, domestic, sensual, swathed in the frills and folds of parallel clauses and tactile images, and it affirmed the joys of sexual difference through the display of feminine erogeny, lips, skin, breasts, and vulva. It murmured, in intimate and frankly erotic tones, of excess.

In the 1970s, many of us had purged ourselves of the desire for pleasure, had come to see desire itself as illusory, emanating from a failure to accept the reality of our castration, and available at any rate in the libidinal economy only through lack and otherness. We had donned the armor of non-pleasure and anti-narrative, an armor that was studded with the austere rigors of anti-illusionism, duration and static camera as corrective assaults on the seductions of suture, the starkly puritanical didacticism of text as image, and the deconstructivist deprivations of the "flat" images and performances that characterized the neo-material cinema. We had found our bitter comfort in—as Laura Mulvey put it—the thrill of negation and denial.

At that conjuncture, the soft contours of French feminism offered a warm embrace after our travails on the battlefield. Flaunting female anatomy and the construction of feminine subjectivity as written on the body, risking—as they say—essentialism, reading Cixous, Irigaray, Clement and their commentators had the heady perfume of a floral-scented bubble-bath or the energy-careless comforts of central heating after the penury of the chilly British flat and the ubiquitous pine-scented Vita-Bath. Constructed as my visions are through the images of Hollywood cinema, especially from the golden days of '30s escapism or '50s excess, I imagined them wearing maribou-trimmed pastel robes and wriggling their warm, manicured and polished toes in satin slippers.

This is an interesting moment in feminist fashions, for a number of different manifestations come into prominence on the theoretical runway. As always, the seasonal couture collections provide a variety of optional looks.

In Britain, the severe grey suit of language gradually gives way to the tweedy skirt, cardigan, mauve-print blouse with little flowers and sensible oxfords of the matronly gardener—the image that Laura Mulvey constructed so precisely in *Riddle of the Sphynx*. Annette Kuhn, Pam Cook, and Laura Mulvey continue to tend the plots that they had begun to cultivate in the mid-'70s. Their work is increasingly that of pruning, weeding, and conserving the beds that had earlier produced a rather thorny but fruitful proliferation. Despite Stephen Heath's early attempt (in "Difference," *Screen*, 1978), the luscious blooms of French feminism never really took root in the English garden, even in the face of the central position that the issue of difference occupied universally. I have in mind Annette Kuhn's *The Power of the Image* (1985), Rosaline Coward's *Female Desire* (1985), Pam Cook's *The Cinema Book* (1985), Griselda Pollock's *Framing Feminism* (1987), and Jacqueline Rose's *Sexuality and the Visual Field* (1986). Their work is solid and, in British culture as well as in the film theory courses entrenched at universities, widely influential, as both popular journalism and cultural studies have fully incorporated the terminology and ideological frameworks of the British theoretical revolution of the '70s.

In North America, on the other hand, several divergent trends can be found in the fashionable outlooks of the recent past. From the beginning of the '80s in North America, a puritanical feminism had not only survived from radical feminism but proliferated, coming to fruition in the Andrea Dworkin/Katherine McKinnon/Women Against Pornography grouping which was not, strictly speaking, involved in film theory, but which became a vector of some energy in media and cultural studies.

The issue of pornography was also positioned strongly in debates on the nature of female sexuality and eroticism, the sex trade and the feminist relation to the body. For a few years, feminism was a feisty occupation, with lines drawn between a new-found social/sexual purity on the one hand (the so-called "cultural feminists," who argued that feminine sexuality was properly expressed in caring, mutual relationships which emphasized a cuddly sensuality rather than a limited and rather distastefully focussed genitality—

eroticism, in other words, rather than pornography), and, on the other, those feminists who asserted a plurality of female sexuality including such heretofore forbidden practices as role-playing and S&M. In cinema, representations of lesbian and heterosexual love-making, transgressive sexuality, and kinkiness of all kinds were the material for films which diverged widely in form and ideology, but for which female sexuality was a central issue: Betty Gordon's *Variety*, Donna Deitch's *Desert Hearts*, Elfie Mikesch/Monica Treut's *Seduction: The Cruel Woman*, Jutta Bruckner's *Love at First Sight*, Jackie Burroughs's *A Winter Tan*, Nina Menkes' *Magdalena Viraga*, Sheila McLaughlin's *She Must Be Seeing Things*, and Patricia Rozema's *I've Heard the Mermaids Singing*. The scene from all these films which I remember most fondly takes place in the shop run by the raven-tressed, white-skinned maitresse of *Seduction: The Cruel Woman*. Not an expository scene, it foregrounds fetishism in both representation and signification. The scene features loving close-ups of shoes: very high heels always, and fetish details like metal buttons, chains, and straps. My favorites, turning slowly on a lucite pedestal, were simply high-heeled pumps lined with fur.

7.

Dressing for Success, Punk Fashion, and the Post-Modernist Carnival

In the world beyond the screen, especially in the business world, women were dressing for success, and a similar movement had taken hold among academics, as women's studies in North American universities increasingly became not only acceptable, but intellectually commodified. I know that I felt impelled, at one point, to buy myself a "professional outfit." It was a three-piece suit, with matching jacket and skirt and co-ordinated blouse. Longing as I was for the fur-lined shoes, I never could bear to spend money on the requisite plain pumps with the little heels, so the ensemble was never quite right.

At the same time, punk fashions were at their peak of influence, signifying a post-modern angst and a viable constitution of a social group as transgressive other. As Dick Hebdige writes, "The punks played with and played back the rhetoric of crisis, made the word flesh ... sought to make the sado-masochistic matrix strange" ("Posing ... Threats, Striking ... Poses: Youth, Surveillance, and Display," *Substance* No. 37/38, 1983, p. 85). My delight was total when, for some feminists, the studded belts and gloves, leopardskin prints and leather clothes, and—for the first time in years—high heels, came on the scene in a big way. It was a confluence of sexual politics and subculture fashion which—temporarily at least, as the fashion world turns—seemed a felicitous renewal of the transgressiveness of feminism. I could only agree with Hebdige, who wrote of the punks that "Far from abandoning good sense, they are acting in accordance with a logic which is manifest: that as a condition of their entry into the adult [read male] domain, the field of public debate, the place where real things really happen, they must break the laws which order that domain, which order the distribution of significance within that field, that place. They must exceed consensual definitions for the proper and the permissible. They must challenge the symbolic order which guarantees their subordination ... And there is pleasure in transgression" (Hebdige, 85). Haircuts and make-up came back, along with a punk-inspired post-modernist glamor which seemed the sartorial expression of a new aggression in feminism, a kind of intellectual terrorism founded on the rampaging mobility of the increasingly dominant discourses of feminist theory. It was a knowledge of the pleasure of transgression and the power to shock which we had worn on our bodies in the late '60s, but which we had, apparently, forgotten.

There were other factors at work in this particular fashion conjuncture. In addition to the fade-to-black which was occurring on the British scene, the rise to prominence of the French feminist psychoanalytic movement and, in North America, the sexuality debates which re-focused attention on the feminist relation to the body and sexuality, there was a shimmering new star rising rapidly on the horizon. Post-modernist theory, with its attention to previously unworthy subjects such as *really* popular culture, including the art market, consumerism, fashion itself, and panic sex, served not only as a contributing factor in the recentralization of the body in theoretical discourse, but afforded the terms for a newly-invigorated carnival of theory. Throw out those clumpy old boots of post-structuralism. Get out your dancing shoes. Forget Foucault! Theory was irreverent, pop, sexy, and fun. Feminism was hot and thrilling again.

8.

And Fashion is Fashionable Again

In a recent article, Kim Sawchuk calls for a re-thinking of the traditional Marxist/feminist approach to fashion, which she characterizes as a simple notion of fashion as a reflection of the social onto the body or as a repression of the natural body ("A Tale of Inscription/Fashion Statements," *Canadian Journal of Political and Social Theory*, vol. XI, no. 1-2, 1987, p. 55). Citing Anne Oakley's history of fashion, *Subject Women*, Sawchuk recalls the repeated demands for change to a "plainer, more masculine style of dress" in periods of feminist rebellion (e.g. the early 20th century, as well as the '60s and '70s). In the '70s, fashion was seen as a commodity to be resisted, not only in a refusal of consumerism, but because it reflected the positioning of women within patriarchal capitalism: that is, as the gaze is gender-determined and masculine, objectifying and fetishizing women, through fashion the women turn themselves into objects for the gaze, thus reinforcing the phallic economy of desire (Sawchuk, 54). *Au contraire*, asserts Sawchuk: "To assume that all clothing is reducible to the fashion industry in this restrictive sense, and that all looking and aestheticization of the body is an objectifying form of commodification is simplistic" (Sawchuk, 59). She also rejects the transference of feminist film theory—the mastering male gaze, voyeurism, fetishization, and objectification—to discussions of fashion, which in her argument can be tactile, poetic, and intimately connected to the lived body (Sawchuk, 59).

Sawchuk argues from history that the anti-fashion discourse cannot be so transparently confounded with feminism, for often it has been tied to a discourse aimed at repressing women's potentially subversive sexuality in order to send them back to the home. The social purity movements of the early 20th century, which deplored women's "love of finery," sought to return women to the home, the natural body, and maternal fecundity. Aestheticization of the body—the love of finery—was seen as a sign of irrationality (as well as moral depravity), and thus this argument for austerity in dress valorizes (masculine) rationality and feeds on the existing discourse on women as superficial, duplicitous, and thus a sexual threat to men (Sawchuk, 58).

"It is necessary to abandon some aspects of feminist thought which criticize fashion as 'misrepresentation' of women and advocate a return to the 'natural' body" (Sawchuk, 60). With Baudrillard, Sawchuk argues, we exist in an age which anticipates an image, in an implosion of space between the imaginary and the real.

9.

The Perils of Post-Modernism

Patricia Mellencamp is considerably more cautious in her approach to post-modernism. She takes a few cracks at those post-modernists who champion "feminism's acclaimed marginality and unstated centrality" ("Uncanny Feminism: The Exquisite Corpses of Cecilia Condit," *Framework* No. 32/33, 1986, p. 109). In Hal Foster, for example, feminism is seen as the estranged, unknowable other, along with other races and cultures which are invoked as a desirable dialogue, a discourse of salvation. Here is Mellencamp in full swing on this one: "While many feminists are proudly standing on opposite shores, watching the 'splendid light' of independent films and videotapes, and being invited to the intellectual dance of postmodernism by scholars and the art world, we might heed the alarm of the youngest sister, for there are warnings in the academic air of godly wrath and signs of virulent condescension, brazenly heralding a resurgence of reactionary, anti-feminist positions" (Mellencamp, 106).

10.

The Little Black Dress or the Double Body of Masquerade

However, Mellencamp does—cautiously—embrace Bahktin's theory of the carnival body, as suggesting another potential interpretation of masquerade as a possibility for feminism, rather than the conventional treatment as disguise, lure, or envious lack. Bahktin's carnival body is indivisible, a body without those inner/outer, self/other polarities in which the exterior is inauthentic, a mere cover-up. It is a body of doubled surfaces rather than inner recesses. Bahktin's "double body" and the "double-directed discourses" of parody can be seen as a form of "double representation" similar to the masquerade, the play with mimesis which makes visible what was supposed to remain invisible. Mellencamp examines Cecilia Condit's videotapes, which she reads as a "resubmission" to masculine exploitation taken on willingly, knowingly, like a masquerade restaged as an extravagant, hyperbolic spectacle, and thus challenging the divisions of vision and body while escaping the confines of "discourse" (Mellencamp, 113-114).

We have here the center of an important constellation of ideas which are shaping up quickly this season. As the *Village Voice* fashion supplement pointed out recently, 1987 was the 61st anniversary of the little black dress, heralded by *Vogue* in the fall of 1926 as the staple of any woman's wardrobe. It seems to be no accident that the staple of this season's theoretical wardrobe is also the most feminine of self-representations, the masquerade. The earliest notion of the masquerade involved the taking on of the feminine as a mask, as in Riviere (cited above), to disguise the "masculine" desires beneath. In more recent constructions, such a play on the traditional constructions of femininity affords the opportunity to render visible those very elements of construction, to produce a distance between the body and the socially determined (masculine) discourse of femininity.

Mellencamp is echoing Mary Russo ("Female Grotesques: Carnival and Theory," *Feminist Studies/Critical Studies*, ed. Teresa de Lauretis, Bloomington: Indiana University Press, 1986), who is echoing Luce Irigaray: "To play with mimesis is thus, for a woman, to try to recover the place of her exploitation by discourse, without allowing herself simply to be reduced to it. It means to resubmit herself ... to 'ideas' ... that are elaborated in/by masculine logic, but so as to make 'visible,' by an effect of playful repetition, what was supposed to remain invisible: the cover-up of a possible operation of the feminine in language" (*The Sex Which Is Not One*, trans. Catherine Porter, Ithaca: Cornell University Press, 1985, p. 76).

Russo goes on to cite Mary Ann Doane, who uses Riviere to argue that the masquerade can produce a distance from the image in order to generate a problematic within which the image is manipulable, producible and readable by women. For Doane, this suggests a way around the theorization of the spectator only in terms of the male gaze and masculine categories of voyeurism and fetishistic pleasure. Doane's conclusion concerns the possibility of the masquerade, but her quest begins with female spectatorship and the requirement of "distance" from the image which allows for a pleasurable reading of the image. She hinges her case for the necessity of "distance" on Freud's remark, in "Some Psychical Consequences of the Anatomical Differences Between the Sexes" (1925), that in contrast to the boy child at the first sighting of the female genitals, which involves an initial disavowal before understanding arrives, "A little girl behaves differently. She makes her judgment and her decision in a flash. She has seen it and knows that she is without it and wants to have it" (*On Sexuality*, The Freud Pelican Library, vol. 7, p. 336). In other words, the process of disavowal of castration which prefaces understanding for the boy becomes a lynch-pin in the process of fetishization, the formation of the superego, and indeed in any acquisition of knowledge. It is the "distance" which Doane suggests is necessary for women to manufacture in some other way, since they are incapable of fetishization (Mary Ann Doane, "Film and Masquerade: Theorizing the Female Spectator," *Screen* 23, nos. 3/4 Sept./Oct. 1982, and "Woman's Stake: Theorizing the Female Body," *October* 17, Summer 1981). I must admit that I am skeptical of such an elaborate theoretical edifice founded on what is surely an off-hand remark of Freud's, who later admitted that "This account of how girls respond to the impression of castration ... will very probably strike the reader as confused and contradictory. This is not entirely the author's fault. In truth, it is hardly possible to give a description which has general validity" ("Female Sexuality" [1931], *On Sexuality*, op cit., p. 380). While the assertion of a fundamental asymmetry in the progress of male and female subjects seems essential, Freud's account of the "difference" does seem confusing and contradictory. And it seems doubly insufficient to theorize, as Doane does, an impossibility of "distance" from the image for the female spectator on three little words—"in a flash." And yet this remark of Freud's is, to a significant degree, the basis for much of the work on the masquerade.

Russo finds Doane's discussion of Riviere useful in explaining the asymmetries of transvestism, "which for a woman has always been necessary in some sense in order for her to take part in a man's world. For a woman to dress, act, or position herself in discourse as a man is easily understandable and culturally compelling." To "act like a woman" beyond narcissism and masochism is, for psychoanalytic theory, trickier. This, Russo finds, is the critical and hopeful power of masquerade, deliberately assumed and foregrounded: "To put on femininity with a vengeance suggests the power of taking it off" (Russo, 224).

Russo engages with some very fruitful questions for feminism, before she opts for the masquerade as the most potent form of "acting out" the dilemmas of femininity (Russo, 225). In the opening pages of her article, she had confessed her own desires to "make a spectacle of herself" before citing two divergent models of sartorial deportment for women: "Although the models, of course, change, there is a way in which radical negation, silence, withdrawal, and invisibility, and the bold affirmations of feminine performance, imposture and masquerade (purity and danger) have suggested cultural politics for women" (Russo, 213). But is the model of danger for women ultimately that of the masquerade? I would have thought that the "pleasure of transgression" (Hebdige, op cit.) would be less closely tied to dressing the way women are supposed to dress, even if to an excessive degree.

And Russo herself begins with a more dynamic—at first glance—model in her considerations of Bahktin's notions of the carnival and the grotesque body. Carnival speech and spectacle are heterogeneous, containing the protocols and styles of high culture from a position of debasement. And the political implications of heterogeneity are not just oppositional; they suggest a counterproduction of knowledge, culture, and pleasure (Russo, 218).

For women, Russo argues with Nathalie Davis, there are dangers in the grotesque and unruly body of carnival (Russo, 214). The marginal position of women makes their presence in carnival always potentially dangerous: "In other words, in the everyday indicative world, women and their bodies, certain bodies, in certain public framings, in certain public spaces, are always already transgressive—dangerous and in danger." Like the others, Russo will opt for the masquerade, but not without a brief look back: "The figure of the female transgressor as public spectacle is still powerfully resonant, and the possibilities of redeploying this representation as a demystifying or utopian model have still not been exhausted" (Russo, 217).

11.

Fashion Forecast: The Foreseeable Future

The fashion forecast seems, for this season at least, every bit as limited and limiting as ever. Three models present themselves: Russo's saintly garb of invisibility; cross-dressing (Russo: merely "sanctioned play?"); and the masquerade (Russo: "risking self contempt"). Curiously, the fashionable silhouettes of 1987-88 echo the contours of womanliness which Freud outlined more than half a century ago: "[giving] up her phallic activity and with it her sexuality in general"; "[clinging] with defiant self-assertiveness to her threatened masculinity"; and the "final normal female attitude" (Freud, 376).

12.

The Spectacle of Theory

I was moved to write this article by my own discomfort with the psychoanalytic underpinnings of masquerade as they had been applied to film theory (the "in a flash" model), by my own continuing ambivalence about fashion, and perhaps frivolously, by three recent anecdotes concerning theory and fashion.

The first anecdote involved a visit to the Milwaukee Center for Twentieth Century Studies by Julia Kristeva, one of the truly international stars of theory (she's one of the few whose photo appears on the covers of her books, and recently on their front covers). Her followers showed up at the talk, many of them dressed in the "intellectual terrorist" garb that Kristeva had been known for—short straight hair, mannish shirt, and leather pants. They were unable to disguise their dismay and confusion when Kristeva appeared in (what was described to me as) a Chanel suit with pearls. Indeed, the hapless graduate students were unable to avoid reading her talk in terms of her new apparel. The radical terrorism of Kristeva's usual discourse now seemed traditionally feminine, shockingly corporate, and deeply conservative.

The second was an ironic tale of a struggle with self-representation which backfired. One prominent theorist had been invited to present a paper at an international conference. She had just bought a swanky new dress, and went through a self-reflexive turmoil all across the Atlantic: should she wear the new dress and risk her paper not being heard through the fog of feminine fashionability that the stylish frock presented? But it was her favorite new thing, she pleaded with herself, and a great dress. Finally she decided to wear it. She spent the entire presentation in the female gesture of the '80s—constantly, embarrassedly, adjusting the wandering shoulder-pads.

How are we doing with the masquerade? There are perils here.

The third anecdote involves Kaja Silverman at the International Summer Institute for Semiotic and Structural Studies in Toronto last June. The event was reported this way: "KAJA SILVERMAN was the talk of the town for her fashion statement ... we loved the summer frocks and the party shoes ... but we were blown away by her outfit at the eroticism colloquium ... black-seamed stockings, rhinestone drop earrings and a cocktail dress with black lace atop (at 10:00 in the morning, no less!) ... and this for a paper on male masochism ... PAUL BOUISSAC fumbled repeatedly as he tried to find a place to pin the microphone" (Dave Paparazzi, "Disseminating Scruples," *Borderlines*, 9/10, Fall/Winter 1987/88, p. 4).

Two things are clear from this anecdote, which is embedded in a "life in the fast lane" report on "the rich and famous of the academic conference set." The spectacle of theory and theoreticians as spectacle are the subject of this gossip column, which is hilariously naughty and remarkably on the mark. Check out the "Market Quotes": "...if you're holding IRIGARAY shares, dump them fast before word gets around ... DERRIDA held steady: a solid, blue chip investment; it probably won't yield the same spectacular rates of return as in the past, but as with Xerox, you'll never take a bath ... but adventuresome futures speculators made a killing on SILVERMAN: a relatively new stock, it offers an attractive package to investors who may be considering divestment from Irigaray." I don't want to make too much of this, for this kind of personal gossip has been around for some time in the academic world. Perhaps it is simply more blatant now, because theory has itself been extremely speculative and specular, trading in theories of representation as subject and methodology.

Certainly—and this is the second point from the anecdote—Silverman is deliberately working with the ironies and potential transgression of particular forms of self-representation. Silverman begins her essay "Fragments of a Fashionable Discourse" (op cit.) with a frontal attack: "The image of a woman in front of the mirror, playing to both the male look and her own, has become a familiar metaphor of sexual oppression. Despite this cautionary emblem, I would like to reopen the case on self-display ... The history of Western fashion poses a serious challenge both to the automatic equation of spectacular display with female subjectivity, and to the assumption that exhibitionism always implies woman's subjugation to the controlling male gaze" (Silverman, 139). Ranging through histories of fashion, Hitchcock films, Proust, Dior ads, Lacan, Hebdige on subcultures, and current feminist fashions, Silverman argues for a complex circuit of visual exchange which includes class, male exhibitionism/specularity and Freud's assertion of clothing as a necessary condition for subjectivity. In opposition to the traditional feminist rejection of fashion as oppressively limiting for women, she argues that "if ... clothing not only draws the body so that it can be seen, but also maps out the shape of the ego, then every transformation within a society's vestimentary code implies some kind of shift within its ways of articulating subjectivity" (Silverman, 149). She ends the piece with a defence of her own "sartorial system," vintage clothing as a "sartorial strategy which works to denaturalize its wearer's specular identity." Because "retro" dressing refuses the antithesis of present and past which characterizes new fashion, it "inserts its wearer into a complex network of cultural and historical references," and because it recontextualizes objects from earlier periods, it can maximize, through rereading, their radical and transformative potential. Because it contructs a dialogue between the present and the past, "retro also provides a means of salvaging the images that have traditionally sustained female subjectivity." Finally, Silverman concludes, "It is a highly visible way of acknowledging that its wearer's identity has been shaped by decades of representational activity, and that no cultural project can ever 'start from zero'" (Silverman, 150-151).

The '40s black cocktail dress at 10:00 a.m. for a talk on male masochism: what, indeed, could be more appropriate? As Hebdige wrote of the punks: "They skirted round the voyeurism issue—the politics of visual pleasure, power, and the look. They played with our curiosity and finally refused to submit to our gaze. They turned being looked at into an aggressive act." (Hebdige, 85).

That at least is the optimistic ending.

13.

The Normal Female Attitude

Here is the other ending.

When spectacle is fashionable, and masquerade is fashionable, and fashion is fashionable, and even knowledge that we can't start from zero is fashionable, how do we bring about change? Russo asks, "Are women again so identified with style itself that they are estranged from transgressive effects? In what sense can women really produce or make spectacles of themselves?" (Russo, 217). If we are dressing ourselves, in fact, as women have always dressed, how do we even signify our intentions towards change?

Let us not be left with this, the empty spectacle of the dutiful daughter wearing the father's favorite dress—Freud's "final normal female attitude"— while brazenly proclaiming rebellion.

The Creative Approach
ROBERT STEWART

· · · · · · · · · ·

The notion of creativity is so new in the historical scheme of things that it was not until well into the present century that the word began to show up in dictionaries. Writers and philosophers in the past have had a great deal to say about talent, imagination and inspiration, but only in relatively recent times have these been wrapped together into the phenomenon we call creativity.

The oversight can be traced back to old-fashioned snobbery of the kind that took for granted that the common man was incapable of "creating" anything. The sages of history believed almost unanimously that the universe functioned according to a cosmic pattern in which everything and everybody had a place, with themselves near the top. The place of ordinary souls in the natural order was decidedly not to bring new ideas and works into being. It was to stick to the labors assigned to them in the eternal plan. The closest traditional thinkers ever came to the modern concept of creativity was their concept of genius, which was strongly influenced by snobbery and determinism. The word "genius" derives from the term for the presiding spirits which were supposed to have dwelt within people in ancient Rome. The individuals known as geniuses were thought to be endowed by the gods with transcendental intellectual and/or artistic powers. Like gentlemen, geniuses were born, not made.

If the occasional prodigy like Michelangelo was thrown up out of the masses, the anomaly was conveniently explained by the theory that he was divinely inspired. Otherwise men (almost always men; hardly ever women)

In its tone, this essay will be familiar to many of the hundreds of thousands of people who receive The Royal Bank Letter, *in whose March-April 1988 issue it first appeared. Since 1945, the newsletter has appeared as regularly as a bank statement, preaching such bankerly virtues as hard work, thrift, probity and the minding of one's own business. Until 1977, its essays, which are unsigned, were written by John Heron; since then they have been the work of Robert Stewart (born 1938), a former staff writer at* The Wall Street Journal, The Financial Times of Canada *and other publications, who has widened their scope considerably.*

of genius came from the dominant class. This was scarcely surprising, because they were the only members of society with the education and leisure to make the most of their talents. The bulk of the people had neither the time nor the opportunity to exercise whatever creative ability they might have had. The prospect that there might be a vast untapped mine of talent and intelligence in the population at large was scarcely considered. Neither was much thought given to the possibility that talent might come in degrees, so that people of lesser abilities might be capable of making valuable contributions to the quality of life.

The advent of public education in the western nations in the latter part of the 19th century did little to change this attitude. The method of teaching by rote was not conducive to encouraging youngsters to use their imaginations. The idea that creativity in childhood should be actively nurtured would have been considered next to heresy in the age of "spare the rod and spoil the child." It took the pioneers of psychology to see the plain fact that one did not have to be divinely endowed to conceive original works of art or inventions. William James was moving in the direction of our present conception of creativity when he wrote in his *The Principles of Psychology* in 1890: "Genius, in truth, means little more than the faculty of perceiving in an unhabitual way."

Carl Jung spoke of the "creative man" in his essays in the 1920s and '30s, though he remained somewhat mesmerized by the mystical theory of genius. Nevertheless, he and other writers on psychology helped to refine the concept of creativity we have today. That concept, as it is usually understood, is that the potential for originality exists to a greater or lesser degree in every human. It is like a sixth sense, as inherent in the organism as the other five. If it cannot exactly be taught, it can be cultivated by training, example, and habituation. And it can be brought to bear on work of any scale or nature: an office manager who comes up with a bright new scheme for handling paperwork is being as creative in her field as a novelist is in hers.

Though all this might seem clear enough, the question of what constitutes creativity remains beset by misconceptions. The most basic of these is that it is confined to the arts, an impression which artists themselves do little to correct. It is in the arts that creativity has become a rather derisive term. Critics and professional practitioners cringe at the thought of all the incomprehensible poetry, the graceless sculptures and truly primitive paintings produced in the name of letting the creative juices flow. The opportunity to be creative has been interpreted by some as an opportunity to look and behave like an artist without going to the trouble of actually being one. This leads to another misconception of creativity, which is that it is sufficient unto itself. It is, of course, associated with freedom—the freedom to let the spirit rove in the undiscovered reaches of the imagination. But what Matthew

Arnold said about opinions is equally pertinent to creative endeavors: "It is a very great thing to be able to think as you like; but, after all, an important question remains: *what* you think."

Reporting on his experiences preparing a television series on the subject a few years ago, journalist Bill Moyers wrote: "Two things are implied in the word 'creativity' as I have come to understand it: novelty and significance. What is created is new, and the new opens up paths that expand human possibilities." Without the element of significance, creative efforts amount to no more than self-indulgence. As Ralph Waldo Emerson so nicely put it, "Talent for talent's sake is a bauble and a show."

Among the definitions of "creative" in *The Oxford English Dictionary* is "showing imagination as well as routine skill." The reference to skill is essential to the meaning. A man could compose music in his head like another Mozart, but without the skill to play it or to set it down in musical notation, his artistry would be lost to the world. Sir Joshua Reynolds insisted that he would never have become known as a painter of genius if he had not acquired the requisite technique to take advantage of the artistic breakthroughs made before him. New heights, he said, are reached through a knowledge of what has already been done and a knowledge of how to build on it. "It is by being conversant with the inventions of others that we learn to invent; as by reading the thoughts of others, we learn to think."

The assumption that there is a mystical element in the creation of great works, he said, arises from an ignorance of the process. "The untaught mind finds a vast gulf between its own powers, and those of works of complicated art, which it is unutterably unable to fathom; and it supposes that such a void can only be passed by supernatural powers." Reynolds did not deny that nature gives some people more capacity than others, but he nonetheless believed that strenuous effort is needed to make the best of whatever ability is present. "If you have great talents, industry will improve them; if you have but moderate abilities, industry will supply their deficiency."

Some of the most brilliant figures in history had to toil long and hard to give birth to their masterpieces. Beethoven's musical notebook bears all the scars of agonized creation. Dr. Samuel Johnson, by his own account, wrote "doggedly." The Nobel Prize-winning novelist Sinclair Lewis described the writing process as "painful." As a general rule, creation is "10% inspiration and 90% perspiration," as Thomas Edison said.

Discoveries in science and technology are thought by "untaught minds" to come in blinding flashes or as the result of dramatic accidents. Sir Alexander Fleming did not, as legend would have it, look at the mold on a piece of cheese and get the idea for penicillin there and then. He experimented with antibacterial substances for nine years before he made his discovery. Inventions and innovations almost always come out of laborious trial and error. Innovation is like hockey: even the best players miss the net and have their shots blocked much more frequently than they score.

The point is that the players who score most are the ones who take the most shots on the net—and so it goes with innovation in any field of activity. The prime difference between innovators and others is one of approach. Everybody gets ideas, but innovators work consciously on theirs, and they follow them through until they prove practicable or otherwise. They never reject any thought that comes into their heads as outlandish. What ordinary people see as fanciful abstractions, professional innovators see as solid possibilities. "Creative thinking may mean simply the realization that there's no particular virtue in doing things the way they have always been done,"wrote Rudolph Flesch, the language guru. This accounts for our reaction to deceptively simply innovations like plastic garbage bags and suitcases on wheels that make life more convenient: "How come nobody thought of that before?"

Creativity does not demand absolute originality. It often takes the form of throwing an old ball with a new twist. A concert pianist may play a composition written three centuries ago note-for-note and still find unsuspected values in it. An engineer may devise a fresh application of a principle first propounded by Archimedes. The creative approach begins with the proposition that nothing is as it appears. Innovators will not accept that there is only one way to do anything. Faced with getting from A to B, the average person will automatically set out on the best-known and apparently simplest routing. The innovator will search for alternate courses which may prove easier in the long run and are bound to be more interesting and challenging even if they lead to dead ends.

Highly creative individuals really do march to a different drummer. A study directed by J.P. Guilford, ex-president of the American Psychological Association, found that humans go about thinking in two ways. The most common way is convergent thinking, which spirals inward towards the center looking for answers. The other is divergent thinking, which radiates out from the center, opening up new lines of inquiry. Everybody thinks both ways from time to time, but particularly creative people are in the habit, whether natural or acquired, of thinking divergently.

Small children are divergent thinkers, always liable to take off on a tangent. Any thoughtful adult watching a group of them playing "let's pretend" will be humbled by their sheer creativity. Some psychologists, in fact, try to draw out the creative strain in adults by having them play like children. The practice recognizes the truth in Carl Jung's statement that "the dynamic principle of fantasy is play, which also belongs to the child, and as such ... appears to be inconsistent with serious work. But without this playing at fantasy, no creative work ever yet came to birth."

The poet and essayist Samuel Taylor Coleridge said the genius resides in a combination of a child's sense of magic and an adult's trained mentality. Unfortunately, most children start to suppress their wonderment and adventurousness even before they reach their teens. This happens because of pressure from their peers to conform to group standards. Originality begins to falter as soon as children conceive the fear of looking like fools. In later life, especially within organizations, the people with the greatest mental openness and the most original slants on questions are often regarded as office clowns, whose far-out ideas are good-naturedly laughed out of meetings. Often, too, they settle into the role their colleagues have assigned to them. It is easier to play the eccentric than to fight for one's ideas.

Highly creative people *are* eccentric in the literal sense of the word. They have less respect for precedent and more willingness to take risks than others. They are less likely to be motivated by money or career advancement than by the inner satisfaction of hatching and carrying out ideas. In conventional corporate circles, such traits can look quite eccentric indeed. But while there is an identifiable creative personality which follows these lines, testing has shown that very few people, if any, are without the instinct to be creative. One point on which all the experts are agreed is that many people are not as creative as they could be simply because they tell themselves that they are not the creative type. To act creatively, you must first give yourself permission to try.

Everybody, the saying goes, is a genius once a year; the certified geniuses merely have their bright ideas closer together. It might be added that everybody is a genius while asleep. "Dreaming is an act of pure imagination, attesting in all men a creative power, which, if it were available in waking, would make every man a Dante or a Shakespeare," wrote Frederick Henry Hodge, a founder of the transcendental school of philosophy. Though some rare types are capable of recapturing their dreams, most of us are left with only fragments or vague impressions of our unconscious wanderings. The nearest we can get to the perfectly free state of dreaming is to daydream, which our culture tells us is not a fit thing for an adult to do.

In addition to the social misapprobation attached to daydreaming, modern society makes it somehow anti-social to engage in silent contemplation. It is ironic that, in an age when people have more leisure time than ever before, they spend less time than every exploring their own imaginations. We always have to be *doing* something, if only watching television. Consciously creative persons do not feel uncomfortable "doing nothing." They allow for plenty of quiet time in which to spin fantasies and toy with ideas.

Because creativity is a habit of mind, creative people deliberately cultivate the habit. They train themselves to take a playful approach, thinking up metaphors and similes, playing imaginary roles, and conjuring up scenarios.

Physical age is not a factor. "No matter how old you get, if you can keep the desire to be creative, you are keeping the man-child alive," as actor John Cassavetes said. In fact, young-minded people have an advantage over people who are merely young: they have years of learning behind them. "The real key to being creative lies in what to do with your knowledge," says creativity consultant Roger Von Oech. "Creative thinking requires an attitude or outlook which allows you to search for ideas and manipulate your knowledge and experience."

Van Oech and others in his field see a serious need to develop the latent creativity in ordinary human beings. On the private level, an inability to express themselves causes some people emotional difficulties and even mental illness. On the public level, the exploitation of the creative resources within the population is essential to improving the lot of mankind.

At a time when we are using up our other natural resources at a perilously rapid rate, creativity is the chief renewable resource left to us in treating global problems. If we human beings are wise, we will work to remove the social and institutional barriers to exercising creativity everywhere. We should keep in mind that creation is the opposite of destruction. Creativity offers the hope of new solutions to old problems. By making creativity a way of life at work, at home and at play, we can not only fulfill ourselves personally, but contribute to the building of a better world.

Time, Space and Light: Discovering the Saskatchewan Soul
SHARON BUTALA

. . . .

In the excitement over the unfolding of his scientific and technical powers, modern man has built a system of production that ravishes nature and a type of society that mutilates man.[1]

When I was a child living in small towns and villages, and before that, in the northern bush where our father had a sawmill, Saskatchewan seemed to me to be, not a *place*, but a sort of primeval background to the real world which consisted of *places*, certain points on the earth's surface where real things happened and real people lived: England, California, Egypt, Ontario. Saskatchewan was only a holding area where one waited impatiently till one was old enough to leave in order to enter the excitement of the real world.

It seemed to me then that Saskatchewan had nothing to recommend it except, perhaps, a certain pine forest on the banks of the North Saskatchewan near Nipawin where I had once seen so many crocuses growing that at first they had been invisible, so that we children discovered them as one small clump that expanded and expanded to infinity as we ran from the base of that pine to the next, wildly, chaotically, in childish ecstasy, unable to assimilate such a paradise of those precious flowers, where before we had always had to search for them, and sometimes found none at all.

Or, I allowed Saskatchewan might be a *place* when, near Lake Kipibiskau

---

Sharon Butala (born 1940), who lives near Eastend, Saskatchewan, wrote this as the catalogue essay for the multi-media production The Farm Show, *and later published it in the February 1988 issue of* NeWest Review. *Her most recent novel,* Luna, *also appeared during 1988.*

each summer, our family came upon a field of wild tiger lilies blazing orange red in the hot sun, and were warned by our mother not to pick them so they would always be there.

It was a place, too, the day we rode with our grandfather on a hay rack pulled by horses, ducking to keep from being hit by the branches of willows and aspens, bumping over corduroy roads till we reached a small tree-encircled meadow. There we children ran shouting through the sun-and-dew sparkled grass that reached over our heads, keeping well away from where our grandfather stood in grass to his waist, cutting the hay with a scythe; a thoughtful, rhythmic motion, repeated endlessly, all these years in my dreams, the blade glittering as it rises to strike the sun, falling to disappear with a deep whisper in the thick, unimaginably green grass.

He was our mother's father, reluctantly in Saskatchewan after losing his Manitoba farm to three years of drought and then to the banker, alienated by foreclosure forever from the extended family of pioneers he'd been raised in the midst of, as was my grandmother, a farmer's daughter too, and my mother and her siblings.

It was my father's life-long dream to farm, a dream he knew his finances would never permit. He had been born on a farm, had lived there the first six years of his life, till in 1911 his parents abandoned rural poverty in Quebec for a Saskatchewan homestead, near Bellevue, which drought forced them to abandon, too, during the Depression. Not one of their sons became farmers, although all of them dreamt of it all their lives.

All of that, the pastoral dream, the family history of drought and disloca-tion, is familiar to us. It is repeated in family after Saskatchewan family, and has appeared over and over again in one form or another in our literature— a prairie version of paradise forever lost.

Although we whites have no mythical time, no time before time, in this province, "the farm" is rapidly becoming that. Perhaps this is where the history of the Saskatchewan soul begins, and we are creating it every day in our Eden-like memories and in our "I remember when I was a kid on the farm/my grandfather's farm" stories, and in our desperate but so far losing struggle to hang onto the few family farms that are left.

For only short periods of time since the turn of the century have farm people felt that their way of life was not seriously threatened by poor grain prices, or overproduction, or competition from other countries (always with the proviso that the weather co-operates).

But today, in the 1980s, farm people are fighting a battle as bad as or worse than that fought during the Great Depression, not so much against the elements this time as against the world economic order, and the giant multi-nationals which control the grain trade and which know no allegiances other than to money and power, and against governments that are helpless in the face of them, or are in league with them and, while paying lip service to the ideal of the family farm, have little desire to save it and no real understanding of why it should be saved.

The first has driven farmers to do damage to themselves, to the land and the environment, and even to the way of life itself in their struggle for economic success. The second battle, to get the attention of the government, will be a losing one as long as only about 4% of the population remains on the farm and has, therefore, no significant clout at the polls, and as long as most urban people remain bored by the question, failing to understand that their prosperity rests on the backs of the people in the hinterlands.

The prestige carried by people in modern industrial society varies in inverse proportion to their closeness to actual production.[2]

Perhaps if the eastern government, by the Dominion Lands Act of 1872, hadn't divided the face of the prairie as it did, in huge squares, with the added residency requirement, so that people were forced to settle on isolated farms instead of in places which made the most sense to them aesthetically and from the point of view of comfort and convenience, and the railroads had not contributed heavily to the establishment of towns at fixed points along their lines which suited their convenience rather than the peoples' inclinations, the rural population would not be so easily dispersed today.[3]

In 1905 the Western Stock Growers' Association passed a resolution that, had the federal government paid any attention, would have created a province that ran from the Rockies all the way east to just past Swift Current, along the American border.[4] This land was ranchland at the time, and best-suited to that use and, had the government agreed, would probably have remained as such instead of being plowed up as it soon was. Over half the area in question is the Palliser Triangle. Had it remained grazing land hundreds of farmers might not have seen their heartbreaking labor come to nothing, and their hopes, and even their lives, crushed during the Depression.

The corporate and bureaucratic scheme of settlement laid out by distant powers forced a way of life that was not natural to those living on the land and it probably laid the foundation for many of today's ills. But all this is hindsight and not of much use in solving today's problems.

Although much lip service is paid to the family farm as an ideal way of life, the farm population in Saskatchewan has been declining steadily since 1936, with the result that this life is actually only a memory for many of us, and for many others, is an experience that belongs to our parents or grandparents, for we are slowly developing a wholly urban population. It is predicted, in fact, that by the year 2003, 90% of the population of the three western provinces will be urban, with the rest of the population clustered in "corridors" between cities.[5]

In fact, this trend to urbanization is world wide. Elaine Morgan says in *Falling Apart: The Rise & Decline of Urban Civilization*:

> The current figures on global urbanization are devastating. In 1960 two-thirds of the world's population made their living on the land. At the present rate of implosion, by the end of this century the ratio will be reversed and two-thirds of the world's people will be living or trying to live in cities.[6]

Millions of people have been displaced, left to fend for themselves as best they can, usually by moving to the city, an environment they do not understand and one in which they are not well-equipped to function. One way to look at what is happening in Saskatchewan is to see it as a part of this trend. And what will become of the land and of the food it produces, or used to produce, if it falls into the hands of governments or corporate farmers? We don't know the answer, but the question should keep us awake nights.

As farmers have been forced off their land, it has been bought by others, usually the closest neighbors, with a resulting steady increase in farm size. Larger farm size along with the shortage of labor created as rural people moved to towns and cities, or went to work in the oilfields or the mines, forced increased mechanization onto those left behind, the use of bigger, more efficient machinery (and the increase in debt that went with it). Efficiency became the watchword and in order to achieve maximum yield, chemical herbicides and pesticides and fertilizers came into widespread use. In order to put every available square inch into production, windbreaks were plowed up, sloughs drained, and old farm buildings burned and buried to get them out of the way of giant cultivators.

Soil degradation, always a problem where mechanized farming is the rule, has become one of frightening proportion. "Erosion by wind and water, compaction, salinization, acidification, loss of organic matter ... [eats up] millions of acres of our best farmland."[7]

In the north, thousands of acres of trees were uprooted and cleared away, opening the land to problems of drought and erosion that it never suffered from before, and in the south our heritage of fragile native grasses has been virtually eradicated, leaving behind a barren landscape that in places sickens the heart to see. The beauty of the prairie landscape, a gift that belongs to all of us, is being destroyed, and even the wildlife finds it hard to survive. There is no avoiding the fact that family farmers are doing this.

The industrialization of farming has driven thousands off the land; it poisons our water and our air; it turns our fertile land into desert and, in the end, as events show, it has not led to the promised prosperity. According to Senator Herb Sparrow, it has not even led to increased efficiency. Sparrow claims that the number of bushels per acre has actually dropped, in spite of improved seed, better equipment, and herbicides and pesticides:

> You can break up areas around sloughs and have expanded land by removing brush on fence lines that protected the soil. When you take all these factors into consideration, you're not getting as much per acre.[8]

There is, too, another point of view about life on the family farm which, since it comes from ex-farm people themselves, can't be ignored or brushed away. For these people the good memories are by far outweighed by the bad: the unrelenting, unbelievably hard physical labor; the continual poverty; the struggle to acquire amenities of living that urban people took for granted—all-weather roads, telephones, electricity and the labor-saving devices like washing machines that come with it; the lack of freedom in that wherever there was livestock it was impossible ever to leave the farm for more than 12 hours at a time, year after year, and there were no days off; the threadbareness of lives lived without food for the soul—without music or art or poetry or the theater; the stifling of all dreams and ambitions that had nothing to do with farming; the omnipresent, eternal worry about money and the threat of foreclosure.

All of this drove many away from the farm, and forced most of the rest who wanted to stay into a desperate determination to survive and to improve conditions by making more money, by becoming more "efficient" (as governments, banks and universities were urging them), which meant getting bigger, buying bigger machinery, plowing up every inch.

And yet, although all of this dismal picture is perfectly true, the myth, in the true sense of the word, grows. There must have been then, there must be, something about farm life that remains beautiful and good, and that is the true source of the myth of the family farm as the ideal way of life.

Ask a farmer and he will tell you that he likes the freedom, even though he knows as well as urban dwellers do that in terms of finances that freedom is illusory, since farms are roped and tied by bankers, and would fail in minutes without heavy government subsidies. There has always been, though, and it's no small matter, the freedom of choice to establish one's own daily and weekly schedule, the lack of which is one of the most irksome aspects of salaried work. And growing food is work that satisfies, as paper-shuffling can never do.

Then, too, there is still, in rural areas, a powerful and intimate sense of community which stems from the relative lack of mobility of rural people and the tendency to marry someone from one's own community, so that large, extended families result. These families continuously impinge on any one family's life and its consciousness and self-definition in a way that happens less often in urban centers. And the community itself is, for an individual born there, a web of relatives, friends, and lifelong acquaintances in which he/she feels securely placed. Even what appears to the city dweller as a sea of emptiness, the spaces between farms, does not seem that way to the farmer. His/her farm is part of a map of neighboring farms, community leases, abandoned farmsteads, railroad crossings, hamlets, villages and towns, and he/she knows this spacious terrain as intimately as the city dweller knows the few blocks of his/her own neighborhood. The loss of this community, with the loss of the farm, must be like losing one's arms or one's legs.

Both of these, freedom and community, are ingredients in this "something that is beautiful and good," but they are far from all of it.

This "something" has to do with the scent of the prairie air untainted by the fumes of hundreds of vehicles and of factories and the neighbors' dinners, it has to do with the silence, the perfect quiet, of the early mornings and evenings broken only by natural sounds—birds, insects, the songs of coyotes or timber wolves, or water running over stones, or the wind in the grass.

It has to do with space, the space that each person has or can easily find simply by stepping outside the house or the barn, with the distance between neighbors, with the view that runs for miles, unbroken by skyscrapers or complexes of buildings, and with the great round of open sky above.

It has to do too, with living within a more natural flow of time; the changing seasons, the births in the spring and seeding, to the reaping in the fall; it has to do with proximity to the monthly changes of the moon and all the beliefs that go with those changes; it has to do with setting one's working day to fit the rising and setting of the sun, and watching the nightly turning of the stars. All of this was so, at least until industrialization began to change this more leisurely pace to the urban sense of hurry and of the rapid passing of minutes.

Even light is part of this "something." The farmer worked all day out of doors in the natural light of the sun, and was always free to enjoy the brilliant, clear and nearly constant prairie light, which soothed one's soul and which working under the steady hum of fluorescents can never do.

But there is a way not included within terms like space, time or light, in which we become attached to the land.

It is easy to underestimate the power of a long-term association with the land, not just with a specific spot but with the span of it in memory and imagination, how it fills, for example, one's dreams. For some people what they are is not finished at the skin, but continues with the reach of the senses out into the land ... such people are attached to the land as if by luminous fibers and they live in a kind of time that is not of the moment but, in concert with memory, extensive, measured by a life-time.[9]

Lopez, in *Arctic Dreams: Imagination and Desire in a Northern Landscape,* talks about a "spiritual landscape," that exists for long-term permanent inhabitants of a place, that is not apparent to the visitor or the short-term or part-time inhabitant. Those who have lived on a place for long periods see it as more than trees, hills, stones, dirt and grass, and more even then the place where such-and-such happened. It is a sense that the earth lives and has a soul and that its soul can and does commune with the human soul. It is this sense out of which place comes and it is also the one out of which the myth grows.

The field of tiger lilies I saw a child has been gone for a long time. On Saturday one of our neighbors who lost his farm this summer held his sale. He had been on that place since just after the war and he and his wife are no longer young and they have lost everything.

The Saskatchewan we all knew as children, the one that is embedded in our souls, is disappearing. We cannot save it entirely, but (through a device such as guaranteed annual income), if we could make it possible for people who want to live this way to return to small farms of perhaps a quarter section each, they might save our heritage. On small places it is possible to care for the land inch by inch and to return it to a more natural state, to give it back its beauty, its productivity, and its peace.

But of even more importance, such a system would allow us to keep and develop more deeply our ties with nature, for which our souls yearn, and which, inevitably, strengthen our humanity.

Notes

1. Schumacher, E.F., *Small is Beautiful* (London: Abacus, 1974), p. 246.
2. Ibid., p. 125.
3. Lehr, J.C., "In Whose Image? The Landscape of the Prairies," in *Face of the Prairies: 2003,* ed. Fred A. Curtis (Regina: Community Planning Association of Canada Saskatchewan Division, 1985), p. 275.
4. Breen, David, *The Canadian Prairie West and the Ranching Frontier 1874-1924* (Toronto: U.of Toronto Press, 1983), pp. 137-38.
5. Gordon, G.E. "Prairie Settlement," in *Face of the Prairies: 2003,* ed. Fred A. Curtis (Regina: Community Planning Association of Canada Saskatchewan Division, 1985), p. 161.

6. Morgan, Elaine, *Falling Apart: The Rise & Decline of Urban Civilization* (London: Souvenir Press Ltd., 1976), p. 214.

7. Sparrow, Herb, "Profile: Senator Herb Sparrow, Concerned About Our Soils," in *Agri-Mart*, Thursday, 29 October 1987, p. 2.

8. Ibid., p. 2.

9. Lopez, Barry, *Arctic Dreams: Imagination and Desire in a Northern Landscape* (New York: Bantam, 1986), p. 250.

The Punjab in Turmoil
CATHERINE PIGOTT

• • • • • • • • • •

AMRITSAR—The narrow lanes of shops around the Golden Temple, Sikhism's holiest shrine, are jammed with rickshaws and shoppers. Scruffy kids hawking temple postcards and pictures of the gurus pester strangers. Not far from the Amritsar International Hotel, half a dozen Punjab and Haryana Roadways buses career in and out of the station every minute, the drivers all sitting on their horns.

At dusk the scene falls silent. In Punjab, a state in the northwest corner of India that is home to nearly 80% of the country's 13 million Sikhs, buses are not allowed on the roads after 6 p.m. The state's most recent bus massacre, on 6 July 1987, left 19 passengers dead—most of them Hindus. Members of a Sikh terrorist group claimed responsibility.

India's most troubled state continues to live under the ceaseless pressure of militant politics and acts of terrorism. Violence shows no sign of letting up, in spite of a recent police crackdown and the suspension last May of the democratically elected state government by Prince Minister Rajiv Gandhi. More than 1,200 people were killed in Punjab last year in attacks blamed on Sikh militants seeking an independent nation. They call this nation Khalistan—land of the pure.

Almost 60% of those killed by extremists are fellow Sikhs suspected of being government agents or police informers, estimates Prem Kumar, a newspaper editor in the state's capital. Moderate leaders prepared to compromise on the issue of Khalistan are also targets.

To journey into the Punjab today, into the geographical and spiritual heart of this envisioned homeland, is to find a community divided against itself, splintered into fragments. Three-and-a-half years after the Indian army stormed the Golden Temple to arrest Sikh militants lodged inside, many Sikhs express a deep uncertainty, not only about their future in India, but

In 1987, Catherine Pigott (born 1959) spent several months in India on a grant from the Canadian International Development Agency. The experience resulted in this piece of reportage, which appeared in The Whig-Standard Magazine, *Kingston, Ontario, on 20 February, 1988. She was a* Whig-Standard *staff writer at the time.*

their place in the world. "Where will we go?"a young Sikh asks. "In India, we are 'Hindu-killers.' Outside India, we are 'terrorists.'"

What's happening in Punjab is the single greatest threat to the world's largest democracy.

The Sikhs' desire for greater autonomy in India is not new. They raised the first call for a homeland at the time of independence in 1947, when the Muslim country of Pakistan was carved out of India. "There has always been the feeling that the Muslims got Pakistan, the Hindus got Hindustan [India] and the Sikhs got nothing," explains Khushwant Singh, a prominent historian and journalist.

5 June 1984—the day the Indian army bombarded the Golden Temple in a move code-named Operation Bluestar—has been called "the foundation stone of Khalistan." Indira Gandhi's Congress Party had been supporting and subsidizing a fundamentalist Sikh preacher, Sant Jarnail Singh Bhindranwale, to provoke division among her growing Sikh opposition in Punjab. But the Congress plan went out of control. Bhindranwale became a magnet for fanatical, armed separatists, drawing them to him and launching a reign of terror in the state. When Mrs. Gandhi ordered her troops to invade the Golden Temple and arrest him, more than 1,000 devotees, many of them women and children, died in the crossfire. Bhindranwale's body was found in the basement of the demolished Akal Takt, the shrine where he had taken refuge. Five months later Prime Minister Indira Gandhi was gunned down by two Sikh bodyguards. News of the assassination unleashed a brutal three days of anti-Sikh riots in Delhi. Sikhs were burned alive. Their long hair was cut off and left beside their charred bodies. More than 2,000 Sikhs, almost all of them male, died in the fierce backlash.

Feelings of outrage and injustice have hardened throughout the world Sikh community. Events in 1984 and since are proof for many that Sikhism will be desecrated again—and ultimately wiped out—unless Khalistan is established. One of the groups that claimed responsibility for the June 1985 bombing of Air India Flight 182, which killed 329 people, was the Babbar Khalsa, whose avowed goal is an independent Sikh state. The group's founder is a Vancouver-based Canadian Sikh. But a growing number of Sikhs in India have a concern they say is far more critical than getting Khalistan: lack of leadership in their community has reached the point of crisis. "Even those of us who claim to know our own community are terribly confused," says Dr. S. Singh Bal, vice-chancellor of Guru Nanak Dev University in Amritsar and a scholar of Sikh religious history. "I am ashamed of the entire thing."

There are three rival factions of the Akali Dal, the Sikh political party. The elected committee that oversees the affairs and the $12-million budget of all Sikh *gurudwaras* (temples) in Punjab has two presidents: Gurcharan Singh

Tohra, who was at the helm for 14 years and is now in jail, and acting president Harinder Singh Tarn Tarni. Harinder is under increasing pressure from militant groups who have seized control of most Sikh temporal and religious organizations.

Parallel pantheons of high priests further confuse the rank and file. On 22 Oct., after a special council, the outlawed Panthic committee told newspapers they no longer recognized Darshan Singh Ragi as head priest and had replaced him and three other high priests with underground leaders.

The five-member Panthic committee has undertaken the task of uniting the terrorist groups—no easy mission. Police reports list as many as 31 different groups using violence to achieve Khalistan. Conflicting claims of leadership come from Canada, the U.S. and Britain, where a Khalistani "government-in-exile" carries on a campaign for independence. "We can't find anybody who has the power to unite us. Our very social and cultural existence is in danger," says Professor M.S. Taj, a political science lecturer and registrar at Amritsar's leading Sikh school, Khalsa College. "The central government has finally achieved its purpose in Punjab."

Taj, a teacher for 20 years, recounts episodes from the Sikhs' martial history in his classes. When we had no one else to fight off, he tells his students, we fought among ourselves. "This is the tragedy of the Sikhs. They are united only when they are in danger."

Sikhs fought back successive waves of Mughal invaders from Afghanistan during the 18th century. More than half of those who died in the struggle for freedom from British rule in this century were Sikhs, although they make up less than 2% of India's population. When facing a common enemy, Taj says, "we have at times reached very near to the definition of a nation in cohesion and unity. But during this crisis, we are more divided and fragmented than ever before."

. . . .

Sikhism, the world's newest major religion, is barely 500 years old. Guru Nanak, the religion's founder and the first of 10 Sikh gurus, forged a system of belief that drew on Islam and Hinduism, yet differed from them in almost revolutionary ways. The Sikhs believe that there is only one God and He is truth. Guru Nanak, born in 1469, adopted the Hindu concept of reincarnation, but denounced the worship of idols. He rejected the Hindu caste system with its notion of "untouchability." He instituted what is still a mainstay of Sikhism's religious munificence—the guru *ka langar*, or guru's kitchen, where followers of all faiths eat together to break down barriers of caste.

• • • • • • • • • •

The teachings of Guru Nanak and the first five gurus were strictly pacifist, but the martyrdom of Guru Arjun, the fifth guru, turned Sikhism into a militaristic religion. Facing persecution from Muslim rulers on one hand and absorption back into Hinduism on the other, Sikhs became an army of the faithful.

The 10th and last guru, Gobind Singh, baptized a new order of Sikhs—the Khalsa, or pure ones. They swore to wear five emblems of purity and loyalty: unshorn hair and beard; a comb, to symbolize neatness and self-discipline; a steel bangle on the right wrist; soldier's breeches; and a dagger *(kirpan)*. The vows were sealed with a sip of sugared water stirred with a double-edged sword. "When all other means have failed, it is righteous to draw the sword," Gobind Singh told his army. He taught the Sikhs to preserve and defend their identity at all costs. All male Sikhs took the surname Singh, meaning lion, and all the women the surname Kaur, princess. They took up the cry *"Raj karega Khalsa*—the Khalsa shall rule!"—a cry still spoken by Sikhs.

Before he was assassinated in 1708, Guru Gobind Singh decreed there would be no other guru after him. The Sikh Holy Book, the *Granth Sahib*, would provide spiritual guidance in place of a living guru. The affairs of war and politics would be in the hands of the *Panth*, the community of the Khalsa and their followers. Sikhs think of their religion as one of the most democratic in the world.

"Perhaps Guru Gobind Singh injected too much democracy into Sikhism," says historian Dr. S. Singh Bal. He says the tradition of gathering together to take a decision has been abused. "We feel that our entire structure of formal institutions is being undermined." He points to pressure within the community to resort to more militant rhetoric in order to gain power. In the confusion, Sikh democratic institutions "have been made meaningless."

Bal, who is protected by an armed guard wherever he goes, believes that 90% of Sikhs would oppose Khalistan, but political self-interest and fear of speaking freely suppress opposition. Sikhs thought they had an exalted position in this country and now that is gone, Bal says. "As a Sikh, I would first blame my own people." He brings a slightly yellowed photograph from another room. "That's me in London. I was clean-shaven when I was married." The man in the picture, with dark, close-cropped hair, a Clark Kentish suit and not a trace of beard, bears no resemblance to Dr. Bal now, whose appearance is unmistakably Sikh. He is grandfather, and his beard is white and flecked with grey. He wears a powder-blue turban.

"I've got to aim at some social recognition here in Punjab," he says. Without long hair and a beard, "Hindus won't own me, Sikhs would disown me." He sometimes adjusts the six meters of cloth wound around his head as he speaks. "The issue of distinctiveness is becoming even stronger now, and the outward signs have become the most important. Our adherence to religious practices is increasing while faith in the institutions is shaken."

• • • • • • • • • •

"We have worn our *kirpans*, and we have grown our beards. Now where do we go?"

Rajbir Singh has been on a journey since the Delhi riots of 1984. Several days after Mrs. Gandhi's assassination, he walked out of his engineering college in Delhi and headed for a Sikh ashram in the southwestern corner of Punjab. He spent the next three years in the austere, isolated religious commune, serving the sick, scrubbing cooking utensils, sleeping little and pouring over the holy books.

"After Operation Bluestar, this no longer was India. India didn't exist anymore," Rajbir, 24, says in a calm, even tone. He comes from a family of wealthy industrialists and was educated at the best convent schools. When he saw how easily his religion could be swayed and then smashed, he went looking for a meaning beyond the turmoil that was threatening Sikhism. He re-emerged four months ago and joined the family's automotive parts business. He wears a neatly tied white turban and a tailored buttoned-down shirt. Sitting in his uncle's palatial living room in a posh Amritsar neighborhood, he says he's at peace with the spiritual and the secular. "There is something good about all of this," he says of the events before his retreat. "It completely shattered us. Now we have to lay new foundations on something that is going to be far more permanent, far more sane."

Rajbir recalls the hold Jarnail Singh Bhindranwale had on the people of Punjab. "The whole Sikh community suddenly became aware of religion, and in order to convince ourselves that we are religious, we followed him." Now, Sikhs see themselves as the most despised minority in India and abroad. "We can't go any further down the road he started us on. We are realizing that if we go on supporting militants, they are going to break up the system, and we can't live with that change. I would not like to burn my house when I have to live in it."

His uncle, a textile manufacturer and dried fruits importer, says he is among the more than 30% of Punjabi Sikhs who have business interests in other states and countries. "The Sikh economy is such that it is dependent on the integrity of Indian unity." As for Khalistan, he says, "We know that, economically, it's suicidal."

• • • • • • • • • •

"It's hate. It's anger. Nothing positive," Khushwant Singh says of Khalistan. It's because of such statements—which are proclaimed in his columns, probed in his books and even broadcast on CBC Radio—that his Delhi residence is under guard 24 hours a day. A soldier encircled by sandbags is posted at the door. Inside, the 73-year-old historian sits near the fireplace, a blanket over his knees, reading the latest potboiler on Punjabi politics.

"It's been one crisis after another. Sometimes one almost thinks the community has a death wish." The central government has not fulfilled even one accord made with the Sikhs, he says. "Anyone who tries to ask for a settlement of some kind to restore peace is immediately dubbed as a traitor, so one is completely lost."

More than three full years after the Delhi riots, no arrests have been made and no charges laid, although ringleaders have been widely identified. "The terrorists will keep getting recruits," he says. "Crime unpunished breeds criminals. How can we face young Sikhs and say we will settle with this government?"

• • • • • • • • • •

They wouldn't reveal their exact ages, but the oldest face among them couldn't have been more than 22 or 23. A couple of them looked about 16. "The boys," holed up in Room 47 inside the Golden Temple, sit close together and press towards a tape recorder. They say they feel insecure in this place, but they're not leaving.

Malkiot Singh's soft-spoken voice is at times hard to hear. "The battle started from here, it is continuing from here, and it will end up here," he says through an interpreter. He is, according to police classifications, a "category A, hardcore terrorist," with a reward of nearly $10,000 on his head.

His saffron turban, the color of martyrdom, is wrapped carelessly. He wears the traditional Sikh loose knee-length shirt. His face, like the others, is young, unlined. They are members of the Khalistan Commando Force, one of the larger groups involved in the killings of more than 100 police and civilians a month in Punjab. "We want independence," says Malkiot Singh. "We want Khalistan at any cost."

The question, "Why do you want Khalistan?" is, for them, unanswerable. Questioning must begin from the assumption that there will be a Khalistan. In their world of absolutes, there is no question. This is something they will die for—and kill for.

But they do have a vision of this homeland—more mythical than concrete. Its heart will be the Punjab, but it will stretch over Himachel Pradesh and Haryana to the city of Delhi, where, they believe, Jarnail Singh Bhindranwale will someday return to raise the Khalistani flag atop the Red Fort. Khalistan will be ruled by the Sikhs, but the government will be "secular," they explain. Each religion will be allowed to flourish. There will be no discrimination.

Room 47 and the dozens of other windowless rooms that line the marble walkway around the temple's holy pool were built to house some of the

20,000 pilgrims who used to come every day. Since 1984 numbers have fallen off sharply. The 400-year-old shrine that every Sikh prays to be able to see in his or her lifetime now receives about 600 visitors a day, temple information officers say. The flow of donations has slowed to a trickle, and youths from militant factions often swipe what offerings are made. The temple remains in the grip of armed militants, surrounded by an outer ring of paramilitary security forces. Police records in Amritsar are full of terrorist offences committed either inside the rooms or at one of the adjoining buildings in the complex. Crimes include murder, torture and extortion. At least one of the rooms is reported to hold an ample stash of arms.

Journalists started to identify rooms with particular extremist groups, so the numbers were covered with stickers. But the nearest devotee can easily direct you to Room 47. While most terrorists have their bases out in villages or, some reports say, across the border in Pakistan, the Golden Temple still serves as a sanctuary for them. It is a rallying point, a symbolic center from which statements are proclaimed. Major terrorist leaders still come and go from the place. Bhan Singh, secretary of the once-powerful Shiromani Gurudwara Prabandhak Committee that controls the Golden Temple and all other Sikh shrines, says officials can do nothing about it. "All the doors are open. We can't interfere."

"We will achieve Khalistan, whether it is achieved through guns or through talks," says Nihal Singh, Malkiot Singh's associate. "It is up to the government to decide. We are ready for both options." If Rajiv Gandhi is willing to negotiate on the formation of Khalistan (and there are no signs that he is), Nihal says through an interpreter, "we are ready to give up violence."

The commando members say militant groups are united under the 11-member Council of Khalistan, which includes six overseas Sikhs, two of them Canadian. Mr. Gandhi can negotiate with them, the boys say. For its part, the government says no talking until peace has been restored in Punjab.

One of the younger boys brings steaming tea in steel bowls. They describe their life here. "We are like brothers," Nihal says, slurping the tea so as not to burn his lips on the hot metal. "We do not recognize our real brothers."

The room is without furniture. There are mats and bedrolls on the floor, and clothes and towels hang from nails in the whitewashed walls. They get their meals from the *langar*, the free kitchen, inside the temple complex. The continuous, sing-song recitation of the guru Granth Sahib, accompanied by harmoniums, is piped into their rooms on speakers 14 hours a day.

Malkiot Singh says the army assault on the temple in 1984 sealed his commitment to religion and to terrorism. Every day he and the others go to the Sanctum Sanctorum to pray before the Granth Sahib. They bathe outside in the holy pool twice a day.

"Our guru is our source of strength," they say. Before leaving the temple to pick up guns or assassinate "an informer," they offer prayers in the Sanctum Sanctorum. "We seek the blessing of our guru that the operation we are going out on should be successful." They believe the survival of Sikhism is at stake.

They invoke names from a long line of warriors and martyrs whose portraits hang one floor above their rooms in the Central Sikh Museum. The pantheon includes Baba Deep Singh, one of the great heroes of Sikhism, who swore to defend the Golden Temple during the time the Afghans ruled Punjab. Tradition has it that Baba, decapitated in a fray with Afghan general Ahmad Shah Abdal, fought his way to the temple with his head in one hand and his sword in the other. Pictures of the headless martyr are as common in Sikh houses as pictures of the gurus. The Sikh museum also displays a picture of Beant Singh, the guard who shot Indira Gandhi and was then killed on the spot. The words under his face read, "Long live the martyr, the man who restored the honor of the Sikhs."

"The Sikhs know how to fight," Nihal Singh intones, and the boys show the daggers they wear slung across their chests. "During the independence struggle, Sikhs were in the forefront, and we achieved independence for India. Now, we can achieve it for ourselves."

Khalistan Commando Force members deny that their group kills innocent people. All targets, they say, are government agents and police informers: people who have betrayed the Sikh religion.

The boys come from villages in the countryside and were educated in local schools. They refute claims that they are becoming isolated from the majority of Sikhs. "We have mass hold in villages," Nihal says. "People don't support us openly, but in heart they are with us. If the government wants to know the extent of the support for Khalistan among the Sikhs, it can hold a referendum in Punjab."

Support for the militants has grown because "the government is letting loose unprecedented repression against the Sikhs," he says. "The government has started a fratricidal war among the Sikhs."

• • • • • • • • • •

Julio F. Ribeiro, senior superintendent of the Punjab Police Force, brushes aside the suggestion of "false encounters" with a sweep of this leather baton. Reports of his men killing off terrorist suspects don't seem to disturb him.

Ribeiro's equation to smash terrorism is simple: "They ambush ours, we ambush theirs. Our chaps and their chaps—it's only between us. And we are not going to get killed first." He has just addressed villagers in Amritsar district, an area prone to terrorist activity, on taking responsibility for their own defence. The rifle butts and roving eyes of his bodyguards outside can be glimpsed between the flaps of the tent. He brushes a fly from the rim of his tea cup. "I've lost 111 men in the last four months."

Ribeiro, one of the three most heavily guarded men in Punjab, admits that at least 12 innocent people have been shot since police began a policy of retaliation for the killings of policemen in early 1986. An Amnesty International report has charged that police deliberately kill suspects, sometimes after capture. A committee appointed by the state of Punjab found that security forces were taking innocent people into custody and killing some of them. Ribeiro is straightforward. "We have said we are sorry. No innocent man has been killed except due to mistakes of judgment."

Stories of youth being shot "in police encounters" and "while trying to escape" are read by most Sikhs to mean a gross violation of human rights. Ribeiro calls the escapes "a bad habit that has grown" and says suspects linked to terrorist activities "take great pride in escaping."

Since president's rule (a form of martial law) took effect in May, about 300 extremists have been killed by police and nearly 5,000 are behind bars, according to estimates made at the end of December. Ribeiro says there are not enough police to prevent escapes when large groups of detainees are being moved.

Ribeiro, a tall man, strides up and down a line of 50 young men who stand expectantly, shirts off, waiting to have their chests measured. They step forward one at a time, take a deep breath and pray they will meet the 34-inch chest requirement for a job on the Punjab Police Force. Four months ago Ribeiro launched a large-scale recruitment drive into the villages, directly challenging traditional terrorist recruitment bases.

His speeches on village self-defence now include a call to farmers to send forward sons, nephews and brothers for employment. His assistants stand by with application forms and measuring tapes. The minimum height is 5'7", and boys must be high school graduates. Anxious parents, both Sikh and Hindu, watch from a discreet distance.

"We've picked up about 60 today," says Ribeiro's deputy. This is their third stop. It's getting dark. New blood is badly needed, he says. More than 50 corrupt officers were recently dismissed. Sikhs form a majority of the 15,000 active officers and, he says quietly, divided loyalties and the lure of bribes eat away at morale.

• • • • • • • • • •

A Khalsa College student, Bhagat Singh, pushes his glasses back on his nose and tries to explain. "Imagine one child of the family is not getting love from the parents. What will he do? First, he'll try to get affection, but he won't succeed. Then, the idea will come in his mind that he should separate from the family." The 24-year-old commerce student, son of an

Amritsar businessman, says almost all students support the idea of Khalistan. "In India, we are without hope. Unemployment is only for Sikhs."

Amritsar's Khalsa College is a showpiece of the Sikhs, India's most prosperous community. It was founded in 1892 as part of a renaissance movement in Sikh religion and culture, and alumni records read like a who's who of Sikh politicians, historians, industrialists and top military brass. The elegant Victorian buildings, separated from the road by a wide stretch of lawn, were built with funds raised by Sikh landlords and peasants who gave 3% of the land revenue tax they paid to the raising of the college.

"This college is the center of the hopes and aspirations of the Sikhs," says registrar and professor M.S. Taj. Virtually every reform movement, from the fight to gain control of their temples in the 1920s to the struggle for independence in the 1980s, has found a stronghold in the college. Student strikes and demonstrations regularly paralyze its academic life.

The students seated around a table in the room behind the principal's office are sons and daughters of judges, lawyers and professors. They plan to do graduate studies next year—to go into banking, enter medical school. And they are the source of the call for Khalistan.

At least 70% of the student body supports the All India Sikh Students Federation, Bhagat Singh says. Some students argue the figure is higher. The main goal of federation leaders is the achievement of Khalistan. Its members were responsible for many of the attrocities committed in Bhindranwale's name. It has now split into two factions and its leaders are underground.

Balwinder Singh, a graduate student in economics, lists the names of classmates being held in detention. "There are about 15 students in the Jodhpur jail who are innocent," he says. "We have so many examples." He repeats the common belief among Sikhs that many terrorist acts are in fact the work of the Indian government—a deliberate attempt to defame the Sikh community. In the face of this "injustice," he goes on, speaking sometimes in English, sometimes in Punjabi, the geographical boundaries of Khalistan mean nothing. "Khalistan is the shape of our anger."

Beyond the anger, Prof. Taj reflects, Khalistan becomes a multi-purpose tool. For some, it's a strategy—a means of political existence they dare not relinquish. For others, it is the key to belonging, an identity. It is, ultimately, an escape. "I do want there to be a Khalistan, and power will be in the hands of the Sikhs," says Gurjeet Singh, a fourth-year science student. "We will create an ideal rule." He searches for a way to explain what "ideal rule" will be. "I will give you the example of America."

The state of Punjab the students see is too small to contain them. They believe they are capable of much more. New investment in Punjab has nosedived. People in other parts of India are afraid to come here and do business. Most landholdings have been carved up into fragments and farming can't absorb more people. Young Sikhs say they are victims of prejudice when competing with Hindus for jobs. Jaswinder Singh, a fourth-year science student, says his job prospects in India are hopeless, but "we will be well-settled in Khalistan."

And there's one trump card left. "Three of my uncles are in America," Jaswinder says, thumbing through his address book. "I'm just hoping for my chance to go." A minute earlier he had proclaimed that all Hindus should be banned from Punjab to make way for Khalistan. "This politics—it's just a formality," he says lightly. "What I want is a green card." He's got to get somewhere somehow, he says, with an eagerness verging on desperation, be it Khalistan or a one-way ticket out.

• • • • • • • • • •

The first trucks loaded with the furniture, children and jumbled possessions of Hindu families started to roll out of the village six days after the killings.

Outside Narinder Kumar's house, young men heave the family's belongings into the back of a battered lorry while women prepare tea for the mourners who have come to sit with his widow. Usha, 28, left alone with three children under the age of eight, crouches under a thick shawl. "Right now I just have too much anger to know my feelings," she says. They decided that day they would leave Dhapai, and the Punjab, for good.

Everyone sits on the ground when something sad has happened. About 15 women, most of them Sikh, sit close to Usha and begin the hundredth re-telling of what happened five nights earlier, on 27 Oct., when Narinder Kumar, 33, was shot dead as he stood behind the counter of his small shop. Half an hour later the gunmen returned and killed his 70-year-old father Megh Das.

"They were shouting slogans. We heard them: 'Blood for blood! Blood for Khalistan!'" a white haired woman recalls. Five men, all Hindus, died between 5:30 and 6 p.m. that night. According to villagers, four armed men entered the village, two from each side. One Sikh pleaded with them to spare the life of his clean-shaven brother, the village pharmacist. The Sikh was spared, the pharmacist and a customer slain. Sikh separatists have been blamed for the attacks.

Usha, who doesn't know what kind of work she can do to support a family, came to Dhapai eight years ago when she was married. The Kumars had lived here for generations, villagers say. Dhapai, just over an hour's drive from Amritsar through acres of wheat, sugar cane and mustard seed, is a prosperous farming community of about 2,500 people. Less than 4% were Hindus—about 12 families—and the October killings finally drove them out.

Two years ago, a woman in the group of mourners remembered, the

Hindus nearly left the village en masse, fearing a backlash after the storming of the Golden Temple and the Delhi riots. The rest of the villagers assured them that they would be protected. No such promises are being made now, she says. "We can only console. We can't protect."

Ram Lubhaya, 35, who was alone in his shop when he was fatally shot, had already built a house in the neighboring state of Haryana. He was only waiting for his customers to pay off their debts, racked up during the October religious festival of Diwali, before moving his family out of the Punjab. "All Hindus are leaving this place," says his mother. They would stay for the ceremony that marks one week after the cremation and then they would go.

• • • • • • • • • •

As much as 80% of terrorist activity in the Punjab is concentrated in the northernmost districts of Amritsar and Gurdaspur, where Dhapai is situated. These areas surround the militant nerve center of the Golden Temple, and both districts border on the sensitive frontier between India and Pakistan. "For generations we were living together," a Sikh landowner remarks as he stands in front of the cracked and peeling wooden doors of the Hindu temple, the oldest building in Dhapai. "The personal ties are still there." The temple doors are closed, chained and padlocked. "It's very, very sad," he says. "I cannot give them any guarantee that I can protect them."

Dhapai and villages like it, where the Hindu community is no more than a dozen families, are vulnerable targets, says Amritsar District's deputy commissioner, Sarabjit Singh. It's easier to kill a few and drive the others out. Dhapai is now virtually a pure Sikh village, and the Punjab is one step closer to Khalistan, so the reasoning goes.

Although an estimated 80% of India's Sikhs live in Punjab, even here they are barely a majority. More than 40% of all Punjabis are Hindu. The founder of the Sikh faith, Guru Nanak, was a Hindu, and the great majority of the guru's followers came from the Hindu community.

Most Hindu families in northwestern Punjab not only revered the Sikh gurus, they often brought up their eldest son as Sikh and married their daughters to Sikh men. (These practices continued until recently.) The Golden Temple at Amritsar is central to the ethos of all Punjabis, Sikh and Hindu.

Close to the core of the crisis of identity among Sikhs is a gut fear that the colossal Hindu majority—85% of India's population—will slowly swallow all other religious minorities on the sub-continent. And when Hindus describe Sikhism as a "sect" of their own religion, Sikhs recoil from what they see as the looming threat of re-absorption into everything their gurus sought to liberate them from.

The exodus of Hindus from Dhapai ended relationships that go back, some of them, more than 300 years. "As individuals, we love each other," the Sikh landowner explains. "As communities, we hate each other." He points out padlocked doors and abandoned houses as he threads his way down a narrow lane. There is nothing the government can do, nothing the village can do, and nothing a village defence committee can do to stop it from happening again, he says. Nothing, except to give Sikhs a homeland where they'll be free from the forces of Hindu chauvinism. "Hinduism," he says in a controlled, almost muffled voice, "is eating us alive."

• • • • • • • • • •

A procession of plenty. Fleets of trucks, their cabs festooned with tinsel and illuminated pictures of Guru Gobind Singh, roll out of Punjab bearing loads of wheat and paddy. This state grows more than half the food that feeds India's 800 million people. Its history is one of spectacular agricultural advancement paralleled by a bullet-ridden chronology of political instability. Eighty per cent of Punjabi Sikhs work in agriculture and nurse a fierce attachment to the land. "For we Jats, to dispose of our land is to dispose of our prestige," says a young farmer in Amritsar District. "We are cultivating whatever we have."

Although the majority of holdings are not more than five acres, marriages are made and unmade, internecine feuds provoked and murders committed over land. Jats, the landowning class of Sikhs, hold political sway in the countryside. The bulk of landless laborers are Sikh converts from the "untouchable" Hindu castes.

The Punjab was the center of the Green Revolution that made India self-sufficient in food production in the mid-1970s. Jat peasants revolutionized their farming methods, first doubling and then trebling wheat yields by using tractors, new varieties of hybrid seeds, fertilizers and insecticides. The Green Revolution was followed by a similar increase in rice yields.

• • • • • • • • • •

Punjab, an area that composes only 11½% of the entire country, now produces 50% of India's rice and 60% of its wheat. "No other class could have done it," a prosperous Jat farmer explains. "We are the only eastern religion with a work ethic."

The well-ordered, irrigated fields of rural Punjab could almost be taken for farm country in eastern Ontario. Well before 7 a.m. the sounds of the tubewell pumps and tractors starting up can be heard, vying with the sonorous notes of the pre-dawn prayers from the *gurudwara*, broadcast across the fields on loudspeakers. One almost expects a box of cornflakes to appear on the farmhouse kitchen table. Instead, the Punjabi farmer begins his day with *roti*, round, unleavened bread, and *sog*, an iron-rich paste made of boiled mustard plant leaves, washed down with butter and hot buffalo milk.

"You will not find the real Punjab in the cities," says Raghbir Singh, a landowner and science teacher at a Khalsa school in Tughalwal village, about 10 miles from Dhapai. He expresses a certain contempt for "citified" Sikhs, those who venture out to the countryside with their beards tied up in handkerchiefs to keep the dust out. Raghbir says with a level gaze that these are not real Sikhs. In the cities, he tells a visitor, "you have seen Sikhs as traders, as slaves, not as rulers." Jats, who see themselves as the owners of Punjab, resent Hindus for seeing themselves as the owners of India. "We have merchants, traders, ruling us, and the traders don't want the farmer to share in the government," Raghbir says, fingering the beard that curls onto his chest. "They only want us to feed India. They do not want us to participate."

He spreads his fingers and drives his fist into his palm. "One hundred twenty one Sikhs hanged in the freedom struggle. Hundreds more dying to defend Hindus." The counting of the dead and wounded continues. The number and names of the persecuted are recited in prayers. "Now we want the fruit of that," he says, "but we are getting nothing."

Raghbir and the other teachers, also farmers, want higher prices for their produce, a greater share in river waters for irrigation and electricity and full possession of the capital city they share with Haryana. They talk about "political independence," but veer away from speaking the word "Khalistan." They can't say what shape it will take or who will be leader. "He will be born. He will come."

In the villages there is sympathy for "true terrorists," Raghbir says, draining his glass of tea. "The true terrorist kills the sinners," he says, his voice deep, professorial. "He is someone true to the religion." Those who kill innocent civilians "are not true Sikhs," but government agents in turbans, paid to defame and disrupt the Sikh community.

"The government must negotiate with the militants," he says. The All-India Sikh Students Federation, the Panthic Committee, the Khalistan Commando Force—they are the ones leading the struggle with the central government, he says. "If the militants are satisfied, we will be satisfied. Otherwise, there cannot be peace in Punjab."

• • • • • • • • • •

Peace, Sadhu Singh says quietly, is what people in his village want most. "We are tired of the agitation. People don't want it anymore. You can only keep up agitation for so long before exhaustion sets in." The burning village issue now, the young farmer says, "is the sowing of our wheat and the harvesting."

In Sadhu Singh's village of 4,000, where the houses of the landed families and the hovels of the landless "Mazhbi" Sikhs are separated by a wide pond, life's rhythms revolve around the growing season and the four *gurudwaras*. Gurbachan Singh, 60, has been the *granthi*, or village priest, for 25 years. He is a poor man, landless, with a matted beard and a carelessly tied turban. "I preach only what is in the Holy Book. Only that," he says through a translator. He gestures to the Granth Sahib, covered with a red cloth and resting under an awning in the dim interior of the gurudwara. "The Guru is sleeping," he says, almost in a whisper. In the morning, he opens the book with an elaborate ritual. He brushes the pages with a whisk made of white yak's hair and reads out the rich Punjabi poetry put down by Guru Nanak four and a half centuries ago, teachings that have become the compass needle of village existence.

Sadhu Singh sits in a lawn chair in the sun and tries to remember what drew him back to this place. Behind him is a comfortable Jat house with a fortress-like wooden front door. Roses and flowering bushes border a porch worn smooth from several generations of use. The servants have watched children grow up and are now caring for grandchildren. Sadhu's father has been the village headman since 1949. His grandfather held the post before that.

Sadhu returned from Delhi University almost five years ago to manage the family's landholdings, more than 60 acres in all. He wanted to modernize the farm and start sports and social clubs. "I had ideals." In his argyle sweater and North Star running shoes, and with a neatly-trimmed beard, he seems in the village, but not of it. He's now 30, married and a father. Restlessness has set in. "Out here you don't have to be progressive. Psychologically you become backward, cloistered."

Religious sentiments run strong and deep here, he says. Within an hour's drive are two bastions of Sikh fundamentalism: the Golden Temple in Amritsar and Darshan Parkash gurudwara at Chowk Mehta, a center for training preachers once headed by Bhindranwale. Some of the village boys, with limited education and facing unemployment, have been drawn into terrorist organizations. One was killed in an encounter with police last month. Disillusionment with the Sikh political party, the Akalis, may also fuel sympathy for the militants, Sadhu says.

He doesn't know who is harboring terrorists, but says they must have some support in the village. Some Hindu families are sending their children out of Punjab, so if something goes wrong, they'll have somewhere to go. Sadhu is cautious, even afraid, when he speaks. "There is suspicion to voice your feelings. You worry about reprisals from the government or the terrorists."

• • • • • • • • • •

The author Khushwant Singh says that among Sikhs, "There is a growing sense of revulsion against the terrorists," a widespread feeling in the community that they have to pay the price for the actions of a few. Between Hindus and Sikhs, he says, there is "definitely a healing process going on."

On 23 January, 13 Hindus were gunned down in three separate incidents in Punjab. Ten were shot dead by suspected Sikh separatists in Barnala while walking to a public park early in the morning to practise yoga. The Khalistan Liberation Force, a group fighting for a separate Sikh homeland, took responsibility for the massacre. The three others who died, two Hindu politicians and a shopkeeper, brought the January death toll to 75. In 1987, 1,230 people died in separatist violence in Punjab, more than double the total of 560 killed in 1986.

"Punjab is in turmoil," Waryam Singh Bhagowalia says in a dry voice, settling himself stiffly in a straight-back chair. "Very few of us know what Sikhism is." A 69-year-old veteran of the Quit India independence movement under Mahatma Gandhi, he spent a total of three years in jail between 1932 and 1942 for defying British rule. He was a Congress member of Punjab's legislative assembly for 30 years. "When I was in jail, I was dreaming of what free India would be like," he says, smoothing the folds in his loose, flowing shirt. "We haven't taken a step toward it. In practice, it does not exist."

Sundial Renaissance
MICHAEL WEBSTER

· · · · · · · · · ·

First, let us understand that there is no such thing as time. Oh, there are days and lunar cycles and seasons and years, but all the rest—seconds, minutes, hours, weeks, months, decades, centuries—are made up. They are arbitrary divisions of the indivisible that have no foundation in nature. Of course, that has not stopped almost every culture since the Chaldean from defining time by enumerating its passage. Indeed, a common measure of a civilization's progress is its refinement in fractionalizing the day. In the latter part of the 20th century, we in North America pride ourselves on the parsimonious exactitude with which we dole out our minutes and seconds. One has only to ask a stranger on the street for the time to see how digital chronometers are replacing the last vestiges of vagueness—"Oh, about 10 to 3"—with precision—"The time is 2:49." As a whole, our culture sneers at the impracticality and perceived inaccuracies of such antique timekeeping devices as keywound clocks and sundials.

This does not mean that sundials have outlived their usefulness. Certainly, they are limited: they do not work at night or on cloudy days, nor are they accurate underwater to depths of 50 feet. But there is a certain earthy appeal to the notion of sun time, a kind of connectedness with the rhythms of the universe that makes sundials especially appropriate to outdoor situations where other forces of nature are apparent. A garden, for instance. Surrounded by the phenomenon of green growth from soil, water, air and sunlight, a sundial stands like some photosynthesizer of eternity, less a symbol of humanity's triumph over nature than a humbling reminder of the immutable forces that mold our lives. "A sundial fits beautifully among plants and flowers," writes Rene R.J. Rohr in his book *Sundials: History, Theory and Practice.* "A rose bush is its ideal neighbor: life for the sober dial on its moss-covered pedestal or the shimmering rose depends on light. But one lasts long; the other quickly fades."

Six years ago, Michael Webster (born 1948) abandoned life as a construction worker to go to work on Harrowsmith, *where he is now the managing editor. This piece appeared in the May-June 1988 issue.*

Working sundials may be purchased, but the factory-made models found in garden centers are strictly decorative. To be functional, a sundial must be custom-made for each site; a dial mass-produced in California will not serve Canadian sun-readers well. (However, it took the Romans a century to realize that a sundial plundered from Sicily in the First Punic War was not keeping accurate time.)

Of course, custom-made dials are available, but they can be expensive. An attractive homemade dial is not beyond the abilities or resources of most homeowners, and the result can be a wonderful addition to a backyard garden or a thoughtful adjunct to a favorite thinking place or lookout point. Among the dozens of types of sundials, three—the equatorial, the polar and the horizontal—distinguish themselves by simplicity of design, ease of construction and accuracy. Aside from the usual complement of shovels and trowels and hammers and saws, the only special equipment needed is a protractor (the larger the better—try an art-supply store) and a faint recollection of high school geometry.

Before people began building sundials (no later than 1500 B.C.), they followed the apparent progress of the sun by pounding a stick into the ground vertically and watching its shadow. We call such a stick a gnomon, from a Greek word meaning "indicator" or "one who knows." The length of the gnomon's shadow, measured in foot-lengths, became a measure of the day. It was more accurate to say, "You watch the sheep until the shadow is 6 feet long" than "I'll be back when the sun is about yea high."

It was the Babylonians who divided the shadow's progress into 12 equal parts, which we now call temporary hours. They liked the number 12 because, being divisible by one, two, three, four, six and 12, it is easy to work with mathematically. They also divided the sky into 12 astrological signs, and later, the Egyptians divided the year into 12 months. It was the Egyptians, too, who divided the night into 12 parts and began distinguishing one day from another at midnight. (The Babylonians started each day at sunrise, the Israelites at sunset.)

There were disadvantages to the temporary hours of a vertical gnomon, chief among them that one-twelfth of the period between sunrise and sunset varied according to the length of daylight. Even at Mediterranean latitudes, the changing seasons brought unacceptable differences. Farther north, in a city such as Ottawa, a nine-to-five office worker keeping time with a vertical-gnomon sundial would be in the office for fewer than six clock-hours in December but almost 11 clock-hours in June.

Sometime in the first century B.C., though, sundials became practical timekeeping machines in the modern sense. It was discovered that if the gnomon is tilted so that it is precisely parallel to the Earth's axis, it will mark out the hours consistently. That is, the sundial will read 9:30 a.m. at 9:30 a.m., whether the sun has been above the horizon for five hours or for two. To be parallel to the Earth's axis, the angle of the gnomon must change with changes in latitude. At the equator, the gnomon is flat (parallel to the Earth's surface); as one climbs higher on the globe, its angle increases at the rate of one degree for every 69 miles travelled.

This new accuracy inspired a burst of inventiveness that filled the ancient world with thousands of sundials. As with most change brought about by technology, though, there were grumblers, of whom none was more eloquent than the Roman playwright Titus Maccius Plautus: "Let the gods damn the first man who set up a sundial in this city. For our misfortune, he has chopped up the day into slices. When I was young, there was no other clock but my belly. For me, it was the best and the most accurate clock; at its call, we ate, unless there was nothing to eat. Now, even if there is an abundance, we eat only when it pleases the sun. The city is full of sundials, but people crawl around half-dead with hunger."

But progress is rarely, if ever, stopped by public opinion. Sundials continued to chop up the day even after the development of reasonably reliable mechanical clocks in the 15th century, when Galileo invented the pendulum. Indeed, sundials were in even more demand so that the new shaft-and-gear machines could be accurately set. As late as 1900, clocks in many French railway stations were still regulated to a uniform time with sundials. It is only recently that chronometers capable of keeping better time than a sundial have been widely available. Now, of course, many of the digital wristwatches that children wear are more accurate than the finest scientific instruments of the previous century.

One of the disadvantages of such electromechanical precision is a loss of understanding of the precepts behind the measurement of time. Before we can build a sundial, we need to review some basics. Everyone knows that the Earth orbits the sun once every 365¼ days and that the Earth is spinning in a west-to-east direction at the rate of one revolution every 24 hours. This is why the sun appears to rise in Newfoundland before it does in British Columbia. And since the Earth turns 360 degrees in 24 hours, it spins at the rate of 15 degrees of longitude every hour (360 divided by 24). For our purposes, though, it is easier to imagine it is the sun that is doing the moving. It will be no great astronomical or philosophical faux pas to speak of the sun rising in the east, crossing the sky at a speed of 15 degrees an hour and setting in the west—in an everyday sense, this is how most people think of it anyway.

An equatorial sundial is so named for two reasons. First, it represents a slice of the Earth taken at the equator, rather like the middle section of a sliced lemon. Like the lemon slice, it has a center, from which the gnomon protrudes, and spokes that radiate to the circumference. On the sundial, the spokes are marked at 15-degree intervals, each one representing an hour.

The noon spoke points directly north, the six a.m. spoke points west (where it will catch the shadow of the gnomon cast by the sun rising in the east), and the six p.m. spoke points east. Second, when properly installed, the face of the dial—usually a lemon-slice-like disc—is exactly parallel to the Earth's equator. Fortunately, this is easy to set up: simply set the dial on a level surface, and raise the south side to an angle equal to the co-latitude (90 degrees minus the latitude where the sundial is situated). Consult a good atlas or topographical map, and be as accurate as is practical—right to the minute, if possible. The gnomon, perpendicular to the center of the dial, represents the Earth's axis and therefore points to Polaris, the North Star.

Note that because the dial is a miniature of the Earth's equator, the sun will shine on its top surface (representing the northern hemisphere) for half the year and on its bottom, or southfacing, surface for the other half. For year-round use, then, equatorial sundials require a gnomon protruding from both sides, rather like a silver dollar skewered by a toothpick. The placing of hour lines on the underside is the same as on the top, with six a.m., noon and six p.m. facing west, north and east, respectively. However, since the sun will shine on the upper surface between the vernal and autumnal equinoxes (23 March to 23 September), which at Canadian latitudes includes most, if not all, of the gardening season, many builders of backyard equatorial sundials choose only to prepare the upper surface.

A polar dial, with its wide, rectangular face and rectangular gnomon, is the oddest-looking of the three sundials but is perhaps the easiest to construct. It is unusual in that the edge of the gnomon, or style, which casts the shadow, is parallel to the dial face and that the hours lines are parallel to each other, rather than convergent. Nevertheless, it is as accurate as the other designs, its only drawback being that its usefulness is restricted to the hours between seven a.m. and five p.m. The dial is tipped from the horizontal to face the sun at an angle equal to the latitude of the site, and the style's shadow progresses from left to right during the day. Because it faces the sun, the dial face can be used year-round

• • • • • • • • • •

A horizontal dial is the one most people imagine when they picture a sundial. The dial face, either round or square, is flat, and the hours are numbered clockwise around its perimeter; the gnomon is upright and usually triangular, although it can be any shape as long as the style diverges from the face by an angle equal to the latitude of the site. These features make the horizontal dial accurate, easy to read and simple to install correctly. The cost of that convenience is that the hour lines, which radiate from the bottom of the style, are more complicated to draw. Nevertheless, the horizontal dial can be read at any time of the year and at any time of the day, as long as the sun is shining—or, with less accuracy because the shadows are less sharp, on any cloudy but bright day. It is probably the dial that most gardeners will choose to build.

All three sundials will allow one to tell time the way people have for hundreds of years; however, just as many other things have changed in the past century, so has our way of measuring time. The two modern refinements that affect sundial performances are time zones and daylight saving time (DST). The latter is relatively easy to accommodate, at least in a garden sundial. Many sundials list only standard time and leave dial-watchers to "spring forward" mentally in the summer months; others list two sets of numbers. But since DST is in effect from the first weekend in April to the last weekend in October, which covers most of the pleasant weather in this climate, gardeners would be better served by labeling their dials only for DST. This requires no changes in layout except to label the six a.m. hour line "seven a.m.," and so on. Note: although the noon line is now "one," it is still the noon line and must point to solar north.

The concept of time zones, for which Canadian engineer Sir Sandford Fleming is largely responsible, accounts for the fact that when it is sunrise in Winnipeg, it is midmorning in St. John's and the dark of night in Vancouver. In principle, 24 time zones encircle the globe, and clocks are set back one hour for every 15 degrees of longitude west of the Greenwich meridian; in practice, the time zones follow convenient political boundaries. This means that clocks 500 miles apart are often set to the same time, and although the sun is directly over Regina 30 minutes later than it is over Winnipeg, residents of both cities stop for lunch at the same time. The difficulty with sundials is that they measure local time, the time in any given location (and all places directly north and south). At most Canadian latitudes, local time differs by a full second in places less than 1,000 feet apart in an east-west direction. It can be argued philosophically that local time is "real" time, in that it is the time in one's own backyard and not in one's neighbor's, but a time-piece not adjusted to standard time would have limited use.

Fortunately, homemade sundials can easily be "set" to account for standard time. To understand how, imagine a sundial erected on a longitude divisible by 15: along the meridian, standard time and local time (clock time and sundial time) agree. But local time changes four minutes for every degree of longitude (four seconds for every minute of longitude), so if the sundial is moved one degree to the west, it will be four minutes slow compared with a clock. To correct the dial, we would leave the gnomon where it is and rotate the hour lines one degree to the west (counterclockwise). This means the 12 o'clock line would be pointing one degree west of north, and the sundial would again agree with a clock set to standard time. Similarly, if the dial were moved one degree east, it would be four minutes fast, and hour lines would be moved one degree east (clockwise) to set the dial for standard time.

The same principle applies to every backyard in Canada. Suppose, for example, I want to erect a sundial in front of the *Harrowsmith* office in Camden East. The longitude is 76, 51, and it is in the Eastern time zone, which is standardized to 75 degrees west longitude, just east of Ottawa (52, 30 for Newfoundland time, 60 for Atlantic, 90 for Central, 105 for Mountain and 120 for Pacific). The site is 1, 51 west of the standard meridian, so I must move all my hours lines 1, 51 west, or counterclockwise. The result is that my noon line—which still must point to solar north, though it will not appear on the finished dial face—now marks about 12:08 (actually 1:08, because I would also set the dial for DST). So my sundial will agree with my watch from April to October, whenever the sun shines.

• • • • • • • • • •

The adjustment to standard time is made in degrees with a protractor. At one point in calculating where to place the hour lines, one uses a protractor to mark out 15-degree increments, each of which is, or will establish, an hour line. It is at this point that the adjustment is made—if, for instance, a sundial is situated five degrees east of the standard meridian, the seven a.m. line would be marked at 20 instead of 15, and so on, with noon at 95 and six p.m. at 185 (neither the six o'clock line nor the noon line would appear on the finished dial). This will move the hour lines east, or clockwise, the correct amount.

All of the above *sounds* a lot more complicated than it actually is. The basic rule is simple: for every degree west (or east) of the standard meridian the sundial is situated, rotate the hour lines one degree west (or east).

With the sundial erected in the garden and the dial adjusted for standard time and daylight saving time, it would seem that one should be able to relax and enjoy the simple pleasure of rising from one's knees after an afternoon of installing tomato transplants and telling at a glance if it is time to put a roast in the oven or pick up the kids or whatever. There is, however, one further complication, and though its effect on sundial time is minimal, the concept itself is mind-boggling: the day is not 24 hours long, as your mother told you and as I, until now, have pretended. Rather, four days in a year (16 April, 14 June, 2 September and 25 December) are 24 hours long, and the rest are longer or shorter. Remember, this is entirely separate from seasonal changes in the length of the daylight period; it concerns the supposed 24 hours from one high noon to the next. One day can differ from the next by as much as 30 seconds, and these half-minutes accumulate until, at its extremes, a sundial is slow or fast by a quarter of an hour.

The explanation for this phenomenon is reasonable but complex, and even experienced astronomers who understand it thoroughly make a face when asked to explain it to the uninitiated. Readers interested in following it up can find the explanation in a library book on basic astronomy; suffice it to say that there are two factors involved. First, Earth's orbit around the sun is elliptical rather than circular, which causes the Earth to travel faster in that orbit when it is near the sun and slower when it is farther away. Second, because Earth's axis is tipped to the plane of its orbit, the sun's rate of progress across the sky varies throughout the year. Over the course of one orbit—356.25 days, or one year—the variations cancel each other out, so the *average* day length is exactly 24 hours. This is known as mean solar time, and it is the time that our clocks keep.

Sundials, however, monitor apparent solar time and are therefore "slow" or "fast" except on the four days a year when the two times agree. Arguably, of course, it is the sundials that are always accurate and the clocks that are right only four times a year, but our civilization is geared to work on 24 hours a day, and we have to adjust to the average. The variations between sundial time and clock time are predictable and can be shown on a graph known as the equation of time. Stood on end and drawn as a loop, the equation of time becomes an analemma, the elongated figure eight that used to appear in the Pacific Ocean on world globes.

An equation of time shows that the extreme differences are in November and February, which will not affect the garden sundial. Even in the moderate regions of Canada, the months between frost dates are those in which the sundial is not terribly inaccurate. A sundial is three minutes fast at the end of May, six minutes slow around 1 August and eight minutes fast in the third week of September. Many gardeners will accept these minor variations— Does it really matter if it is 1:23 or 1:26?—but those who insist on precision can paint or inscribe an equation of time on the face of the sundial. A glance at the shadow and a simple calculation based on the date will give a reading accurate enough to set a digital watch by.

Armed with a knowledge of the intricacies of sundial time, you may decide that the easiest way to mark the hour lines is to build a sundial, with the gnomon properly aligned with the Earth's axis, and spend a day marking where the shadows fall at the stroke of each hour. Provided you do it on either 14 June or 2 September, when sundial time agrees with clock time, this method will work—thereafter, the dial will always show standardized DST, plus or minus the equation of time. Of course, it would be a shame if one waited weeks for the appointed day and the sun did not shine. Such are the pleasures of sundial time.

The traditional building materials for sundials are stone and bronze, but those who lack sculpting skills or molding equipment need not be discouraged. Sundials may be made from virtually any material that can be left outside: metal (steel, copper, aluminum), wood (lumber or plywood), glass (frosted, clear or stained) or Plexiglas, acrylic and other plastics. Hour lines can be etched, scribed or painted on the dial face. A 12-inch disc or square of five-eights marine-grade plywood, for example, makes a suitable face for an equatorial dial. A length of quarter-inch hardwood dowel set in the disc so that two-and-a-half or three inches protrude from the center is all that is needed for a gnomon—it must be absolutely vertical, though, so use a drill press to make the hole. The hour lines can be painted onto the disc over a couple of coats of a good-quality, nonglare exterior paint, or for a more permanent job, they can be cut, carved, routed or burned into the wood before painting.

A polar dial, with its rectangular dial face, is another candidate for plywood or lumber construction. A 24-inch length of hardwood two by six (or 30-inch length of two by eight), properly protected from the elements so that it does not warp, makes a suitable face. The gnomon can be a piece of sheet metal set firmly in a sawcut, a length of T-bar screwed in place or another piece of plywood or lumber mortised into the dial face or held by dowels or screws. The possibilities are limited only by the imagination.

A horizontal dial offers the most varied use of materials. The flat, compact face lends itself to anything from a slab of poured concrete to a bas-relief-carved piece of exotic hardwood, a sheet of hammered copper or brazed steel or perhaps a piece of plywood with hand-painted calligraphy numerals. The gnomon, too, lends itself to a full range of material choices—fit it on the dial absolutely upright, and file or rasp the top edge until it is exactly straight and angled precisely equal to the latitude. Weld it, screw it, dowel it, mortise it—whatever is appropriate—but remember, if it has any appreciable width, divide the dial face into halves along the noon line and separate them by the width of the gnomon.

In order to orient the shadow-casting edge of the gnomon with the Earth's axis, the noon line of the dial must follow a meridian of longitude; that is, it must point to the true north pole. There are several methods to determine true, or solar, north in one's garden. One is to find magnetic north with a compass, then add or subtract the magnetic declination for the site, a figure available at most libraries and weather offices. Another is to pound a six-foot stake into the ground so that is absolutely perpendicular, and mark the stake's shadow, which points to solar north precisely at solar noon (midway between sunrise and sunset, times broadcast on most television weather reports). Yet another is to align two perpendicular stakes or markers with the North Star on any night the stars are shining.

After solar north has been so carefully calculated, it would be a shame to lose the alignment through a movement of the dial caused by inadequate construction. It is not enough to nail the sundial to the top of a fencepost. To retain any degree of accuracy, the attitudes of north-south alignment, perpendicularity of the gnomon and angle of latitude must be maintained. This requires a pillar sturdy enough to withstand the ravages of weather changes, the assaults of children and the occasional bump with a wheelbarrow full of compost—a length of well casing set in concrete, well below the frost line, for instance, or a sono-tube filled with concrete. Wood set in concrete is less acceptable because it tends to swell as it absorbs moisture from the wet concrete, then shrink as the concrete dries, resulting in a slight but significant looseness that gives new meaning to the term time warp. Ancient sundiallers set their timepieces on a slab of marble, and although that may be impractical these days, a pedestal of stone or brick on a deep concrete footing is attractive, sturdy and traditional.

Whether the dial face is flat (horizontal dial) or is tipped to the north (equatorial dial) or the south (polar dial), it is wise to cap the pedestal with concrete, and because it is all but impossible to trowel the cap to the exactly correct angle, set at least four bolts in the concrete before it dries. Align the noon line to point to solar north, drill holes in the dial face that slip over the bolt thread, and use washers or double nuts to make fine adjustments to the angle of the dial face as it is bolted to the pedestal.

Why I Love Opera, & Find It Irresistibly Funny
GEORGE JONAS

· · · · · · · · · ·

My fascination with opera goes back to a Turkish lady called Fatime. More precisely, it goes back to a contest between my uncle's sense of balance and Fatime's abdominal muscle.

I should warn readers who expect a salacious story that they will be disappointed. No lady's abdominal muscle held much interest for me at the time, perhaps because I was six years old. My parents had asked me to join them at a dinner party for Fatime, a retired diva, who was visiting us with her husband. We often had operatic visitors, because my father (who had been a baritone at the Viennese Opera before giving himself up to the world of business) seemed to enjoy them, but Fatime's party was the first I was invited to attend.

As I remember it (later my mother and father were to dispute some details), the party began with Fatime standing against the wall in the blue salon. As a rule, my parents entertained only cultural guests in the blue salon. Business guests were usually herded into the dining hall, underneath Beethoven's deathmask, where the seating arrangements were more formal. But that night it was only Fatime with her husband, along with my uncle and aunt, and maybe two or three other people. This was probably why I was allowed to take my meal with the guests, though of course I was served at a separate table.

Fatime spoke German fearlessly, albeit with an intriguing Turkish flavor. Her rich alto was booming across the room. "Belly is rock, rock is belly," she declared, as if she were quoting Keats. "The voice is all belly. You say to me, a singer has the voice by the throat? I reply: Ha-ha! I show you."

George Jonas (born 1935) established himself as a poet, playwright and radio producer in Toronto before he became well known for books about crime and the law, such as By Persons Unknown *(1977, with Barbara Amiel) and* Vengeance *(1984). The following piece is from* The Idler, *January-February 1988.*

Her glance fell on my unfortunate uncle. "I want that you push me!" she commanded. "Not where you sit like mushroom, but standing on legs like real man."

I looked up from my plate. Clearly, the conversation was taking an interesting turn. Fatime, her splendid abdominal muscle wrapped in a minimum of silk, was resting her back against the wall. "In belly," she instructed my uncle. "Not poke-poke-poke like chicken, but push! Make a ball with your, how you call them, fingers."

"With your fist, you know, there's a good man," suggested the Freiherr von X., whose name I no longer recall, but who had the rare fortune to be married to Fatime. "I often do it at home. You won't get any peace until you push her."

"You push like chicken," Fatime said to her husband, not without tenderness. "Maybe he push like man."

My uncle certainly had the bulk; what he may have lacked was the heart. He was a manufacturer of red as well as yellow bricks, born as Geza Stiglitz, but by then the possessor of a much more melodious name. My father, a man with some capacity for mental cruelty, had nicknamed him "Stiglitz the Nimrod" many years earlier, soon after learning that Uncle had joined a rather exclusive hunting club. This was not because my father objected to people shooting—or even to people named Stiglitz—but only because he objected to people named Stiglitz shooting for social reasons.

My uncle, who was strictly a social shooter, hesitated for a second, then essayed a tentative push against the undulating silk. "Ha!" said Fatime derisively. "My nanny-goat push more, when little girl in Anatolia. Push like you give birth to locomotive."

A suggestible man, my uncle paled. "Please, dear lady," he whispered, "I'm quite heavy, I could hurt you by accident."

"Push!"

My uncle closed his eyes and began to push. He was pushing, stiii cautiously at first, then in earnest. Finally, he was driving his fist into Fatime's abdomen hard enough for the carpet to begin sliding under his feet.

"Good, just hold table with free hand," Fatime advised him contemptuously. "Now I will sing you."

My father, who must have known what was coming, had already seated himself at the piano. The black Bechstein roared to life, and so did Fatime's abdominal muscle. "*Stride la vampa!*" she began ominously, in the accents of Verdi's gypsy lady, her famous rôle in Vienna and Milan. Frightened and hopelessly off balance, with the rug slowly slipping out from under his feet, my uncle was no longer in a position to withdraw his fist. "*Sinistra splende sui volti orribili,*" Fatime insisted, staring into the middle distance. "*La tetra fiamma che s'alza al ciel!*"

Picture, if you will, the situation from my point of view. I was not particularly backward for my age, but until then I had led a rather sheltered life. It was my first operatic dinner party, and I was anxious to make a good impression, but it was a challenging spectacle for a six-year-old. There was Stiglitz the Nimrod, as red in the face as any of his bricks, balancing his entire bulk upon the belly of a well-dressed Turkish lady, who by then was screaming "*Grido feroce di morte levasi!*" at the top of her lungs.

Any healthy boy could see that it was to be a race between the aria and the heavy Persian rug, which was sliding as slowly but as inexorably as a glacier from under my uncle's feet. Fatime, unperturbed, looked quite ready to go the distance. My father would eventually explain that Uncle did have an outside chance, because Azucena's tale was not a long one by Verdi's standards. But my uncle, who had never been exposed to *Il Trovatore*, had no way of knowing that. His expression soon began showing that abandonment of all hope that the Italian travel writer Dante Alighieri remarked upon in connection with one of his trips.

A brick manufacturer leaning at a 45-degree angle is not a dignified sight, and it doesn't help matters when he appears to be coaxing dark and powerful musical notes from the belly of a fat lady in silk. My behavior didn't help, either. The fact is, I pointed my finger at them and began turning purple.

Later my father called me an annoying child. It was not a supportive comment but it was not inaccurate. To say that I laughed would not begin to describe my reaction at the end of Azucena's lament. I howled. I hooted. I'm afraid I actually stomped my feet, while my poor Uncle slid slowly to the floor, still hinged, as it were, to Fatime's belly by one fist.

· · · · · · · · · ·

My musical education had commenced some years before this incident. My father believed that any civilized child should be able to play Clementi's *Sonatina* by the age of four, but my disgraceful behavior at the dinner party convinced both of my parents that Herr Miller's piano lessons were insufficient. Opera especially, my father felt, had to be approached in a different light. "For example," he said to me, "ignorant people look at *Lohengrin,* and they say that you can't rely on German swans running exactly on schedule."

"Well, of course, any fool knows that you can't rely on German swans. The great Leo Schlezak discovered that at the Metropolitan in New York when they dragged his own swan offstage before he could mount it, causing him to step into the river. But it made no difference. Schlezak, a tenor of great dignity drunk or sober, simply asked '*Wann kommt der nächste Schwann?*' as if he were at a train station in Berlin, and everybody knew that he was still Parsifal's son, damn it! You don't measure opera by puny standards!"

Perhaps it should be noted that this phase in my life occurred in the spring of 1941. Though Hitler was already preparing for Operation Barbarossa, the Molotov-Ribbentrop pact still held. Initially, the pact had deeply disturbed everyone in our liberal circles, except my father, who thought that it was a perfect treaty between two identical systems. "Isn't it logical for the Nazis to be allied with the Communists?" he kept consoling his suicidal friends. "Isn't it natural? The unnatural thing would be for the great democracies to be allied with either one of them."

As it turned out, my operatic education continued against the backdrop of just such an unnatural development. "So, Stalin is now a friend of Roosevelt's," my father offered, "yet some people find it incredible that Azucena should throw her own baby into the fire instead of the old count di Luna's. Well, Azucena was a simple gypsy, while Roosevelt, for instance, is a man of education. He is Felix Frankfurter's buddy. Yet, if you ask me, if Roosevelt doesn't watch out, he could end up throwing his baby into the fire by mistake, as easily as Azucena."

Opera does arouse a certain kind of enthusiasm in people, my father explained. He gave the example of an incident that had happened at the Budapest Opera, when Anna Medek performed there shortly after the turn of the century. The orchestra was conducted by the famous Toccani, and at the end of the first act a gentleman set up a rhythmic chant, shouting "Medek! Toccani!" over and over again. He obviously liked the performance, and he may have forgotten that in Hungarian the words he kept yelling amounted to a statement of his intention to defecate without delay. "Go, by all means," someone said to him at last. "But why must you announce it?"

My father likened the incident to the Nuremberg rallies. "You shouldn't stretch the parallel too far, of course," he cautioned, "but it's a fact that many people don't know what they are shouting when they get carried away."

Operas were absurd, but they were majestic; it was silly for people to criticize them in the name of reality, my father suggested, when reality was just as absurd and often devoid of any majesty. "I've known some modern realists," he mused, "who walked out of *Tosca* because of Scarpia's behavior in the second act. Well, perhaps Scarpia does act a little melodramatically—but then I've watched the selfsame realists sitting glued to the radio, listening to Mussolini speak."

Some years later—this is an aside—my father and I were watching a newsreel showing the bodies of Mussolini and his mistress hanging by the heels from a pole outside a gas station. "Scarpia?" I asked him. *Sotto voce*, but with the wicked smile of someone proved correct by history itself, my father sang his reply: "*E avanti a lui tremava tutta Roma!*"

One could sympathize with Madame Tosca's curtain line: by 1945, indeed, it was hard to imagine all of Rome trembling before a charred side of beef, in trousers, hanging from a pole. However, in 1941 the curtain was still a long way from falling.

I continued my operatic education while the fall of Moscow seemed imminent to many realists who considered operas absurd. My father was virtually alone in the view that Hitler would have had second thoughts about invading Russia if he had known, in addition to his favorite composer Wagner, the operas of Borodin. The German high command should have especially listened to Prince Igor's great baritone air, "*Oh dahtye, dahtye mnye svobodu,*" which gave some indication of how Russians might react to the idea of foreign, as opposed to domestic, servitude. My father immediately sang Igor's aria for me, in a comic version, of course. He accompanied himself on the black Bechstein, roaring with laughter, until my mother bade him stop.

Soon after our musical soirée, my socially ambitious uncle Nimrod was taken to a labor camp called Bor, quite famous in its time, in Nazi-occupied Serbia. Fatime and the Freiherr von X. began holding séances as the best means of communicating with their only son, Martin, who had disappeared at the Russian front. Except for the *Götterdämmerung,* I don't remember hearing any opera. The music on the radio was mainly brass in those years. The Gestapo had discovered other uses for piano wire.

Where the Hell is Ebeye?
KIM ECHLIN

· · · · · · · · · ·

The day I met Hope, she was burying her third child. We were gathered in a two-room plywood shack that was home to 24 people. They slept in shifts. The child, Matthew, was laid out on a white cloth on the floor, fragrant with flowers. In the coral yard outside, Hope's brothers were getting drunk.

Matthew was just past his first birthday—naming day—when he developed diarrhea. Hope was out playing bingo. In less than 36 hours he was dead of dehydration.

Four men carried the child's coffin to the graveyard on ocean-side. Sun-bleached gravestones, one tight against the next, cut white silhouettes against the grey shacks and the Pacific sky. Small children crowded curiously over the box, fanning flies from the tiny still face with scraps of white cloth. Matthew's grandmother, a bent old woman missing her right big toe, leaned against the headstone. Her granddaughter brought her a pair of plastic thongs to wear for the ceremony. Women drifted into the coral graveyard.

The men leaned on a fence outside the death circle. One of them wore a green baseball hat that said: *Where the hell is Ebeye*. A pastor stepped forward. In seven days time they would gather again when the cat rose out of the ocean to take the child into the sea. The pastor prayed.

· · · · · · · · · ·

Ebeye is on the Kwajalein lagoon in the Marshall Islands between Hawaii and Japan. Military people call the lagoon the "catcher's mitt of the Pacific." It bristles with the most sophisticated radar tracking equipment in the world. The tracking system is called KREM: Kiernan Re-entry Measurement Site and is located on the island of Roi Namur at the north end of the atoll. KREM tracks MX missiles launched from Vandenburg, California.

In earlier travels, I had sailed in the Marshalls and heard the traditional stories of the outer islands. I heard too about testing the first hydrogen

Kim Echlin (born 1955) works at CBC television as an arts producer for The Journal, *and is currently writing a biography of Elizabeth Smart. This essay is taken from the Winter 1988 issue of* Border/Lines.

bombs at Bikini. Back at home again, I began to read about Kwajalein and Ebeye. I read that the people were living a kind of living death on this lagoon. They called Ebeye the "Calcutta of the Pacific." I didn't believe it. So I went to see.

When you arrive on Kwajalein they line you up against a wall and a military man barks out the rules of the island. Drooling dogs sniff your bags. You try to find your balance in the exotic, disorienting heat of the equator. Even your toes are hot. On Kwajalein, a small group of American military personnel supervises 3,000 civilian workers—top technicians, scientists and maintenance staff and their families. The base has been developed by the United States since World War II to fulfill a dream best expressed by Senator Barry Goldwater: "We want to be able to drop a nuke into the men's room at the Kremlin." The week before I arrived, one of the missiles from California hit Kwajalein's own electrical generator. The official army statement: "The missile was right on target."

Across the lagoon, 20 minutes away, is Ebeye—78 acres in size, home to 10,000 people. Some people have been moved to Ebeye from other islands around the lagoon for security purposes. Many have moved there from the outer islands to try to get work. Here the days are as long as the nights. Ebeye is one of the few places in the world you can see the Southern Cross and the Big Dipper in the sky at the same time. At noon children nap in any narrow band of shade, under any scrap of cardboard or corrugated metal. There are no trees. There is no space. Yet people continue to arrive and the birth rate is 1.5 per day. About 9% of Ebeye's population gets on the barge each day to commute over to the base at Kwajalein where they work as laborers and maids.

There are Americans who have lived on the Kwajalein lagoon for 20 years and never set foot on Ebeye. Those who go to Ebeye—mostly young men— go there to drink and find women, to forget a loneliness that stings worse than salt. That's how Hope got pregnant.

• • • • • • • • • •

They nailed the coffin shut dark over the sweet hibiscus flowers and the child's face too innocent to bury. Tears rolled down Hope's cheeks as she stared into the unforgiving coral.

The child's father had never seen the boy. He was a Filipino worker stationed on Kwajalein. Some strange intuition had made him send a message to Hope that very morning—his first in a year. He wanted to see her. He wanted to see his son.

After the funeral Hope walked down to the barge. "What am I going to say to him? I'll say I buried the child this morning ... What if he blames me? ... but one thing sure, I won't get pregnant again this time ..."

The dissonance of mourning twisted her smile, "But if I do, well that happens, that's life too mum."

We stood together looking across the lagoon to Kwajalein. The flat coral skyline was broken by white satellite dishes and sleek high-tech towers. They cut the endless Pacific blues of sea and sky with the same salt-white gleam as the white gravestones on the other side of Ebeye.

Almost Heaven: Kwajalein

When I arrived on the lagoon I spent the first few days on the American base before going to stay on Ebeye. A tour of an American military testing facility is a study in public relations. Double talk here is the *lingua franca*, necessary or not.

Kwajalein is a community designed to be a middle American utopia. Walden III. There are no private cars—everyone rides bicycles or takes a shuttle service. People play tennis, softball, golf. On weekends, they sail, swim, sun. The highest per capita density of scuba divers in the world is on Kwajalein. Healthy young people live out their adolescence in this invented island paradise. There is almost no crime. The television diet is CNN and the movies are Hollywood. People wear t-shirts that say: *Kwajalein: Almost Heaven.*

But utopias are built on dreams of conformity. They hide whatever threatens their perfection.

A few years ago Kwajalein was suffering morale problems. Ebeye workers were striking. Greenpeace got on the island and strung up anti-nuclear signs. A group of Marshallese landowners staged "sail-ins" to draw attention to their concerns over land payments and living conditions on Ebeye. Maids were forbidden on the island. A new colonel was brought in to straighten things out.

Everyone says that life is better under Colonel Chapman. Marshallese domestics are back on the base. The curfew for Marshallese on Kwajalein has been eased and Marshallese are allowed once again into the snack bar. One hundred Marshallese a day can visit Kwajalein. They line up for passes. Friday is the best day to go because that's lawn sale day. Marshallese aren't allowed into the department store but they can go to lawn sales.

During my visit, I was assigned a public relations officer and permitted access to the base. I visited the *Yokwe* Club. I sat in the outdoor bachelor's club. I listened. The two biggest problems: isolation, boredom. I met a young man from Texas who had arrived 18 months ago. He was so lonely you could feel it in his breath.

"It's good to talk to someone new. Out here there's hardly any women and after you talk to the guys a while you know just about what they're gonna say.

What do I do? Watch videos, work out in the weight room.

"No I've never been to Ebeye. It gets pretty wild over there I heard. A lot of drinking, people fighting over women. One guy who lives there got beat up pretty good with a two-by-four I heard. Guess I don't need that. Those people are just lazy. Why don't they clean the place up."

I visited the Protestant chaplain and learned that it was his first time in the Pacific too. The young man ushered me into his small office littered with books and papers. He described his mission in a mid-western drawl.

"I was hired principally because I can do counselling," he said. "The problems I deal with ... marriage counselling, isolation ... many of the young men here are away from home for the first time.

"As far as the Marshallese go, well, we want to *share* with them, we have a policy of *cultural exchange*." He lingered over the new words issued direct from Colonel Chapman.

"What can the Marshallese share?"

There was a long pause in the room. The clock ticked. He blushed in the cold blast of air-conditioning.

"Well ... they can share their singing."

"When you go to Ebeye do you participate in their services?"

"I don't go to Ebeye. I'm hired by Global ... that's the contractor that takes care of all the day to day concerns of the island ... our restaurants, supplies, the department store, recreation, the church. My responsibility is to the people here ... that's what I was hired for."

The young man shifted in his seat. Man of god. Hired by Global.

• • • • • • • • • •

The chaplain's attitude was consistent with each culture's different notion of story-telling—oral and written. The Americans feel there is no reason to be curious about the Marshallese people or language or history because the Marshallese themselves have never recorded their history. It is the classic tale of technological cultures consuming non-technological cultures. Americans would say casually "They're losing their culture" as if it were a small coin dropped into the ocean. They always perceived the Marshallese as most satisfactory when they appeared to share the aspirations and manners of middle-class Americans.

Most Americans on Kwajalein are afraid to visit Ebeye. They make frequent comparisons with Tijuana. Their idea of cultural exchange is to observe quaint customs and sell handicrafts in the airport store. They see Ebeye as an unsolvable problem which has little to do with them. They blame the Marshallese for lacking in initiative and for being dirty. They prefer cliched and comfortable notions of poverty learned from their ghettos back

home. They are afraid to step across the lagoon to see their own leased island
from another point of view.

Across the Lagoon

People on Ebeye call one end of the island *Rocktown* and the
other end *The Dump*. You can walk from Rocktown to The Dump in about 15
minutes. Tucked into the shadows of shanty housing are pinball machines.
Through doorways blue kung-fu videos flicker on TV screens. Budweiser
consumption is high, but there is no social drinking. You drink to get drunk.
You drink to forget. Young people hang around the corners of the rows of
houses, all day, all night. Over 50% of the population is under 15 years old
and there is no public high school. Teen suicide is the highest in the world.
Boys and young men join gangs: The Octopus, The Sharks, The Leskan
(Spear-mouths), and The OKK. OKK stands for Olim (no money), Konta
(begging), Kicko (hustling girls).

Dribo Dribo is the Ebeye probation officer. He studied social work at
Washington State University. Giant cockroaches skitter across the concrete
walls and floor of his office in the police station. He wants to talk. Softly.
Slowly.

"What are the charges? Assault and battery. Burglary. Vandalism. They
want money to go to the restaurant. They have no way to get money.

"The girls have groups too—Jinlij (T-shirts) and Jeite (runaways). One of
my cases was a 14 year old girl who ran away and started living with a boy. Her
grandmother called me to find the girl but she didn't want to go back. She
told me her grandfather raped her. In your country I would tell authorities
and we'd charge the old man, but I couldn't do it here. I talked to her
parents. I got them to take her back. I told the old man to find some way to
tell his wife the girl wasn't coming back. I couldn't break the old lady's
heart."

Everyone knows everyone on a small island. People are related to each
other. Dribo Dribo's training in Washington doesn't work here. He says, "I
have to work between the law and the traditional way."

Dribo Dribo shares with every other Marshallese a political matrix which
is bound to the centuries-old law of the *irooj*—the traditional leader. The
irooj divides up goods and responsibilities in the community. His word is law.
But the new written law of the Marshalls, the 1986 constitution formed under
a Compact of Free Association with the United States, contradicts tradition.
The new written law was created by American lawyers. It is based on the
American traditions of the nuclear family, individual liberties, competition
and free enterprise.

To spend time on Ebeye is to acquire a fluency in contradiction—the body uncomfortably trying to scratch its own bones. Dribo Dribo, raised in Marshall custom, trained in American ways, looks uncomfortably over his shoulder at the long shadow of the *irooj*.

The Kabuas

In the late 19th century a Marshallese *irooj* called Kabua exchanged the right to trade copra (dried coconut) for gold, a German ship and a German captain's uniform. Copra is the principle commodity traded in the Marshalls—first with the Germans and Japanese, now with the Americans.

The Kabua family is the oldest and most powerful family in the Marshall Islands. They are traditional leaders—the *irooj lap-lap*. Today Amata Kabua is president of the first Republic of the Marshall Islands and his son, Imada Kabua is the *irooj* of Ebeye. They own a lot of land and traditionally the family has produced great navigators. More recently their power has come from negotiating with the American government over compensation payments for nuclear testing and land lease and rental moneys. The family is extremely wealthy. They often visit Hawaii. They are known for their lavish evenings in Waikiki hotels. Mike Kabua is the youngest son. He has built a tiny, private world on Ebeye. It's a club. It's called Mike's.

Inside Mike's, the dirty beaches, the crowded shacks pressing up against the scarred skyline disappear like bad memories. It could be any club in the world. The walls open to an enclosed patio. In a back room men gamble at a Chinese game called *pokai*. Thousands of American dollars pass across the table. Inside Mike's place the colliding fantasies of Ebeye and America appear in fixed relief.

Mike Kabua is 42. During the day he wears dark glasses, dark green army fatigues and gold rings. His face is pock-marked. He is unmarried.

We sit out on the patio. "I built this whole place from an idea in my head. There were no written plans. Next year this trellis will have more plants. I leave this side open, I like to be able to see the sky."

Mike is called away to oversee new carpeting for the gambling room. He has told me before how much he likes to see the sky. The old Marshallese night sky holds the secrets of navigation. Stars and wave patterns showed the ancient navigators where they were and where they were going. When Mike returns he calls for a bottle of white wine—rare on Ebeye. He has a Filipino businesswoman named Gigi with him and we drink. No one can refuse the hospitality of an *irooj*. He is flattered when Gigi tells him he "has class." Our talk turns to travel—an empty litany of place names.

"I've been everywhere in Europe, I was all over the United States—often in Washington. I was in Vancouver and Niagara Falls. In Buffalo they had a celebration for me and they gave me a key to the city. I asked them if it would open all the banks of America."

We laugh. We talk about Mike's native island of Ebon, the southern atoll where he grew up. I told him a myth I heard there of the lovely, proud woman who bathes each evening on the reef—she makes the sunset streak orange and red, the most beautiful sunset in the Marshalls. Mike answers, "I was raised on Ebon by my grandparents and I learned to fish there. I heard the old stories ... but I feel them pulling away ..." He pulled his two hands invisibly against each other in the air. "Culture is always changing but I see this change with sadness ..."

Michael Kabua doesn't know how to navigate and he doesn't fish much anymore. His dream, when the bar is finished, is to start a market to sell fish and local foods to Kwajalein. Give the people a way to make money. Mike Kabua was sent to business school in Orange County before he came back to settle on Ebeye. When I asked him who he sees in Honolulu, he answered with a sly grin, "Imelda Marcos."

The traditional leadership of the Marshalls has been particularly unprepared for the world to move in. From their first encounters with the Germans they quickly used their power to acquire the foreign goods which in their culture signalled social status and prestige. The German captain's uniform and the American bar take on a multiple significance. Nothing about Ebeye seems fixed. The buildings themselves seem ready to blow away into the sky. And as the traditional leadership tries to fix things—divert local money, hold onto their land—new problems are created. Take, for example, the legendary stainless steel trailer at The Dump.

The trailer used to belong to a respected *irooj* called Lejallin. Lejallin died some years ago but traditional custom dictates that no one may enter the home of a dead *irooj*. In the days of woven huts, the house blew down in a year or two and then the land could be used once again. But a stainless steel trailer doesn't blow down. It resists even the merciless salt of the Pacific and Lejallin's trailer stands untouched. Lots of stories have grown up around the trailer. Stories repeated because they express the hidden fears and desires of the people. It is said that money is hidden in the trailer. Once two young boys went inside to get the money. One boy became sick and died and the other was so fearful he hanged himself. Lejallin's trailer is still there, taking up precious land, and I was shooed away when I went to look. Stories usually express a couple of sliding truths. On Ebeye the *irooj* still commands respect, still carries the power of tradition. But today the young people on Ebeye are beginning to defy the customary privilege of their leaders. Like the two young hero-rebels of the whispered myth, they are daring the forbidden and entering where only their *irooj* have gone before. How far they will go, how far the *irooj* can allow it, or control it, has not yet been tested.

Politicians Are Good Liars And Bad Liars

The elected mayor of Ebeye is a young radical called Alvin Jacklick. I visited him in a spacious, air-conditioned office that also houses the Kwajalein Atoll Development Association (KADA). This group has fought for control of land rental payments made to the Marshallese government each year by the United States. Alvin Jacklick wears a t-shirt and leans back in his leather chair. A wide desk separates us and behind him are pictures of his family and a model outrigger canoe. It is an office that foreigners understand. Jacklick was elected in 1983 after four years of voluntary work in the Kwajalein administration office. Alvin Jacklick understands the difference between an oral and a written tradition. His language has the foretold quality of someone who believes he knows the end.

"I grew up on the ocean. My father was a navigator, and an engineer trained by the Japanese. I sailed all over the atoll and to other atolls with him—to Likiep, to Majuro.

"In 1970, I wanted to go to school at the University of Washington in Seattle. They stopped me in Honolulu because the Marshallese government hadn't sent my papers. But I got through anyway.

"What made me different? I wasn't dependent on my parents. I wanted to replace the magistrate on Kwajalein. A few days before I left I went to him and said, 'Murph, I'm going to school in Seattle for four years. When I come back I'm going to replace you.'

"Murph said, 'I never heard a Marshallese guy talk like that.' Then he pulled out his wallet and gave me everything that was in it—$300—and he said, 'I want to thank you for saying that to me.'

"In our traditional way, the child is dependent on the grandparents and everyone is dependent on the *irooj*. But what do I do if I'm a young man on Ebeye with two or three children. Should I have to go to my grandfather and ask for $10 to feed my family? In the extended family everyone is dependent on the head of the household."

The covey of new young leadership on Ebeye is staking out its power with an inexperienced, nervous intelligence. They talk openly of the failure of the irooj system. They eat lunch with American lawyers, drink at Mike's place with visiting officials. Alvin Jacklick calls himself a politician, and when I ask whether the radical changes he proposes will work he winks ironically, "Politicians are good liars and bad liars ... The time will come for the Marshallese people to decide between the traditional power of the *irooj* and the freedom of democracy. A lot of young people now reject the traditional leaders."

"Will it work?"

"The question remains to be answered."

Under Alvin Jacklick the island has already got a sanitation system, running water and a desalination plant. Jacklick intends to take over public safety and the miserably understaffed departments of education and health before the end of the year.

The nervousness of the new leadership comes from trying to sail a new kind of vessel. As I made ready to leave, Jacklick repeated a Marshallese proverb. "*Jela turin jela* ... this means knowing beside the real knowing, to pretend to understand what you really don't. It's a dangerous quality in leadership."

Alvin Jacklick has contemplated power. In the United States. In the Marshall Islands. Alvin Jacklick grew up on the ocean. He knows how shifting winds and hidden currents change the course of a ship. The navigator learns about the waves and the stars from the old men before he sails alone. But when he sails alone, it is he who must bring the ship safely back home.

Poorest Of The Poor

Outsiders often see Ebeye as a nightmare romance of the tropics, a *Heart of Darkness*, a place in which any outrage can be tolerated and a place no one would choose to live. But to believe this is to miss Ebeye.

Plenty of people have *chosen* Ebeye as home. There is Ben Barry, a black American from Texas. He chose Ebeye 20 years ago. He escaped marriage and kids and a living death in a factory in southern Texas. He was hooked on heroin in the Korean war. He kicked it and became a sailor. He worked a stint on the Kwajalein base then moved to Ebeye. Today he deals *pokai* in the back of Mike's place. The Kabuas take care of him. His story is still punctuated with trying to comprehend the incomprehensible—the racism he suffered at home. "How come I stay here on Ebeye?" says Ben, "I been a lot of places and this is the first place on earth ever took me just the way I am."

There is Father Hacker. Father Hacker is a Jesuit from Buffalo, New York. He was a Second World War prisoner in a Japanese camp. After that he came to the Marshalls. He's built two churches and two different congregations— one on Majuro, one on Ebeye. He preaches in Marshallese each Sunday to a crowded church. He worked closely with the Marshallese Bible translation project. He has a boys' marching band and he runs a small school. When I asked him if he thought the Ebeye children were growing up in two worlds he spluttered impatiently, "Of course they don't live in two worlds, they make it one world."

There is Bobby, the Filipino who will sell you anything. Bobby is one of those outsiders who imagines Ebeye as a kind of colonial opportunity to be tapped. Bobby commutes to his job on Kwajalein each day but on Ebeye he also runs a *jeepnee*, a garishly painted Filipino bus. He was importing power boats from Denver while I was there and opening a restaurant and toying with the idea of a water taxi service to and from Kwajalein. Bobby was on the make. Ebeye was the place he chose to make it.

Ebeye has its liminal groups too. A few Vietnam vets who scratch out a living and hang around bars with the mile long stare. Marshallese from the outer islands who come and live off their relatives and ride around and around in taxis. The people who live in the Shelter.

The Shelter is a large echoing concrete building that used to be a recreation area for the public school. There was a fire in 1982 that swept over The Dump end of the island and threatened to raze the whole place. People ran out of their shacks and watched as the flames leapt from one house to another in seconds. Only the ocean itself could stop the flames. Small buckets flew from hand to hand. A few men started ploughing down the tiny rooms of birth and life and death with construction tractors. In this way they stopped the fire.

Half The Dump got destroyed in that fire. Some people never rebuilt. Maybe the sight of the fire burned away their desire. They huddled in corners and stayed in The Shelter. They marked out space with large mats. They ran a long cord in through the door and plugged in their televisions. They played bingo. Children began again to be born. Infant mortality here is the highest on Ebeye. The kids who survive are neither from The Dump nor Rocktown. They are from The Shelter. They are malnourished. They don't go to school. On Ebeye, they are the poorest of the poor.

School Days

There is one small private high school on Ebeye—run by the Seventh Day Adventist Church. Facilities, teachers, space are all inadequate.

The principal's wife told me this story. One day a boy came to her and asked to be admitted. They were overcrowded and she couldn't allow him in. Each year they turn away students. When the boy went home his father beat him. That night the boy hanged himself.

Tell Me A Story

There is a precise point at which the Americans on Kwajalein and the Marshallese on Ebeye fail to connect. It is in their sense of story-telling. For Americans, raised on television serials and Aristotle, each story must have a beginning, middle and end. But for the Marshallese, raised on oral narrative, stories are constantly shifting and adapting, told, retold, modified, only the most sacred details remain fixed. The law of the ocean is eternal and moving. If the Marshallese people believe that the effects of nuclear testing will never end, it is because their sense of history has taught them to believe that time has no terminal point. Western myth tells of holocausts and revelations that play out the end. But Marshallese myth depicts history as a continuum of human stories, of gods and tides and wave patterns forever interconnected. And the ongoing, unanticipated effects of western nuclear weapons on Marshallese bodies and culture substantiate *their* view of history. There is no end.

Marshallese people talk, incomprehensibly to the Americans, of a time when the Americans will leave their lagoon. The Germans have come and gone. The Japanese have come and gone. Why not the Americans?

The Americans, on the other hand, know that a conclusion must be reached—the denouement played out. Fixed as Americans are on the narrative of the melting pot, they do not understand that assimilation is not even considered by most Ebeyans. Nor do many Americans understand that their presence in the lagoon is still at the deepest level construed by Ebeyans as a temporary condition, a political option shaped by continuing compensation payments and leases for the land and lagoon.

The latest twist in the plot is to assimilate a limited number of Marshallese children into the American school system on Kwajalein.

In 1987, five Marshallese children were chosen to use the educational facilities of Kwajalein. They leave Ebeye on the morning barge with their teacher, Atota, and spend half a day in the kindergarten and half a day in the nursery school. Next year they will go on to first grade and a new group of five will enter the system. If the program continues there will be 75 Ebeye children in the American school system on Kwajalein by the time the first group reaches 12th grade. But when they go home to Ebeye each night, they return to an island with no public high school, where most of the population has nothing to do but wait.

Kathy is the nursery school teacher on Kwajalein. She is an enthusiastic observer of the children's progress.

"It's a great opportunity for them. Of course there were cultural differences at first. You saw this morning with our reading books. They had trouble identifying the pictures of the elevator, of the banjo. But they'll adapt.

"What improvements would I like to see? Well, there is one thing. I'd like to forbid them absolutely to speak Marshallese on the island. When they have a problem they always go to Atota, the teacher's aide, and speak Marshallese. We don't know what's going on, they don't learn how to *cope.*"

The American melting pot. Get them young. Forbid their language. Like most people on Kwajalein, Kathy has never taken the free 20-minute barge to the island across the lagoon. She has never been to Ebeye.

Ugly Riballe—Go Back To Kwajalein

Riballe means "clothes-wearer" and is used for whites. It survives from early mission days. I met one young Marshallese man who was mistaken for a *riballe*. His name was Qew.

Qew was visiting the island as a translator for a documentary film maker. He had been away studying in California for five years. He dressed and talked like a Californian. Lots of people didn't recognize him as Marshallese when he was with Americans. One day we walked by a group of shouting children and he laughed.

"Know what they just said to me—they said, 'Ugly *riballe*, go back to Kwajalein!'"

Qew was worried about what to do when he finished school. As we sat eating sashimi in his uncle's restaurant, he paused and looked around the room—six small tables and Pacific pop music rattling out of the speakers held by a nail to the wall. "All I know is I'd like to come back but I don't know what I could do here now. My friends all drink too much. Americans are the stupidest and the smartest. They've brought the best and worst. Now, what can we do with it?"

• • • • • • • • • •

The most peaceful time of day on Ebeye is twilight. Small children hush their crying. The long struggle of each day to get to evening is finally over. The fears of the night have not yet set in.

I liked to go down to the wharf at twilight. Men and boys fished each night. They shared bait and lines and gazed out on the water. They watched the evening barge come in. Workers came home carrying coolers of ice. Small boys ran around the wharf and little girls tipped their chins forward and twirled their braids in a circle around their heads. Handstands were the latest fad among the children. They clustered in small groups flipping upside down.

The West has created a myth of the idyllic Pacific paradise. The West loves *Robinson Crusoe*. It buys Gauguin's paintings of thick women with flowers in their hair. It produces *South Pacific* for Broadway and takes the middle classes to Pacific Club Meds. It is ironic that the West has never met the people of the Pacific.

When I left Ebeye, Qew saw me off at the barge. I stood on deck looking back at the island until it disappeared into the dusk of the blue lagoon. The island where I'd heard a thousand stories jumbled together like shanty housing. The island where I'd seen ten thousand faces waiting. The barge bumped against the dock and I felt the dull thud of Kwajalein. I felt the dull thud of turning away and already I was half-way home.

If Kennedy Had Lived
RAY ARGYLE

· · · · · · · · · ·

There he was, striding along the beach, splashing water as he went, as alert at 70 as when he was president, his hair now turning gray, his face a bit puffy maybe, but smiling still, displaying all the charisma and character that propelled him into the White House in 1960, saw him survive an attempt on his life in 1963, and returned him in 1964 for a second, magnificent term as President of the United States.

When he walked on the Florida beach, tourists still crowded around him, calling out, "How'ya doin', Jack!" He didn't often mix in public these days, but he still obviously relished the public acclaim he had known for more than 40 years. He divided his time between the Kennedy compound at Hyannis Port, the family's Florida home at Palm Beach, and his town house in Washington. By 1988, he had become the unchallenged "elder statesman" of American public life.

John F. Kennedy's two terms in the White House put him at the apex of American life during one of the most triumphant and tragic decades in the nation's history. He nurtured a civil rights revolution that brought millions of blacks into the political and economic mainstream. He supported the women's movement, and sympathized with the spirit of the Woodstock generation even if he couldn't join the restless young people who sang of a new approach to life at rock concerts across the nation. He was unable to save Vietnam from communism, but neither did he permit the U.S. to be drawn into a long, hopeless struggle which he knew it couldn't win. And he suffered the personal tragedy of losing a brother to an assassin's bullet, just as he saw such historic figures as Martin Luther King Jr. die in the crucible of the social revolution that marked the 1960s.

America almost lost JFK that day in Dallas, back on 22 Nov. 1963 when that crazy Lee Harvey Oswald took a shot at him from the sixth floor of the Texas

Ray Argyle (born 1929) worked for British United Press and later managed the syndication service of the old Toronto Telegram. *He is now chairman of Argyle Communications in Toronto and the publisher of* Video Scene, *in whose August 1988 issue this piece appeared.*

School Book Depository. Oswald's first bullet creased Kennedy's scalp, but spared his life. The gunman's second bullet took the life of the man who rode beside Jack and his wife Jackie on that otherwise pleasant late fall day, Texas Governor John Connally.

Another Texan, Lyndon Baynes Johnson, was sworn in as acting president as JFK underwent sensitive but blessedly brief surgery that afternoon in Parkland Memorial Hospital. Johnson never had to carry out anything more than the most routine of presidential duties; JFK returned to the Oval Office early in 1964, his zest for life reinforced, if anything, by his Dallas experience. A centimeter's difference in the trajectory of the bullet that hit JFK would have cost him his life.

It was public knowledge that President Kennedy had always been fatalistic about the possibility of an assassination. Now that he had survived an attempt on his life, he was determined to move quickly on his major priorities: economic growth, a full measure of civil rights for all citizens, and a resolution of the nuclear arms race. He felt he was being given a second chance, and wanted to build on the momentum that flowed from the outpouring of public support over his narrow survival.

On 12 July 1964 President Kennedy signed into law a Civil Rights Act that, among other things, guaranteed all citizens the right to vote. He saw the discrimination that Negroes (as they were still referred to) had to live with and judged, correctly, that until they became a voting force to reckon with, progress would be slight.

The presidential election of 1964 was never in doubt. The Republicans nominated an Arizona senator, Barry Goldwater, but on 3 Nov. JFK and Vice President Johnson carried all 50 states, winning a record 63% of the popular vote. There remained one piece of unfinished business, however: on 6 Dec. 1964, Lee Harvey Oswald was sentenced in a Dallas court to concurrent terms of life imprisonment for the killings of Gov. Connally and Officer J.D. Tippitt. A few years later, Oswald would die in a prison brawl.

Vietnam was already a divided country when John F. Kennedy took office in 1961. The old French colony of Indochina had been cut in half—communist and non-communist—at the Geneva peace conference of 1954.

In a debate in the Senate that year, young Senator Kennedy set out the views that would guide him in his future presidency. It would be "dangerously futile and self-destructive," he declared, "to pour money, materials and men into the jungles of Indochina without at least a remote prospect of victory."

Kennedy had learned from the Bay of Pigs fiasco that U.S. military intelligence could not always be relied on for either accurate information or sound judgment. He knew he would have to take personal responsibility for whatever decision he reached in Vietnam, just as he had taken personal responsibility for the Bay of Pigs and the Cuban missile crisis.

His suspicion of the soundness of U.S. military intelligence was put to the test early on that July morning in 1964 when North Vietnamese PT boats attacked the U.S. destroyer *Maddox*, just off the North Vietnamese coast. Many of the president's advisors sought to use the occasion to justify a full-scale American assault.

As Kennedy gathered his cabinet about him, Vice-President Johnson emerged as the loudest voice for action. "Damn those Viet Cong Commies, let's get Congress to pass a resolution authorizing the use of American forces," Johnson argued. He was supported by the Joint Chiefs of Staff. Kennedy hesitated, ruling that no decision would be made for 24 hours. He recalled his own experience as a PT boat commander. Somehow, the official version of the attack didn't ring true.

The next day, when expanded reports of the encounter reached the White House situation room, the reality became clear: the North Vietnamese had mistaken the *Maddox* for South Vietnam ships which were engaged in a shelling and sabotage mission against North Vietnam coastal towns. The North Vietnamese realized their mistake as they neared the *Maddox*, cut off their attack and beat a hasty retreat. President Kenndey decided that no direct U.S. retaliation was warranted.

Kennedy was determined to keep Vietnam out of the 1964 presidential campaign. He pledged that no American army would be sent there. But it was the growing dilemma over Vietnam that haunted Kennedy's days and nights in the White House.

The first U.S. bases in Vietnam were attacked by the Viet Cong within hours of the expiry of a brief New Year (Tet) cease fire in February 1965. A month later, the arrival of 3,500 Marines at Da Nang brought U.S. troop strength to 27,000. Gen. William C. Westmoreland, who had been named U.S. commander in Vietnam, reported that the military situation had become so desperate as to require the immediate commitment of a full American armored division. Kennedy made the fateful decision to send another 50,000 men to Southeast Asia.

"No one can pretend that South Vietnam is fighting for anything less than its very survival," President Kennedy told the nation in a TV broadcast from the Oval Office on 20 March 1965. Speaking with his familiar cadence, he told Americans: "The struggle raging across that embattled and ancient land stirs in our hearts the same sense of sympathy and outrage that Americans felt when Nazi bombers dropped their lethal cargoes on a defenseless London 25 years ago. Only this time, we shall not wait for the enemy to come to our shores, as we waited a generation ago. We shall go to his."

President Kennedy's rating in public opinion polls soared in the days after his speech. But it was a speech he would always regret. The arrival of American fighting men in South Vietnam raised the morale of the South Vietnamese government and its army. But the presence of the U.S. Army in fact made no real difference to the military situation.

The communists were steadily winning more territory, and at home, the very constituencies from which President Kennedy had been drawing his greatest support—young people and blacks—turned on the administration.

His struggle to gain passage of a tougher Voting Rights Act in 1965 could not be won, Kennedy realized, if at the same time he made public his uneasiness about American involvement in Vietnam. The most powerful conservative forces in the nation were already arrayed against him. Around the cabinet table, JFK and his brother Bobby found themselves increasingly isolated. Apart from George Ball and Adlai Stevenson, no high ranking Administration official was prepared to concede that Vietnam was lost. But as U.S. casualties mounted and attitudes on the campuses and in the ghettos hardened against the war, Kennedy knew he had to act.

JFK recalled for one cabinet meeting the words he had used when being interviewed by Walter Cronkite on 2 Sept. 1963: " In the final analysis it's their war," he had told Cronkite, " they're the ones who have to win it or lose it. We can help them, we can give them equipment, we can send our men out there as advisers but they have to win it, the people of Vietnam against the communists ... I don't think the war can be won unless the people support the effort ..."

Throughout 1965 and 1966, it became increasingly clear to Kennedy that the people of South Vietnam were not supporting their government and that the continued presence of U.S. troops would do nothing but ensure more death and desolation, as well as dividing public opinion at home.

The first anti-war "teach-in" had been held at the University of Michigan on 24 March 1965. It was followed by a demonstration of 25,000 students in Washington. Soon, campuses across the country saw the burning of draft cards and in some cases, the waving of Viet Cong flags. The demonstrations both troubled and impressed Kennedy. Trying to deal with both the crisis in Southeast Asia and the threat of another "long hot summer" in the ghettos of America, Kennedy turned increasingly to his brother Robert for advice. It was at Bobby's urging that JFK returned to the campus of American University in Washington in May 1966 for his famous "generations divided" speech.

"It has been written that old men make wars, but young men must fight them," President Kennedy said. "We see in America today the spectacle of our generations divided, not over economic or racial issues, but over a vision for the future of our country. We cannot proceed securely into that future without bridging the chasm that today splits families and communities across America. We will benefit little if in the name of defending freedom abroad, we squelch the spirit of dissent at home."

It would be March 1967 before President Kennedy would be able to make his momentous announcement of a "freeze" on the deployment of additional American forces, and an 18-month staged withdrawal as the South Vietnamese "assume responsibility for their own defense." The U.S., Kennedy said, would continue to arm the Saigon government. Within six months of the final U.S. departure, however, the Communists would overrun the south, renaming the capital "Ho Chi Minh City."

On 4 April 1968, the 39-year-old civil rights leader Martin Luther King was assassinated as he stood on a balcony outside his motel room in Memphis, Tenn. The ghettos of American cities erupted in violence.

King's assassination touched Kennedy—who himself had narrowly survived an assassin's bullet—as had no other event in his lifetime. JFK led the mourning for King, and appealed to blacks in the inner cities to curb their outrage.

"Our priority as a nation must be to achieve justice, tranquility and economic opportunity for all our people, without regard to the color of their skin or the homeland of their forefathers," President Kennedy told Congress on 16 May 1968, in a message carried by satellite around the world.

Kennedy added: "America cannot aspire to the leadership of the forces of freedom and justice around the world when it denies those principles to one in 10 of its citizens at home. I am today sending to Congress a message calling for the enactment of a Civil Rights Manifesto which future generations will rank with the Bill of Rights as a sacred document by which Americans will measure their commitment to equality as well as their dedication to liberty."

President Kennedy also sought to ease the tensions of the arms race before he left office. He negotiated a "World Recovery Pact" with the Soviet leaders, Bulganin and Kosygin, before leaving office in January 1969. The treaty, which called for a 10% annual reduction in arms expenditures and diversion of the funds into Third World development, was never ratified by the Congress because of disagreement over means to verify the promised arms cutbacks.

In 1968, with President Kennedy's two terms having run their course, the U.S. faced the decision of choosing a new occupant for the White House. Despite the many achievements of the Kennedy years, the American withdrawal from Vietnam haunted the Democratic Party, as the "loss" of China a generation earlier had been blamed on a Democratic administration.

A maelstrom of controversies surrounded Kennedy's final days in office. Lyndon Johnson was determined to win the Democratic nomination; Robert Kennedy was just as determined to deny him the prize. Against the president's advice, Bobby Kennedy campaigned for the Democratic nomination. On 6 June, the very night of Bobby's triumph in the California primary, a second Kennedy became the target of an assassin's bullet. This time, the gunman fired from close range, and did not miss his target. Robert Kennedy died two days later; his assassin, Sirhan B. Sirhan, would go to prison for life.

The Democrats chose Johnson and his hand-picked running mate, Senator Hubert H. Humphrey of Minnesota. But the 1968 election went to the Republicans. Richard M. Nixon, joined by the formerly obscure governor of Maryland, Spiro Agnew, won 43.4% of the popular vote on election day, compared to 43% for the Johnson-Humphrey ticket. The balance went to George Wallace, the staunchly segregationist Alabama governor.

Vietnam behind him, Nixon concentrated on expansionist economic policies at home and followed up JFK's efforts in foreign affairs. He handily defeated a Humphrey-McGovern ticket in 1972 but never finished his second term, resigning in disgrace 9 Aug. 1974, in the wake of Watergate disclosures.

Democrat Jimmy Carter had little difficulty defeating Nixon's successor, Gerald Ford, in 1976 and served two terms, his eight years marked by economic stability and absence of inflation. (Economists said the U.S. disengagement from Vietnam saved the economy from dangerous overheating that would have led to rampant inflation.) On Carter's retirement in 1984, Republican Ronald Reagan, the old movie actor, came to office after having served two terms as governor of California. He announced early in 1988 that he would not seek re-election, giving age and health as his reasons.

One of Kennedy's greatest achievements came from the vigorous leadership he provided for America's venture into space. He remained a strong advocate of the space program even after the landing of men on the moon in 1969 and the disaster of the space shuttle *Challenger*.

For John Kennedy, the years following the White House were among the most fulfilling of his life. He became president of Harvard University in 1971, putting him conveniently close to the Kennedy Library in Boston, which he watched over closely.

All his life Kennedy had been fascinated with journalism. He worked briefly as a correspondent for International News Service and covered the founding of the United Nations in 1945. Thirty years later, he returned to that craft as editor of a new daily newspaper, *America's Day*. The paper, often criticized for the brevity of its news reports, soon became respected for the quality of its editorial page where President Kennedy would daily dictate a long, thoughtful analysis of a current issue in American life.

On 18 June 1988, President Kennedy was in the study of his Georgetown townhouse when he suffered a massive stroke. He died within minutes, at the age of 71. His state funeral a week later, attended by heads of state from around the world, was unmatched in American history.